*Recharging Judaism*

# Recharging Judaism

## How Civic Engagement Is Good
## for Synagogues, Jews, and America

RABBI JUDITH SCHINDLER

*&*

JUDY SELDIN-COHEN

*With reflections by Ruth Messinger,*
*Rabbi Jonah Pesner, and Meir Lakein*

*Foreword by Dr. SUSANNAH HESCHEL*

CENTRAL CONFERENCE OF AMERICAN RABBIS
New York, New York

RJP, a division of CCAR Press
355 Lexington Avenue
New York, NY 10017
(212) 972-3636
www.ccarpress.org

LIBRARY OF CONGRESS CATALOGING-IN-PUBLICATION DATA
Names: Schindler, Judith, author. | Seldin-Cohen, Judy, 1961- author. |
  Heschel, Susannah, writer of foreword.
Title: Recharging Judaism : how civic engagement is good for synagogues,
  Jews, and America / Rabbi Judith Schindler & Judy Seldin-Cohen ; with
  reflections by Ruth Messinger, Rabbi Jonah Pesner, and Meir Lakein ;
  foreword by Dr. Susannah Heschel.
Description: New York, New York : Reform Judaism Publishing, a division of
  CCAR Press, [2018] | Includes bibliographical references and index.
Identifiers: LCCN 2017048547 (print) | LCCN 2017051056 (ebook) | ISBN
  9780881233094 (ebook) | ISBN 9780881233087 (pbk. : alk. paper)
Subjects: LCSH: Social justice--Religious aspects--Judaism--United States. |
  Judaism and social problems--United States. | Social service--Religious
  aspects--Judaism.
Classification: LCC BM645.J8 (ebook) | LCC BM645.J8 .S33 2018 (print) | DDC
  296.3/8--dc23
LC record available at https://lccn.loc.gov/2017048547

Printed in the United States of America. All rights reserved.
10 9 8 7 6 5 4 3 2 1

# Contents

Foreword by Dr. Susannah Heschel     vii

Preface     xi

List of Tables and Figures     xix

### Part I: Recharging the Synagogue

1. Let Us Travel Upstream: Volunteerism as the First Step in Civic Engagement     3
   *A Secular Glossary*     18

2. A Minyan on the Move: The Power of Community outside the Synagogue     27
   *Why Ten Constitutes a Minyan and the Pertinence of Prayer*     45

3. Responding to Complaints on the Journey: The Teachings and the Realities     53

REFLECTION: *How Civic Engagement Recharges the Synagogue*     77
   Rabbi Jonah Dov Pesner, Religious Action Center of Reform Judaism

### Part II: Recharging Ourselves as Jews

4. Listening to the Call: *Sh'ma*     85
   *The Refugee Crisis through a Jewish Lens*     95

5. Finding Our Jewish Voice: Alone I Cannot Sing     103
   *Is a Blessing Appropriate for Civic Engagement?*     119

6. Living Our Values: Protecting the Earth that Sustains Us     125
   *An Environmentalist Reinterpretation of the* V'ahavta     141

REFLECTION: *How Civic Engagement Recharges Jews*     145
   Meir Lakein, JOIN for Justice

## Part III: Your Guide to Plugging into Civic Engagement

7. Rabbis, Lay Leaders, and Congregations:                153
   A Threefold Cord Is Not Readily Broken
       *Cautionary Tales*                178

8. Blueprints of the Tabernacle: God Is in the Details     183

9. The Cycle of Civic Engagement:                          199
   The Work That Fills the *Mishkan*
       *The Power of Partnerships*      221

REFLECTION: *How Civic Engagement Is Good for America*     227
   Ruth Messinger, American Jewish World Service

## Afterword: Moving Forward

10. *Vayisu*: And They Journeyed . . .                     233

Glossary of Hebrew Terms                                   243

Abbreviations                                              247

Sources Consulted                                          249

Index                                                      257

# *Foreword*

### Dr. Susannah Heschel
Eli Black Professor of Jewish Studies,
Dartmouth College

"LET THERE BE a grain of prophet in every person," my father, Rabbi Abraham Joshua Heschel, once suggested to an interviewer. We may not be prophets, but we are descended from them, inspired by their example and striving to believe and to act as they taught.

This wonderful book inaugurates a new era in Jewish life, bringing us together, as clergy and laypeople, to recharge Judaism. Note how innovative this project is: rabbis used to be called *Seelsorger*, ministers of the souls of their congregants and expected to refrain from social or political concerns. Note, too, that congregants used to sit back in their chairs and watch while rabbis and cantors led the service— "vicarious praying," my father called it.

Today is different. We are partners and we are Jews of passion. To pray and keep silent on the injustices of our world is blasphemy— and utterly un-Jewish. There is no seclusion in Judaism; there is demand, and the response must be vitality. "Some are guilty, but all are responsible," my father declared.

Who are the prophets, and what is the prophetic Judaism that guides us? For a long time, from the 1860s to the 1920s, Protestant scholars of the Bible thought of the prophets as "ecstatics," people who suffered from fits, after which they would make proclamations. Jewish theologians, by contrast, focused on the message of the prophets, which they formulated as "ethical monotheism." My father's question was somewhat different: What is the prophetic experience? What manner of man is the prophet? He saw in the prophets people of extraordinary depth and exquisite sensitivity to the sufferings of others. While we may criticize injustices in our society, to the prophet "injustice assumes almost cosmic proportions." Beneath the outrage lies the prophet's awareness of "the silent sigh" of human anguish.

The prophet is attuned to human beings and to God simultaneously; "God is raging in the prophet's words," so that calm and patience become intolerable. My father asked: How can I pray when my government is dropping napalm on children in Vietnam, when crimes are committed in my name, when all around me there is indifference and callousness?

Prayer is intimately linked to social activism. Today we ask how we can pray when we know that wars are raging and helpless civilians are becoming desperate refugees, with borders closed and fates sealed. How do we chant from the Torah the many verses containing reminders from God that we were once strangers in the land and dare not oppress strangers in our midst—and yet we know that hateful and often murderous racism prevails in our land? After all, what do the prophets denounce? War crimes, economic exploitation, the suffering of widows and orphans. To be disengaged with the suffering of other human beings is to be disengaged from God.

How do we find hope in a time of despair? How do we have faith in Isaiah at a time when the words of Jeremiah express our mood of desolation? Let us remember that the ultimate expression of God is not wisdom, magnificence, land, glory, nor even love, but rather justice. Zion, Isaiah declares, shall be redeemed by justice, and those who repent, by righteousness. Justice is the tool of God, the manifestation of God, the means of our redemption and the redemption of God from human mendacity.

Who will speak for me? asks God. Who will remember the covenant of peace and compassion? Can we abandon despair and find the inner resources to respond like Isaiah, who said, "Here I am, send me" (Isaiah 6:8)?

With this book, we are recharging Judaism and ourselves. The alliance between rabbi and congregants gives a new fervor to our work and allows us to recognize that there can be no faith without justice—for all humanity.

To live a life of moral grandeur and spiritual audacity is a profound challenge; we must all begin by practicing small acts of courage and truth. King David, on his deathbed, told Solomon, "Be strong and of good courage and do it; fear not, be not dismayed; for the Eternal God my God is with you. God will not fail you or forsake you until all the work for the service of the Eternal is finished" (1 Chronicles 28:20, translated by Susannah Heschel). This is the verse my father dedicated to me, and it is our legacy as Jews.

# *Preface*

*R*ECHARGING JUDAISM is unique among Jewish social justice books because it is co-authored by a rabbi and a lay leader. As clergy and congregant, we see the often complicated world of civic engagement from two different viewpoints. We approach the disparate skills and goals of the multiple stakeholders in this work using our own distinctly different educational backgrounds and synagogue experiences. We argue our thesis—that civic engagement is good for synagogues, for Jews, and for America—using ancient and contemporary Jewish texts and our primary research among American synagogues that are deeply engaged in this work. We provide a "how-to" guide with pragmatic advice for congregations newly embarking on this path, and we offer insights to experienced congregations seeking to sustain and evolve their work.

We chose the phrase "civic engagement" to describe this work after much thoughtful deliberation. Social justice is sometimes viewed as a coded word for liberalism or an aspirational goal for a committee that is largely involved in service work. Civic engagement, on the other hand, is the process of addressing an injustice, with the goal of improving our collective future. Civic engagement is non-partisan, although it may involve political processes to change local, state, or federal policies. Civic engagement may entail mobilizing consumers or other stakeholders to use their power to alter unethical or unsustainable institutional practices.

Our goal is to encourage more American synagogues to incorporate civic engagement alongside their traditional offerings of Torah study, worship services, and acts of loving-kindness. Civic engagement connects Jews with Jewish community both inside and outside the walls of synagogue buildings, connecting the loosely affiliated more profoundly and meeting the unaffiliated in the secular world.

As synagogues embrace civic engagement, Jews who are instinctively drawn to this work become confident voicing the teachings of our faith, living Jewish values as they transmit them to the next generation. Civic engagement through our synagogues empowers us to respond as Jews and as Jewish institutions to address the serious challenges facing our country today.

We first became a team as a congregational rabbi and a volunteer lay leader at Temple Beth El in Charlotte, North Carolina. Over the course of more than ten years, we collaborated on such projects as the first Jewish-sponsored site for the Children's Defense Fund Freedom Schools®, the volunteer and advocacy website SolveThePuzzleCharlotte.org for homelessness issues, and the award-winning *Souls* documentaries on student diversity and affordable housing. Rabbi Schindler served the temple as senior rabbi and now as rabbi emerita; Judy Seldin-Cohen co-chaired the temple's Social Justice and Action Committee and chaired its Affordable Housing Committee, served on the temple board, and participated on countless other committees, both inside the temple and representing the temple in the community. This book has been its own special partnership of collaboration, debate, and personal connection.

Thanks to the wisdom of our publisher, *Recharging Judaism* is structured into three stand-alone parts: recharging the synagogue, recharging ourselves as Jews, and a guide to plugging into civic engagement. The book is intended for a diverse group of readers: clergy across the streams of Judaism, synagogue board members, lay leaders, steadfast volunteers, involved and uninvolved congregants, Jewish activists, intrigued secular Jews, and inquisitive non-Jews who see the foundational value of this work. We have chosen to address each segment's interests in depth, recognizing that you, as the reader, will decide when to skim a section and when to read contemplatively. Recognizing that our non-clergy readers have varying degrees of familiarity with Hebrew, we have explained each Hebrew word at its first usage and included a glossary for later reference, if needed.

We are honored to include three reflections by guest authors: why civic engagement is good for synagogues, why it is good for us as Jews, and why it is good for America. Rabbi Jonah Pesner led Temple Israel in Boston on its journey to civic engagement and created Just Congregations as the model for Reform synagogues at the Union for Reform Judaism (URJ). He now leads the URJ's Religious Action Center of Reform Judaism (RAC), serves as senior vice president of the URJ in Washington, DC, and sits on the national board of the NAACP. Meir Lakein, an Orthodox Jew who embraced synagogue organizing in its early stages, was introduced to us through his prior work for the Greater Boston Synagogue Organizing Project; he now is director of organizing at JOIN for Justice, the Jewish Organizing Institute & Network in Boston. Ruth Messinger served for twenty years in New York City government and then as president of the American Jewish World Service (AJWS) for eighteen years. She now serves as AJWS's global ambassador, encouraging clergy of all faiths to speak out for the oppressed in the United States and abroad. She is the recipient of five honorary degrees and many awards and has been named one of the ten most inspiring women religious leaders by the *Huffington Post* and the sixth most influential Jew in the world by the *Jerusalem Post*.

We are grateful for the generosity of Dr. Susannah Heschel in writing our preface. Dr. Heschel is the Eli Black Professor of Jewish Studies at Dartmouth College, a Guggenheim Fellow, and the recipient of four honorary doctorates. She has authored multiple works of her own, in addition to editing and publishing writings of her father, Rabbi Abraham Joshua Heschel (*z"l*).

Most chapters in *Recharging Judaism* conclude with a section that provides a deeper dive into a related topic, in some cases based on Judaic texts and in others stemming from our primary research. These sections—shaded for easy reference—are positioned to answer questions raised for some readers by the chapter, such as why ten constitutes a minyan or the consequences of proceeding without rabbis, lay leaders, and congregations in partnership. You may choose to read each of these additional sections in the order in which they are presented, postpone reading them without losing the thread of our narrative, or skip them entirely.

We sourced our Torah translations from *The Torah: A Modern Commentary* edited by Gunther Plaut (revised edition, 2005). Translations from the Prophets and Writings are from the *JPS Hebrew-English Tanakh* (2003). For Rabbinic texts, we used the online resource Sefaria: A Living Library of Jewish Texts (sefaria.org), and study sheets for these Rabbinic texts are available upon request to the authors (RechargingJudaism@gmail.com). Any adaptation of these three translations is noted. Texts not reflecting gender-neutral language have been amended, and we refer generically to rabbis and lay leaders as "she" or "he" in roughly equal frequency.

*Recharging Judaism* includes words of wisdom from more than seventy-five rabbis, both modern and ancient. The congregational rabbis with whom we spoke were inspiring in their dedication to the work of synagogue civic engagement, and we thank them: Morris Allen, Thomas Alpert, Dena Feingold, Jacob Fine, Dara Frimmer, Karyn Kedar, Asher Knight, John Linder, Sydney Mintz, Gayle Pomerantz, Jack Romberg, Rachel Saphire, Matt Soffer, and Felicia Sol.

We also referenced writings from modern rabbis across the streams of Judaism; we hope that you will be motivated to read more of their works, listed in the sources consulted. This book would not be possible without the words of our sages throughout the centuries on whom our understanding of Judaism rests; we encourage you to explore their writings as well.

Over the span of two years, our primary research included discussions with more than fifty people representing eighteen synagogues in interviews that frequently lasted an hour or more and often included follow-up phone calls or emails. One of the most gratifying parts of writing this book was interviewing not only the clergy but also the synagogue lay leaders. We are deeply appreciative that each of these congregants—most of them total strangers—shared with us their wisdom and personal stories. Our gratitude goes out to the following: Sara Albert, Honey Kessler Amado, Ted Busch, Susan

Drucker, Lara Ettenson, Abby Flam, Steve Fox, Rochelle Friedlich, Paula Galowitz, Dr. Linda Glazner, Fran Godine, Janet Goldenberg, Janet Hirsch, Barbara Hyman, Raizel Kahn, Harriet Lavin, Barry Moline, Dr. Nick Morse, Stephen Phillips, Mike Rosen, Cindy Rowe, Susie Selbst, Debra Silverman, Neil Silverston, Mike Sims, Marsha Stickler, Yonatan Thull, Judith Trachtenberg, Julie Weinberg, Jean Wolman, and Lisa Zucker. In addition, we are especially grateful for the Jewish community professionals who shared their time and their expertise with us: Diana Einstein, Joy Friedman, Kelly Goldberg, Anna Hanau, Meir Lakein, and Sue Worrel.

The unequivocal message from the lay leaders we interviewed is that civic engagement has been a meaningful connection to their synagogues, sometimes the most important one or even the only one. For example, Barry Moline had been involved in the religious school at Temple Israel in Florida because of his children, but his civic engagement work expanded and strengthened his ties to the synagogue. Lara Ettenson described herself as culturally Jewish, explicitly not religious, attending High Holy Day services at Congregation Emanu-El in California with the primary purpose of accompanying her mom. Yet Ettenson has now become a temple leader—building her synagogue's social justice capabilities, serving as chair of its Tzedek Council, sitting on the temple board, and representing it on the RAC Commission for Social Justice. Mike Rosen told a similar story of indifference to worship services; his passion for social justice now brings him to Temple Emanu-El in Texas nearly every day and also to a seat on his temple board. Janet Goldenberg at Temple Beth Elohim in Massachusetts, a key leader in the temple's successful work on gun violence, said she might not have stayed affiliated with a synagogue but for the advocacy work.

We began this journey with a book concept entitled *Bagels and Bacon* based on the challenges we faced in our Jewish social justice work in the Bible Belt. The insights offered by every reader who previewed our writing from that first concept until the present have guided its evolution to the book you are now reading. We are grateful to those who read a few chapters and to others who read the entire draft. Without them, this book would not have been possible, although all errors are our sole responsibility. Thank you to Sara Albert, Rabbi Tom Alpert, Chris Bishop, Jeff Cohen, Rabbi Lucy Dinner, Rick Glaser, Dr. Linda Glazner, Rabbi Dusty Klass, Meir Lakein, Stuart Matlins, Mary Nell McPherson, Melissa Raphael, Steve Raphael, Ellen Reich, Neil Silverston, Rabbi Matt Soffer, Anita Strauss-LaRowe, Rabbi Micah Streiffer, Annabelle Suddreth, Jane Vance, and Sue Worrel.

There are many others who helped us in large and small ways on our path to publication. Their contributions included sharing background stories that were not specifically quoted, finding sources, checking facts, providing advice, and much more. Thank you to Mickey Aberman, Rabbi Allen Bennett, Teresa Blackwell, Elyse Bodenheimer, Sister Simone Campbell, Jodi Cohen, Talli Dippold, Rabbi Jonathan Freirich, Lisa Garfinkle, Jeff Garis, Debora Gluick, Kelly Goldberg, Matt Grob, Rabbi Yossi Groner, Brittany Hanlin, Dr. Maria Hanlin, Dr. Susannah Heschel, Ben Hill, Daniel Infeld, Rabbi Rick Jacobs, Rabbi Asher Knight, Steve Kupietsky, Nicole Lamparello, Holly Levinson, Rabbi John Linder, Dr. Michael Meyer, Dr. Marty Perlmutter, David Perry, Rabbi Jonah Pesner, Rabbi David Powers, Butch Rosen, Alan Rosenberg, Rabbi Jennie Rosenn, Cindy Rowe, Rabbi David Saperstein, Susie Selbst, Harper Seldin, Dr. Maury Seldin, Sarah Seldin, Ben Shorstein, Mark Shorstein, Janna Siller, Rabbi Joel Sisenwine, Jake Sussman, Cantor Mary Thomas, and Rabbi Dr. Shmuly Yanklowitz. In cases of potentially controversial or embarrassing stories (e.g., the section on cautionary tales), we neither identify nor thank the person who shared his or her story—though we are especially grateful to each of you.

We thank our publisher, Rabbi Hara Person, who generously met with us in the hotel lobby during the 2015 RAC Consultation on Conscience, guided us to a book concept worthy of a publishing contract with CCAR Press, and skillfully edited and expedited the final manuscript. We also thank all the others at CCAR Press who helped guide this book through to completion: Debbie Smilow, Sasha Smith, Ortal Bensky, Rabbi Dan Medwin, Carly

Linden, copy editor Debra Hirsch Corman, designer and typographer Scott-Martin Kosofsky, and CCAR chief executive Rabbi Steven A. Fox.

Our deepest gratitude is to each other and our families.

Rabbi Judith Schindler is grateful to her co-author—without whom this book would not have come to fruition—the anchor grounding this work and the study partner who debated every word. Her greatest measure of gratitude goes to her husband, Chip, whose steadfast love and support have made all her work possible, and to her boys, Maxwell and Alec, whose patience and encouragement allow her to follow her dreams.

Judy Seldin-Cohen thanks her three children (equally), her parents, her sister, her son-in-law, her soon-to-be son-in-law, and her grandson for their understanding that this book absorbed time and attention that might otherwise have accrued to them. She is awed by the wisdom and energy of her writing partner, whom she is finally comfortable addressing solely by her first name. But her greatest appreciation is for her husband, Jeff Cohen, who read every chapter at least four times, who bravely and gently provided edits and other feedback, and who lovingly reminded her to enjoy the journey.

# List of Tables and Figures

TABLE 1: CBCO Affiliations of Temples Referenced — 22

TABLE 2: Responses to "What's Essential to Being Jewish?" — 56

TABLE 3: Comparison of Millennials' to Total Responses to "What's Essential to Being Jewish?" (top three responses) — 59

TABLE 4: Say "Yes" to Your Blueprint for Civic Engagement — 191–192

FIGURE 1: The Ladder of Civic Engagement — 16

FIGURE 2: Third Selma March — 41

FIGURE 3: Frequency of Synagogue Attendance — 57

FIGURE 4: Breastplate of Congregational Diversity — 200

FIGURE 5: Cycle of Civic Engagement — 201

FIGURE 6: The Ladder of Civic Engagement — 237

PART I

*Recharging the Synagogue*

# Let Us Travel Upstream

## Volunteerism as the
## First Step in Civic Engagement

MARRIAGE EQUALITY in Washington state. Gun legislation in Massachusetts. Housing homeless families in North Carolina. Better working conditions for tomato pickers in Florida. What do these causes have in common? Synagogues strengthening their communities and this country through civic engagement.

Every day, synagogues across all streams of Judaism mobilize their members to shelter the homeless, heal the sick, and comfort the bereaved. Some also go further, enlisting congregants to advocate for changes that address the sources of these crises. Not only sheltering the homeless, but also creating more affordable housing. Not only healing the sick, but also improving access to health care. Not only responding to the tragedies of mass shootings, but also preventing gun violence. As more synagogues embrace all the steps of civic engagement, they recharge Judaism, benefiting their congregants, their synagogues, and this country.

Activists of many faiths use the following parable to preach the power of leveraging volunteerism as the first step in alleviating suffering: A villager sees a stranger thrashing in the current of the nearby river. Without stopping to think, the villager jumps into the river and pulls the stranger to safety. Soon a schedule of lifeguards is established, and every few days another villager is hailed as a local hero after pulling another stranger from the river. As more and more resources are devoted to rescues, finally someone stands up and says, "Maybe we should travel upstream and see why so many people are falling in the river." Dr. Martin Luther King Jr. praises this volunteerism—or social service—for allaying hardship, while also exhorting us to address the root causes of that hardship through seeking social justice.

So it is with Jews volunteering in the community. We can line the proverbial river with lifeguards, pulling out strangers who fall into the current of hard times. And we can also travel upstream in civic engagement, enlisting our synagogues to remedy the sources of this suffering.

## The Synagogue Is Not an Island

> Rabbi Shimon bar Yochai taught: People were on a ship. One of them took a drill and started drilling underneath him. The others said to him, "What are you sitting and doing!" He replied, "What do you care? Is this not underneath my area that I am drilling?" They said to him, "But the water will rise and flood us all on this ship." (*Vayikra Rabbah* 4:6)

While we might delude ourselves into thinking that our own vessels are seaworthy, the maxim remains true that we are all in the same boat. Synagogues are not only places for prayer and comfort, but are also part of the fabric of our communities, states, and country. To believe that the synagogue is isolated from the tides outside its walls is to shirk the responsibilities of our faith, hoping that we will stay afloat while others are flailing for life preservers.

Prayer without action mutes the voices of our biblical prophets who have laid the foundation of Judaism. In the opening chapter of the book in his name, the prophet Isaiah calls out against the hypocrisy of ritual without deeds:

> "What need have I for all your sacrifices?"
> Says the Eternal. . . .
> Though you pray at length,
> I will not listen.
> Your hands are stained with crime—
> Wash yourselves clean;
> Put your evil doings
> Away from My sight.

Cease to do evil;
Learn to do good.
Devote yourselves to justice;
Aid the wronged.
Uphold the rights of the orphan;
Defend the cause of the widow.

(Isaiah 1:11, 15–17)

With the destruction of the Second Temple, prayer replaced ritual sacrifice. Yet, neither sacrifice in its day nor prayer in modern times was ever meant to be offered in isolation. The values embedded in Jewish texts and prayers serve as a guide for our lives. These teachings are meant to inspire our actions in the public space, not to be left behind in books and pews.

Civic engagement as a Jewish community ensures that our society is better aligned with our values, charging us to call for economic justice, environmental stewardship, and human rights. The ideals laid out in the Torah and proclaimed by the prophets were a guide for the Israelites when we were settled in our land, and with this sovereignty came a spiritual and moral responsibility. The laws of human dignity and justice are scaffolds that are intended to sustain our society. Recognizing the powerlessness of others, we have laws to protect the most vulnerable in our society—the stranger, orphan, and widow.

Even in exile, we worked to protect the vulnerable among us. The prophet Jeremiah understood that we would be scattered to lands other than our own and instructed us, "Seek the welfare of the city to which I have exiled you and pray to the Eternal in its behalf; for in its prosperity you shall prosper" (Jeremiah 29:7).

When the walls defining Jewish community were expanded during the Enlightenment and beyond, the Jewish commitment to protect and serve others extended its reach as well. As soon as Jews were able to engage in modern society, we worked to bring our voices and vision to the civic structures in which we could participate. Today the Jewish responsibility remains to fulfill ethical obligations along with the ritual. The religious world of Jews is not divorced from the reality outside; it is dependent upon it.

Jeremiah promises us personal benefit from working for the peace of the communities in which we live, acknowledging that our serenity is disturbed by the pain that exists outside our synagogue walls. Our spirituality is thwarted by crises that tear at the fabric of society. Our Jewish community's sense of security is threatened by rising intolerance against any people. And today, those threats against us and against others are increasing. Whether it is homophobia, xenophobia, Islamophobia, antisemitism, or racism, no community is immune from being targeted.

Each congregant brings into the sanctuary the burdens of the weekday world—the unending acts of gun violence and mass shootings to which we tragically have become too accustomed, the news of refugees dying as they flee their home countries, or the droughts and storms that call into question the health of our environment. The synagogue is not disconnected from its community nor unaffected by our nation's policies. The devastating storms outside our synagogues create waves that impact us all.

Viewing the synagogue as merely a sanctuary treats it like an island vacation. Jews who visit find short-lived renewal, and just as returning to work after vacation quickly wearies the rested body and mind, so too the comfort of prayer can dissipate quickly in the weekday world. Yet when the vision uttered in worship extends into civic engagement, Judaism becomes part of our daily lives, and healing continues beyond the hours of prayer.

Congregations engaged in social justice do see their synagogues not as separate from the outside world, but as a powerful source of energy and ideas for sustaining both their secular and Jewish lives. Their congregants learn that long-lasting repair is possible, and both the synagogue and the individual Jew find renewed purpose and are recharged through collaborative and collective commitment to civic engagement.

To recharge our synagogues and ourselves, this civic engagement must offer the potential for meaningful change. Janet Goldenberg, a Massachusetts congregant participating in a Shabbat discussion after Saturday services about gun violence after the Sandy Hook

Elementary School tragedy in Newtown, Connecticut, raised her hand in the follow-up meeting to ask if the work they were contemplating would actually make a difference. "I don't want to do something that just makes me feel good, or [just to] feel like I'm doing something," she explained. "If this work can save even just one life, I'm in 100 percent, but I'm not interested in busy work."

Her perspective is shared by so many volunteers who are already busy with work, family, fitness, neighbors, friends—with their own lives. Unless our labors have the potential for yielding real fruits, wasting time and resources is irresponsible not only for the volunteers whom we recruit, but also for the institutions that we support. Goldenberg's wisdom hinges on discerning the difference between *feeling* like we are doing something and actually *making* significant change.

The efforts of the following four synagogues illustrate how civic engagement, especially in collaboration with other organizations, can yield tangible results for our cities, states, and country. These synagogues range in size from 130 to 1,200 families. They are located in progressive states and in conservative states, in cities ranging from one hundred thousand to a few million in population. Yet, each made a meaningful difference advocating for change as a Jewish congregation.

> Anyone who saves one life, Scripture accounts to that person as if he/she saved the entire world.[1]
>
> (Babylonian Talmud, *Sanhedrin* 37a)

After the Sandy Hook tragedy, Temple Beth Elohim in Wellesley joined with other Boston-area congregations to lobby for a gun violence reduction bill. Four of five key provisions survived when the bill passed the Massachusetts House and Senate and became law under Governor Deval Patrick in 2014. In 2015, local police officers were already pointing to specific people whose lives were saved by the enforcement of the bill.

> Any person who does not have his or her own home is lacking human dignity.[2]
>
> (Babylonian Talmud, *Y'vamot* 63a)

At Temple Beth El in Charlotte, North Carolina, more than one out of six congregant families volunteered in 2009 at agencies serving the thousands of homeless and vulnerable poor in the community. Determined to collectively travel upstream, the synagogue board passed a resolution encouraging the temple, its leaders, and its members to speak out on homelessness and affordable housing in the community.

Temple Beth El's public position led to collaboration with a group of churches, resulting in a $20 million public/private endowment to fund families on a path from homelessness to financial independence. By its third year, the endowment was subsidizing rent and arranging for supportive services for ninety-nine families.

> It is not good that the man be alone.
> (Genesis 2:18)

In yet another example, Temple Beth Am in Seattle joined with eight other Reform congregations to work for marriage equality in Washington State in 2012. Initially supporting the passage of legislation and then a ballot referendum, the Washington State group mobilized public support that led to an early victory for same-sex marriages.[3]

> Woe to those who build their houses with unfairness and their upper chambers with injustice, who make others work without pay and do not give them their wages.[4]
> (Jeremiah 22:13)

In a final example, Beth Hillel Temple in Kenosha, Wisconsin, joined many other American congregations in the Fair Food Campaign to improve pay and working conditions for the tomato workers in Immokalee, Florida. This region in Florida supplies the vast majority of tomatoes for national fast-food and supermarket chains. The Fair Food Campaign resulted in an additional penny per bucket for workers, plus more humane working conditions, although more work remains to be done.[5]

The ideal of economic justice that we seek as a society is proclaimed in Deuteronomy: "There shall be no needy among you" (*Deuteronomy* 15:4). Yet the text also acknowledges that our obligation will remain perpetually relevant: "There will never cease to be needy ones in your land" (Deuteronomy 15:11). These two texts reflect the balancing act required between the perfect and the pragmatic. The first speaks to systemic change ("going upstream") and working toward the goal of justice. The second acknowledges the urgency of helping those who are homeless and hungry now ("rescuing the drowning"). This dual imperative illustrates the need for synagogues to accomplish the social justice work that addresses root causes alongside the social action work that relieves suffering.

Synagogues find that they can bring justice to the communities with which they are inextricably bound by sustainably protecting and saving the lives of others—reducing gun violence, creating affordable homes, expanding the legal protections of marriage to same-sex couples, and advancing more humane conditions for farm workers. Committing to the work of civic engagement acknowledges that our synagogues are not islands—neither impervious to the storms in our communities nor vacation spots for fleeting renewal; our institutions are participants in the secular world in which we live.

### Our Individual Paths to Civic Engagement
What draws Jews to the work of civic engagement? The answers are as diverse as the Jewish people.

Many clergy we interviewed cited Jewish texts that inspired their work. Rabbi Sydney Mintz, from Congregation Emanu-El in San Francisco, was moved by Hillel's words calling us with a sense of urgency to advocate both for ourselves and for others, "*Im lo achshav, eimatai?* If not now, when?" (*Pirkei Avot* 1:14). Rabbi Dara Frimmer, from Temple Isaiah in Los Angeles, cited as her inspiration, "Do not stand idly by [while your neighbor's blood is shed]" (Leviticus 19:16). Rabbi Dena Feingold, from Beth Hillel Temple in Kenosha, Wisconsin, rattled off several texts meaningful to her, starting with the text of Isaiah from the Yom Kippur morning service, "Is this the fast I desire?" (Isaiah 58:5). According to Isaiah, the goal of our rituals of sacrifice and piety is "not to starve our bodies" but to address the evil, oppression, hunger, and poverty we see in our society and world (Isaiah 58:6–7).

Rabbi Matt Soffer, from Temple Israel in Boston, explained his reasoning for choosing the text from the Passover seder "*B'chol dor vador*, In every generation [a person must regard himself or herself as though he or she personally had gone out of Egypt]" (*Mishnah P'sachim* 10:5):

> This text hammers home the obligation [to pursue social justice] more than any other. All the texts that remind us that we were there. We have to read ourselves into the narrative and read the narrative into our lives. The text compels us to absorb the narrative as having been there and finding our way out of it.
> . . . We all have to figure out what is the call of Sinai for all time.

We, the authors, are drawn to this work through the heritage of our families. Rabbi Schindler is inspired by the memories of her grandfather and father, who lived their lives fighting against injustice in Nazi Germany, in America, and globally. Judy Seldin-Cohen cites as Jewish activist role models both her maternal grandfather, who was in the Haganah in the 1930s, and her paternal grandfather, who ran an illegal printing press in czarist Russia in the 1910s.

Lay leaders whom we interviewed were often less specific about their motivations for engaging in this work. Yet they were certain that it was part of their Jewish heritage or a reflection of their upbringing to not only care what happened to others, but to act upon these feelings.

Regardless of the disparity among individuals' motivations, American synagogues have an opportunity to channel this passion for civic engagement with significant benefit to themselves as institutions. In subsequent chapters, for example, you will read about lay leaders whose path to synagogue leadership is defined by civic engagement. Synagogues embarking on the path of civic engagement also recharge us as Jews—teaching us to take the first step toward change and find our Jewish voices—as we work to alleviate poverty, support freedom and equality, and protect the earth that sustains us.

**Our Shared Social Fabric**

Why it is appropriate for synagogues to help non-Jews as well as Jews? Economic justice for all is a fundamental ethic of Judaism, and there is no biblical legal code that speaks more powerfully to this obligation than chapter 15 of Deuteronomy. This text includes both an impassioned call and a clear mandate to lift up the impoverished:

> If, however, there is a needy person among you, one of your kin in any of your settlements in the land the Eternal your God is giving you, do not harden your heart and shut your hand against your needy kin. Rather, you must open your hand and lend whatever is sufficient to meet the need.
>
> (Deuteronomy 15:7–8)

The text explicitly connects the words "needy person among you" with the phrase that follows, "one of your kin," to remind us of our common humanity. From extending loans to forgiving debt to the manumission of indentured servants in the seventh year, the text highlights our responsibility for both relieving the oppressive nature of poverty and maintaining the dignity of those who have fallen into economically desperate times.

The critical question lies in the interpretation of "your kin" (*ache-cha*). Does our obligation extend only to our fellow Jews or to all in our community? The thirteenth-century rabbi Moses ben Nachman (also known as Ramban or Nachmanides) clarifies that our obligation includes all the poor, whether we are a sovereign people or living in exile:

> The meaning of "in your land" refers to all your settlements— in the Land of Israel and outside the Land of Israel. And the meaning of "the poor person in your land" is that this phrase refers both to your poor kin and to all the poor of your land.
>
> (Ramban's commentary to Deuteronomy 15:11)

Many commentators, ancient and modern, struggle to articulate the reasoning behind the commandment to support non-Jews along with Jews. The Rabbis of the Talmud (the central text of Rabbinic Judaism) see poverty as cyclical, and no one is immune from facing that hardship. Rabbi Chiya advised his wife to be quick to feed the poor person who knocks on their door, so that others would respond similarly to feed their own children. Although his wife protests that he is cursing their children, he replies in the name of the Sages that there "is a wheel that continuously turns in the world" (Babylonian Talmud, *Shabbat* 151b).

While we have a covenantal responsibility to help fellow Jews, Rabbi Jonathan Sacks advocates that we are obligated to perform acts of loving-kindness (*g'milut chasadim*) for non-Jews in the same way in order to thrive in a diverse world:[6]

> Civic peace demands more than tolerance, a live-and-let-live attitude to those not like us. *Darkei shalom* [the ways of peace] is an active mandate, not a passive one, doing good to others, and thereby showing that the threads of our common humanity, with their variegated colours, are part of the social fabric we weave together.[7]

This concept of a shared social fabric with non-Jews is critical to our civic engagement work. *Tikkun olam*, "the repair of the world," and *tikkun hanefesh*, "the repair of the soul," are interconnected. The wholeness we seek for ourselves is dependent on our actions in the greater world, and those actions are most effective and sustainable when they are built upon mutuality and relationship.

Civic engagement is not about Jews helping non-Jews, but about our work uplifting us all. In reflecting on the powerful connections developed between Temple Emanu-El congregants and non-Jews with whom they worked closely in Dallas, Texas, Rabbi Asher Knight said, "It was not us doing for them or them doing for us, but all of us working together to make our community better."

Meir Lakein, director of organizing at Jewish Organizing Institute & Network (JOIN for Justice), teaches that Jewish social justice is not simply what we do for others. When our acts of justice are unilateral, we risk marginalization. When we are not in relationship with those for whom we advocate, we risk losing our effectiveness and authenticity. As Lilla Watson, Aboriginal activist and artist, puts it, "If you have come here to help me, you are wasting your time. But if you have come because your liberation is bound up with mine, then let us work together."[8]

The work of civic engagement gives the vulnerable among us the skills to be self-supporting and independent. Both Jewish teachings and modern organizers urge us to work with those falling into the proverbial river of hard times to find sustainable solutions. Engaging with non-Jews is not only our obligation, but also the way of peace for our communities and our souls.

## Modern Streams of Judaism

Jewish tradition teaches that our lives will ultimately be judged on our actions, whether by God or by others. Recognizing the role of Jewish study in inspiring action, the first-century rabbi Shimon ben Gamliel taught, "Study [of the Torah] is not the main thing; [the] doing [of Torah] is" (*Pirkei Avot* 1:17).[9] In Judaism, both study and the actions to which it leads have great value.

The Reform Movement has a long and rich history of linking faith to action, first articulated in the movement's 1885 Pittsburgh Platform, which reads:

> In full accordance with the spirit of the Mosaic legislation, which strives to regulate the relations between rich and poor, we deem it our duty to participate in the great task of modern times, to solve, on the basis of justice and righteousness, the problems presented by the contrasts and evils of the present organization of society.[10]

The Reform Movement established the Religious Action Center of Reform Judaism (RAC) in Washington, DC, to bring the Jewish voice of justice into the debates in our nation's capital. For more than five decades, the RAC has addressed a wide spectrum of legislative and social justice issues with the goal of educating and mobilizing the now more than 1.5 million American Reform Jews. Recognizing the powerful and valuable role of the RAC's leadership, President Barack Obama named Rabbi David Saperstein, the RAC's longtime director, as United States ambassador-at-large for international religious freedom in 2014, in which role he served through the end of the Obama administration.

Albert Vorspan and the late Rabbi Balfour Brickner, respected leaders in the Reform Movement's quest for justice, eloquently described the denomination's deep and strong stance on social justice, which requires "taking some responsibility to do something to right the wrongs that all Americans have done," regardless of your personal experience:

> But you cannot morally say, "This is not my problem," or "I don't know anything about it." These are the excuses most "good" Germans made while our fellow Jews were being slaughtered by the Nazis. What Judaism demands is "Do not profit by the blood of your brother or sister . . ." And your brother or sister is poor, old, black, Puerto Rican, Indian, white and Vietnamese, as well as Jewish![11]

Some may be surprised to learn that all denominations of Judaism call us to actively engage with contemporary society. They erroneously assume that increased ritual observance precludes action on behalf of the secular community. A Modern Orthodox leader, Rabbi Jonathan Sacks is a great thinker, prominent leader, and prolific writer on Jewish perspectives on a range of civic issues, from economic inequality to the need to embrace diversity in our globalized world to protecting the environment. He writes:

> The message of the Hebrew Bible is that serving God and serving our fellow human beings are inseparably linked, and the split between the two impoverishes both. Unless the holy leads us outside toward the good, and the good leads us back, for renewal, to the holy, the creative energies of faith run dry.[12]

Like Modern Orthodoxy, Conservative Judaism also connects our service to God with our acts in this world. The Rabbinical Assembly of Conservative Judaism affirms that ritual acts between human beings and God (*mitzvot bein adam LaMakom*) are inextricably linked to the ethical acts between one human being and another (*mitzvot bein adam lachaveiro*). The Rabbinical Assembly has accordingly taken stands on social justice issues ranging from slavery and human trafficking to the need for a comprehensive energy policy.[13]

Rabbi Harold M. Schulweis was a respected leader in the Conservative Movement in the twentieth century, serving on his local board of the NAACP and helping found both Mazon, a Jewish organization to combat hunger, and Jewish World Watch, an international watchdog group fighting genocide and mass atrocities. In reflecting on the legacy of Rabbi Schulweis, his successor at Valley Beth Shalom in Encino, California, Rabbi Edward Feinstein, said, "Rabbi Schulweis found the presence of God in acts of moral courage, compassion and human decency. He constantly reminded us that we are the hands of God in this world."[14]

The Reconstructionist Movement similarly teaches that working for social justice is one of the ways to find God and that ethical behavior is intrinsic to Judaism. Rabbi Mordecai Kaplan, founder of the movement, argued that Jewish life must provide us with recipes for justice that we make manifest in the world when he wrote, "A theology which is not a plan of social action is merely a way of preaching and praying. It is a menu without the dinner."[15]

Author Rabbi Sid Schwarz, who founded Adat Shalom Reconstructionist Congregation in Bethesda, Maryland, and is still serving there and for close to a decade was a senior fellow at CLAL (the National Jewish Center for Learning and Leadership), describes *tzedek*, the obligation to pursue justice, as a primary purpose of Judaism:

> After three decades of being a rabbi and a teacher in the Jewish community, I found that audiences couldn't answer the question "What is the purpose of Judaism?" . . . I argue that the two primary purposes in Judaism are *tzedek* and *k'dushah*. Both are deeply rooted in Torah. *Tzedek* is the mandate of Jews to extend the boundaries of righteousness and justice in the world, help mend a broken world. *K'dushah* is the notion of our being a sacred people with a sacred purpose. The only way to maintain the integrity of the Jewish idea, of the covenant of Sinai, is for us to be a little bit apart from the rest of world, what I call sacred apartness.[16]

According to Schwarz, being Jewish requires both an active engagement in our society as we pursue justice, *tzedek*, and an embrace of ritual, *k'dushah*. Both are essential.

Rabbis from every major denomination of Judaism affirm that human hands are essential to fix the brokenness of this world in order to bring God's vision of justice to life. The weight that leadership places on this work varies from synagogue to synagogue and from rabbi to rabbi, as well as across streams of Judaism. Yet, the committed Jew understands that Judaism is all-encompassing, involving study and acts of loving-kindness, prayer and practice, the weekday and Shabbat, and the sacred and the secular.

### The Ladder of Civic Engagement

We gain traction on the journey toward social justice by embracing each rung on the ladder of civic engagement (see figure 1). Volunteering our time through social action helps those who are in crisis, allowing us to better understand their pain and their perspective. The next rung, education, enables us to understand the complexity of an issue and identify effective paths to pursue change. Philanthropy is referred to in Judaism as *tzedakah*, which shares the same Hebrew root as the word *tzedek* (justice). *Tzedakah* is an obligatory gift that ensures justice, which stands in contrast to charity, a voluntary gift from the heart.[17] Advocacy encourages systems to be created to prevent those most vulnerable from falling into crisis. Organizing creates power that elevates these issues on our community's agenda. Movements are the fuel that helps us cross the finish line.

Figure 1. *The Ladder of Civic Engagement.*

| Join a Movement |
|:---:|
| Connect with Community Organizing |
| Engage in Advocacy |
| Invest in Solutions through Philanthropy |
| Embark on Education |
| Give Time through Social Action |

Debra Silverman, at Temple Isaiah in Los Angeles, notes the inextricable relationship between social action and social justice work. She explained how all these programs in their religious school are a tremendous draw for the synagogue, citing activities ranging from packing sandwiches in early grades to philanthropy and lobbying in high school years, saying:

> That [social action programming] really helps our congregants connect to what being Jewish means. People feel it deeply, and that is, in part, why people feel connected to the synagogue.... The organizing and advocacy work is more difficult because it requires patience, imagination, and vision. It's a slow process, more difficult than a food or coat collection. That said, we couldn't do social justice—the slower, systemic work—without the social action programs. The programmatic work is the hook.

Service opportunities create the connections that inspire deeper involvement and engagement. Through acts of service, we create a more inclusive community. We build relationships with the constituents we aim to help so that we are working with them rather than for them. Often we have found when a group connects on one level, such as education, they are inspired to expand their work into other realms, such as service or advocacy. Some congregants find fulfillment through a single rung, and their work should be equally valued. While we have laid out the approaches to social justice in the form of a ladder, each rung is of immense importance, and climbing both up and down is necessary for civic engagement.

As you read *Recharging Judaism*, consider the following guide to our terminology:

*Social justice is a goal for our cities, states, and nation.*
*Our journey toward this goal gains traction as we ascend*
*and descend the ladder of civic engagement.*
*Each rung on this ladder is a tactic:*
*social action, education, philanthropy,*
*advocacy, community organizing, and joining a movement.*

Historically, synagogues have taught congregants the Jewish values of social justice through sermons, Torah study, religious school curricula, and adult education classes. They can bring those teachings to life by embracing the journey of civic engagement, offering congregants opportunities to mount any of the rungs of this ladder and accomplish meaningful change in America. Throughout *Recharging Judaism*, we will discuss these Jewish teachings and share instructive examples from synagogues already on this journey.

## A Secular Glossary

Just as familiarity with Jewish texts varies among congregants, so too does experience with civic engagement. Creating common language eliminates some of the friction that slows us down and produces inefficiencies. Throughout this book are teachings from our faith that guide synagogues traveling upstream; below are definitions of secular terms that can help when charting the course.

Direct service is often the first step to alleviate hardship. This is the act of lifting those who are in need and rescuing those who have fallen into the waters of hard times. Congregations also use the terms social service or social action to describe this work, whether it is sheltering the homeless, collecting canned food donations, or tutoring in high-poverty schools.

Religious organizations are the most frequent beneficiaries of American volunteerism; that's where one-third of volunteers spent their most volunteer hours. And, volunteering is significant; one in four Americans volunteered at least once in 2015 with a nonprofit organization.[18]

Many faith leaders speak of sharing our time, treasure, and talents with others. Sharing our time is social action; sharing our treasure is philanthropy. Private charitable contributions to nonprofits in America totaled $373 billion in 2015, funding (in descending order) religion, education, and then human services organizations.[19]

In many instances, philanthropy leads to a recognition that addressing the root causes of our society's problems is, in the long term, the most effective use of charitable giving. The famous philanthropist and business magnate John D. Rockefeller said, "The best philanthropy is constantly in search of finalities—a search for a cause, an attempt to cure evils at their source."[20]

While both social action and philanthropy help the recipient, they have the added benefits of uplifting the one who is helping. Yet both the volunteer and the philanthropist must be continually cognizant of this dynamic and sufficiently self-reflective to ensure that these actions are not sustaining the economic injustice that caused the hardship. Dr. King reminds us of the perpetual obligation to pursue social justice: "Philanthropy is commendable, but it must not cause the philanthropist to overlook the circumstances of economic injustice which make philanthropy necessary."[21]

Social justice aims to eliminate the causes of hardship, working to ensure that human rights are upheld in societal structures. Dr. Lee Anne Bell, a professor at Barnard College, offers the following definition:

> The goal of social justice is full and equal participation of all groups in society that is mutually shaped to meet their needs. Social justice includes a vision of society in which the distribution of resources is equitable and all members are physically and psychologically safe and secure.[22]

The definition of social justice is not universally agreed upon, and many use the term without explicitly defining it. Throughout this book, we will explore the many dimensions of social justice through the lens of Jewish values.

Advocacy is a critical tool for pursuing social justice. B'nai Jeshurun, an unaffiliated synagogue in New York City with a venerable tradition of involvement in its community, offers a helpful definition for this important work on its website:

> Advocacy is an attempt to influence laws, public policy, and resource allocation within political, economic, and social systems and institutions—structures that directly and powerfully affect people's lives. . . . Human rights—political, economic, and social—provide the overarching framework for these visions.

Advocacy enables social justice advocates to gain access to, and
a voice in, the decision-making processes of institutions. It can
change the relationships of power between these institutions
and the people affected by their decisions, thereby changing the
institutions themselves and revitalizing the culture of healthy
democracy and civic participation.[23]

Advocacy as a tool for civic engagement can take many forms, both
for individuals and congregations. One voice can lead to many voices.
One letter to the editor can change many minds. One post on social
media can help to spread facts—rather than fear—among thousands.
Registering voters, calling senators and representatives, raising a difficult issue at a social event, challenging the practice of a business or
corporation—these are acts of advocacy, large and small.

Opinion columnist and author Thomas Friedman believes his edito-
rial columns should serve as either a heater or a light bulb, or both. His
metaphor also applies to advocacy:

"I am either in the heating business or the lighting business."
Every column or blog has to either turn on a lightbulb in your
reader's head—illuminate an issue in a way that will inspire them
to look at it anew—or stoke an emotion in your reader's heart
that prompts them to feel or act more intensely or differently
about an issue.[24]

Advocacy is amplified when multiple voices join together. Enlisting
others to advocate with us is achieved by organizing. Also from B'nai
Jeshurun:

Organizing can be defined as the process of bringing people
together to build relationships, identify problems, and develop
the capacity—the power—to change the decisions and processes
of institutions that contribute to those problems. Organizing
leads to action that is planned and carried out through campaigns: periods of intense and focused effort, with a beginning
and an end, designed to lead to a specific goal that makes a
positive, incremental impact on a problem.[25]

Organizing requires collaboration—joining coalitions outside one's own synagogue—which can be accomplished in many ways. Houses of worship often work together across the boundaries of faith, sometimes along with other community institutions, in **congregation-based community organizing (CBCO)**. CBCO is "a movement that seeks to establish interfaith, cross-class, multiethnic and multiracial grassroots organizations for purposes of increasing social integration and power in civil society and working for social improvement."[26]

Many of the synagogues interviewed for this book belong to CBCOs. Each CBCO has its own name and catchy acronym, and typically they are affiliated with national organizing efforts. In some cases, a regional network is interposed between the local and national levels, such as WISDOM in Wisconsin and Metro IAF in New York City. Table 1 identifies the CBCO affiliations of the synagogues mentioned in this book.

In some instances, organizing and advocacy lack the scale to create the systemic change we seek. Joining statewide or national **movements** can magnify our efforts and propel our initiatives forward. Author Peter Levine, a Tufts University professor at the Jonathan M. Tisch College of Civic Life, writes about the diversity inherent in a successful movement, rarely seen when a single organization leads the way:

> The successful political movements were led by sets of fractious and competing organizations that collectively represented the whole field.
>
> At its moment of greatest glory, the American civil rights movement was led by the Southern Christian Leadership Conference, the Student Nonviolent Coordinating Committee, the NAACP, the Congress on Racial Equality, and the Urban League, with the Nation of Islam operating somewhat to the side. These groups were strikingly different in ideology and theology, structure, demographics, strategy, and regional base. They sometimes competed for the same members and funds. Nevertheless, their network ties were dense and they were capable of highly effective collective action at moments of crisis and opportunity.[27]

## Table 1. CBCO Affiliations of Temples Referenced

| TEMPLE | City/State | CBCO | CBCO Regional/ National Network |
|---|---|---|---|
| Beth Hillel Temple | Kenosha, WI | Congregations United to Serve Humanity (CUSH) | WISDOM/Gamaliel |
| B'nai Jehoshua Beth Elohim (BJBE) | Deerfield, IL | United Power for Action & Justice | Industrial Areas Foundation (IAF) |
| B'nai Jeshurun (BJ) | New York, NY | Manhattan Together | Metro IAF/IAF |
| Chicago Sinai Congregation | Chicago, IL | United Power for Action & Justice | IAF |
| Congregation Beth Am | Los Altos Hills, CA | Bay Area IAF | IAF |
| Mount Sinai Congregation | Wausau, WI | North Central Area Congregations Organized to Make an Impact (NAOMI) | WISDOM/Gamaliel |
| Temple Beth Elohim | Wellesley, MA | Greater Boston Interfaith Organization (GBIO) | IAF |
| Temple Beth Sholom | Miami Beach, FL | People Acting for Community Together (PACT) | Direct Action and Research Training (DART) Center |
| Temple Emanu-El (TEE) | Dallas, TX | Faith in Texas | People Improving Communities through Organizing (PICO National Network) |
| Temple Emanuel | Newton, MA | GBIO | IAF |
| Temple Isaiah | Los Angeles, CA | One LA | IAF |
| Temple Israel | Boston, MA | GBIO | IAF |
| Temple Israel | Tallahassee, FL | Tallahassee Equality Action Ministry (TEAM) [28] | DART Center |
| Temple Solel | Phoenix, AZ | Valley Interfaith Project | IAF |

Professor Levine adds that successful movements create "a shared sense of belonging and identity."[29] This collaboration is characteristic of many successful campaigns for change discussed in this book.

**Civic engagement** is defined by scholar, author, and public servant Thomas Ehrlich as "working to make a difference in the civic life of our communities and developing the combination of knowledge, skills, values and motivation to make that difference. It means promoting the quality of life in a community, through both political and nonpolitical processes."[30]

Civic engagement is not necessarily partisan, but may involve government or community institutions. Rabbi Matt Soffer at Temple Israel in Boston, Massachusetts, elevates civic engagement as an American obligation: "I don't use that word [advocacy] a whole lot. I talk about finding your civic voice. I used the words 'Jewish civics.' Let's take this public. Going public. The statehouse is yours. Finding your story, finding your voice."

Some issues may divide people along political lines, but people with disparate political beliefs can also unite over a single issue that requires civic action. And, in fact, coalitions of diverse voices are particularly powerful forces for change.

## Notes to Chapter 1

1. This translation was adapted to be universal and egalitarian. The original text states, "A singular *adam* was created—to teach you that anyone who causes one Israelite life to be lost, Scripture accounts to him as if he caused a whole world to be lost; and anyone who sustains one Israelite life, Scripture accounts to him as if he sustained an entire world." Given the universality of the term *adam*, "human being," clearly manifest in Genesis 2:7, extending the teaching to one that is universal seems warranted.
2. We translated the word *karka* as "home" instead of "land," as it more accurately reflects today's reality; it is the home that provides dignity, not the land. Similarly, we translated *eino adam* as "is lacking human dignity" instead of "is not a man."
3. "Washington Approves Gay Marriage in Referendum 74 Vote," Huffington Post, November 7, 2012, updated February 2, 2016, http://www.huffingtonpost.com/2012/11/07/washington-referendum-74-gay-marriage_n_2050539.html.
4. We have translated the Hebrew word *hoy* as "woe to those" instead of the NJPS translation "ha!" because it better reflects the cautionary nature of the verse.
5. Steven Greenhouse, "In Florida Tomato Fields, a Penny Buys Progress," *New York Times*, April 24, 2014, http://www.nytimes.com/2014/04/25/business/in-florida-tomato-fields-a-penny-buys-progress.html; Truah: The Rabbinic Call for Human Rights, www.truah.org; Coalition of Immokalee Workers, http://www.ciw-online.org.
6. Jonathan Sacks, *To Heal a Fractured World: The Ethics of Responsibility* (New York: Schocken Books, 2005), 99–114.
7. Sacks, *To Heal a Fractured World*, 109.
8. Lilla Watson, quoted in Geoffrey B. Nelson and Isaac Prilleltensky, *Community Psychology: In Pursuit of Liberation and Well-Being* (New York: Palgrave Macmillan, 2010), 29.
9. Translation from Leonard Kravitz and Kerry M. Olitzky, *Pirke Avot: A Modern Commentary on Jewish Ethics* (New York: UAHC Press, 1993), 11.
10. The 1885 Pittsburgh Platform, CCAR, https://ccarnet.org/rabbis-speak/platforms/declaration-principles.
11. Balfour Brickner and Albert Vorspan, *Searching the Prophets for Values* (New York: UAHC Press, 1981), 64.
12. Sacks, *To Heal a Fractured World*, 9.
13. RA Social Justice Commission, Rabbinical Assembly, http://www.rabbinicalassembly.org/tzedek-justice/social-justice-commission.

14. Rabbi Edward Feinstein, as quoted by Dana Bartholomew, "Valley Beth Shalom Rabbi Harold M. Schulweis, World Leader, Dies at 89," *Los Angeles Daily News*, December 18, 2014.

15. Mordecai M. Kaplan, *Not So Random Thoughts* (New York: Reconstructionist Press, 1966), 23.

16. Sidney Schwarz, *Judaism and Justice: The Jewish Passion to Repair the World* (Woodstock, VT: Jewish Lights, 2006), 3–10.

17. Jews are required to provide life's basics to those who cannot support themselves; these are not optional gifts from the charitably minded. No one is exempt from this obligation; even those who are recipients of support are themselves obligated to help others.

18. Bureau of Labor Statistics, Department of Labor, "Volunteering in the United States, 2015," Economic News Release, February 25, 2016, https://www.bls.gov/news.release/volun.nr0.htm.

19. Giving USA Foundation and Indiana University Lilly Family School of Philanthropy, *Giving USA 2016: The Annual Report on Philanthropy for the Year 2015* (Giving USA Foundation, 2016), https://givingusa.org/giving-usa-2016/.

20. John Steele Gordon, "John D. Rockefeller, Sr.," Philanthropy Roundtable, accessed February 26, 2017, http://www.philanthropyroundtable.org/almanac/hall_of_fame/john_d._rockefeller_sr.

21. Martin Luther King Jr., *Strength to Love*, reprint edition (Minneapolis: Fortress Press, 2010), 25.

22. "What Is Social Justice?" Barnard College, accessed February 26, 2017, http://barnard.edu/reslife/social-justice-house.

23. "What Is Advocacy and Community Organizing?," B'nai Jeshurun, accessed February 26, 2017, http://www.bj.org/community/social-justice/community-organizing-and-advocacy/what-is-advocacy-and-organizing.

24. Thomas L. Friedman, *Thank You for Being Late: An Optimist's Guide to Thriving in the Age of Accelerations* (New York: Farrar, Straus and Giroux, 2016), 12.

25. "What Is Advocacy and Community Organizing?," http://www.bj.org/community/social-justice/community-organizing-and-advocacy/what-is-advocacy-and-organizing.

26. "Congregation-Based Community Organizing," Unitarian Universalist Association, accessed February 26, 2017, uua.org/action/cbco.

27. Peter Levine, *We Are the Ones We Have Been Waiting For: The Promise of Civic Renewal in America* (New York: Oxford University Press, 2013), Kindle edition, 178.

28. TEAM has dissolved, but the examples of the congregation's work are included.

29. Levine, *We Are the Ones*, 181.

30. Thomas Ehrlich, ed., *Civic Responsibility and Higher Education* (Westport, CT: American Council on Education and Oryx Press, 2000), vi.

CHAPTER 2

# A Minyan on the Move

The Power of Community
outside the Sanctuary

JUDAISM RECOGNIZES the power of community. The Talmud
notes that "any expression of sanctity" (*kol d'var sheb'k'dushah*)
requires a gathering of ten Jewish souls—what we call in Hebrew
a minyan (Babylonian Talmud, *M'gilah* 23b). Healing is found,
strength is gained, and celebrations are enriched when we are sur-
rounded by others. A humorous tale captures the inspiration that
can arise from assembling such a quorum:

> Rabbi Paysach Krohn told the story of a rabbi in Jerusalem,
> Rav Yosef Gutfarb, who had been diligent about attending daily
> minyan for decades. Late one night Rav Gutfarb realized he had
> missed the evening service and raced to an all-night synagogue.
> Finding only one person inside, Rav Gutfarb called two taxi
> companies in order to find eight Jewish cab drivers who could
> come to the synagogue address. When the cabs arrived, he told
> the drivers to keep their meters running, but requested that they
> pray in the minyan with him. The drivers all agreed, yet after the
> brief service, every one of them refused to accept Rav Gutfarb's
> money, honored by the experience of the minyan.[31]

Rav Gutfarb creatively assembled a minyan so that he could continue his practice of daily worship. While American synagogue budgets might not support Lyft or Uber bills to satisfy their own minyan
requirements, Rav Gutfarb's ingenuity offers a provocative model.
The eight taxi drivers had not come to the synagogue for the minyan,
but whether out of respect for Judaism or for Rav Gutfarb's commitment to his faith, they refused payment for their metered time.

The "minyan on the move" takes our prayer service outside the synagogue walls, coupling communal prayer with the ethical acts of our faith. Ten people can literally change the world, the Torah teaches us, but it is unlikely that we can make these changes from inside our houses of prayer. The minyan on the move brings our prayers to those places where Jews choose to gather for social justice causes.

When we assemble as a minyan on the move, our prayers and our acts of civic engagement make a difference. Through sharing our personal stories and pain, and through our proximity to others that allows us to hear their struggles, we join together outside our synagogue walls to work toward fulfilling our collective prayers for a better world. As Jews, our memories are part of our identity as a people. We reinforce who we are not only by retelling, but also by reliving journeys toward liberation, as redefined by each generation. The minyan on the move creates new memories that meaningfully connect us to our Judaism, "re-Jewvenating" us.

### Creating Change with a Minyan

Two stories in Genesis teach that ten souls can change the course of history. Commenting on the narrative of Noah, some modern writers claim that God's divine wrath would have been assuaged and the Flood prevented had a minyan existed to stand against the tide of sin. Noah, his wife, their three sons, their three daughters-in-law, plus the Divine Presence constituted only nine. A tenth, posit these voices, could have prevented the loss of so many other lives.

In the second story, Abraham similarly asserted that ten righteous souls should be enough to save Sodom and Gomorrah. When God tells him about the imminent destruction of these two corrupt cities, Abraham speaks out in defense of those who were innocent: "Must not the Judge of all the earth do justly?" . . . And [God] said, "For the sake of the ten, I will not destroy it" (Gen. 18:25, 32). Abraham had started with a petition that God should allow the city to be sustained if even fifty righteous souls existed in Sodom and Gomorrah. Abraham negotiated his way down to ten, yet fewer than ten blameless souls existed and the cities were indeed demolished.

Elie Wiesel, the late renowned author and Holocaust survivor, writes of the "Just Man" who preached endlessly in the streets of Sodom to inspire its inhabitants to change their evil ways. The people of Sodom initially responded with amusement and then with indifference. Wiesel writes:

> The killers went on killing, the wise kept silent, as if there were no Just Man in their midst. One day a child, moved by compassion for the unfortunate teacher, approached him with these words: "Poor stranger, you shout, you scream, don't you see that it is hopeless?"
> "Yes, I see," answered the Just Man.
> "Then why do you go on?"
> "I'll tell you why. In the beginning, I thought I could change man. Today, I know I cannot. If I still shout today, if I still scream, it is to prevent man from ultimately changing me."[32]

The one Just Man of Sodom could not prevent the destruction of the city. Yet if he could have recruited nine others to join him, he could have changed history. Wiesel's message still echoes strongly that we must continue our difficult work to keep the world from changing us. Each of us shouting to make a difference in today's world preserves our own sense of righteousness, but when we lift our voices together, we create the possibility of saving our communities.

Learning from these hard moments in the Torah, how do we as American Jews not protest futilely in isolation, but instead achieve meaningful change by assembling a minyan on the move?

The power of such a minyan on the move was demonstrated when one hundred American women traveled to Jerusalem to fight for pluralistic Judaism in Israel on the occasion of the twenty-fifth anniversary of Women of the Wall (WOW). Since 1988, Jewish women have been gathering at the Kotel (the Western Wall) to pray together on Rosh Chodesh (the new moon), which establishes the first day of the Hebrew month. Sadly, these otherwise joyous worship services on the women's side of the *m'chitzah* (the divider in Orthodox prayer spaces separating men and women) have been regularly disrupted by groups of ultra-Orthodox men and women. These groups deny the authenticity of non-ultra-Orthodox streams of Judaism that accord Jewish women the right to pray aloud in public, wear prayer shawls, lay *t'fillin* (phylacteries), and read from the Torah.

The struggle of Women of the Wall to worship freely has been long and painful due to government obstructionism, which pacifies the ultra-Orthodox element of its political coalition. Each time a court ruled in its favor, the Israeli Ministry of Religious Affairs appealed to a higher court, meanwhile continuing to deny equal rights in worship to women. In 1989, the government passed an amendment to the Protection of Holy Places Law, prohibiting the performance of a religious ceremony at a holy site that is not in accordance with the customs of the place and offends the sensitivities of the worshipers there. The penalty for violating this regulation is six months in jail and/or a fine. This amendment was directed at WOW worshipers and their demands to pray aloud, read from the Torah, and wear prayers shawls and phylacteries. As a result, WOW members were arrested and detained for wearing ritual garb at the Kotel.

Twenty-five years of wins and losses in the Israeli Supreme Court and unfulfilled promises of justice by the Israeli Knesset. Twenty-five years of monthly services disrupted by ultra-Orthodox men—at times, even throwing eggs and chairs at women lifting their voices in prayer. Twenty-five years of Israeli women staking their historic claim, enduring police detentions and arrests. Twenty-five years of empowered Israeli women worshiping with prayer shawls, as do many Jewish women in the Diaspora. As the twenty-fifth anniversary approached, the WOW organizers were buoyed by the international passion for their cause.

One hundred American women arrived in Jerusalem in 2013 to celebrate the anniversary, bringing new energy to the movement. Delegations of congregants and rabbis arrived from Charlotte, Chicago, Dallas, Los Angeles, Miami, New York City, Oakland, and Westchester, collectively sponsoring a gala for the occasion. But it was a group of Reform women in Georgia who contributed in another powerful way. An Israeli police chief responsible for the Kotel security had been visiting Savannah on police business when the women lobbied him for the WOW platform. The Israeli reportedly returned to his duties a "changed man," eager to make the twenty-fifth anniversary successful. According to Lesley Sachs, executive director of WOW, when the ultra-Orthodox attempted to suppress the WOW prayer celebration with powerful audio speakers, they were thwarted with an inexplicable loss of electrical power.[33]

A minyan unites many voices for change. For the Women of the Wall's twenty-fifth anniversary, it was the collective voice of Israeli and American women that helped the celebration move forward. It was this collective voice that contributed to an international passion for this pluralistic cause. And these voices were heard. In 2016, less than three years after the WOW anniversary celebration, Israel's prime minister, the Knesset Cabinet, and the Rabbinate committed to the Mandelblit Plan, creating a place for pluralistic prayer at Judaism's most holy site. The Mandelblit Plan promised that this pluralistic prayer section would be built by the government at Robinson's Arch, administered by a non-Orthodox committee, and accessed through a common entrance with other prayer areas.

Lesley Sachs commented on the impact of the American women:

> All WOW's achievements over the years have been a result of a partnership between supporting Jews outside of Israel and the struggle of WOW at the Kotel. The prime minister is far more sensitive to the disposition and attitude of North American Jewry than to WOW supporters in Israel. It is thanks to the ongoing pressure from supporters in North America that he approached Natan Sharansky to negotiate a solution with the North American Reform Movement, Conservative Movement, Federations, and Women of the Wall. It is the battle regarding the holiest site to all Jews that has united women and free-thinking men from Israel and the Diaspora to work together for change.

A congregant who accompanied Rabbi Debra Robbins of Temple Emanu-El in Dallas to the twenty-fifth anniversary of WOW commented on the 2016 announcement of the Mandelblit Plan: "[The visit] shows me that our individual voices can be heard if we choose to speak up when we see injustice and that by joining in and taking a stand, our collective actions can make history."[34] Another Temple Emanu-El congregant spoke to the connection she feels from participating in the WOW trip: "I am very proud to have been a small part of the struggle. I will always cherish Rabbi Debra Robbins' leadership in bringing Temple Emanu-El members this opportunity."[35]

Sadly, the fulfillment of the Mandelblit Plan remains elusive and WOW's struggles continue today. The international partnership of protest remains an imperative, and in November 2016, American and Israeli leaders of the Reform and Conservative Movements protested the continuing delays by carrying Torah scrolls to the women's side in violation of a regulation set by the rabbi of the Kotel, Rabbi Shmuel Rabinovitch. In June 2017, the Netanyahu government officially froze implementation of the Mandelblit Plan, eliciting condemnation from a broad spectrum of American rabbis, movements, and agencies, including the Central Conference of American Rabbis, the Union for Reform Judaism, the Rabbinical Assembly, The United Synagogue of Conservative Judaism, and the Jewish Agency. American advocacy for egalitarian worship at the Kotel remains the most persuasive counter to the powerful voice of the ultra-Orthodox in Israel's coalition government.

In some people's eyes, opening the Kotel to equality in prayer represents the tip of the proverbial iceberg. Achieving the rights for women to worship in our accustomed ways at the holiest of Jewish places disempowers those who seek to silence women's voices in public spaces and represents legitimacy for pluralistic Judaism in Israel. While many are fighting to expand the rights for non-Orthodox streams of Judaism on other fronts, some American Jews are using the power of communal connection to demand justice through their support of Women of the Wall.

We need not travel thousands of miles with our minyan in order to make meaningful community connections that inspire change. The congregants of Temple Beth El in Charlotte, North Carolina, created a minyan on the move by traveling from the suburbs to the city. For decades, Temple Beth El had declined to participate in the

Charlotte parade honoring Dr. Martin Luther King Jr. because it conflicted with Shabbat morning services. The temple annually hosted a black church's preacher and choir on the Friday night preceding Martin Luther King (MLK) Day, and temple members and the rabbi attended that church's Sunday morning service as guest preacher, choir, and congregation. But on Shabbat, the MLK Parade would proceed without the advertised participation of the synagogue. Our then-understanding of *k'dushah* (holiness) called us to be separate on our sacred day, even though many of the congregation regulars typically went to the parade with unofficial approval from the clergy.

Struggling with the contradiction of tacitly supporting the parade without actually attending, the clergy team had a revelation that a minyan could be held at the MLK Parade site. In 2016, congregants and clergy convened an interfaith gathering at an uptown Charlotte church, where Shabbat was celebrated, Torah was read, and prayers were shared. The young children of Temple Beth El then rode the "Building Bridges" float with the young children of Antioch Missionary Baptist Church and Grier Heights Presbyterian Church (as pictured on the cover of this book). Unity was preached and practiced, and effective lessons were taught by living our Jewish values rather than by solely reading about them.

Raizel Kahn and her four young sons rode the "Building Bridges" float, with her husband walking behind them. A Temple Beth El member, she had not been to the MLK Parade before and was not a regular at Shabbat morning services, but she chose to attend both as part of the synagogue's float delegation. Kahn commented on the relevance of spending Shabbat outside the synagogue:

> The participation made me feel more connected to the synagogue and to the other TBE [Temple Beth El] family we came with. I'm not the most religious person in the world, but I love the sense of community of my temple, and that's what's important to me. The MLK experience was about teaching my kids values and morals, and watching them play with children of different skin color and different religion.

Assembling a minyan at the MLK Parade site resolved the challenge faced by the clergy in wanting to honor Dr. King's legacy on a Shabbat morning. And, just as Rav Gutfarb's taxi drivers found unexpected value in their minyan, congregants unaccustomed to attending worship services appreciated their Shabbat experience outside synagogue walls. The Facebook post of our shared parade float will remain as a powerful reminder of both our joint commitment to fulfill Dr. King's vision of racial equality and our creative celebration of Shabbat in uptown Charlotte with families of different colors and faiths.

Noah lacked a minyan to turn the tide of corruption and prevent the Flood. Abraham could not find a minyan of righteous souls, and so God destroyed Sodom and Gomorrah. Today, civic engagement enables us to assemble a minyan on the move. Through this process, Jews who might not necessarily be drawn to pray inside the sanctuary experience the transformative power of prayer. Jewish community is created in new places as we gather to build a world upon the foundation of justice.

### Communicating Petitions with Our Tears

When our minyan on the move takes us outside our synagogues to petition for change in the face of oppression and injustice, we are often emotionally affected in profound ways. The Talmud suggests that God responds to tears, even when they are shed outside the sanctuary walls.

Rabbi Elazar teaches that the destruction of the Temple nearly two thousand years ago fractured the lines of communication between us and God:

> Rabbi Elazar says: Since the day the Temple was destroyed the gates of prayers were locked, and prayer is not accepted as it once was, as it is stated in the lament of the Temple's destruction: "Though I plead and call out, God shuts out my prayer" (Lamentations 3:8). Yet, despite the fact that the gates of prayer were locked with the destruction of the Temple, the gates of tears were not locked, and one who cries before God may rest

assured that those prayers will be answered, as it is stated: "Hear my prayer, Eternal One, and give ear to my pleading, keep not silence at my tears" (Psalm 39:13). (Babylonian Talmud, *Bava M'tzia* 59a)

According to this teaching, God hears the weeping of those who are hungry and have no money for food. God takes note of the lamenting of those who are impoverished and cannot pay their rent. And God knows of the despair of those who are victims of violence, oppression, and discrimination. In Rabbi Elazar's image of the Divine, God may well listen to us more readily when we hold a box of tissues—or perhaps a protest sign—rather than a prayer book.

In March 2016, Rabbi Judith Schindler led a group of twenty Jewish women from Charlotte, North Carolina, on a Jewish Federation study trip to explore the rich American and Jewish history of Charleston, South Carolina. The first Jew to be killed in the American Revolutionary War, Francis Salvador, is honored by a monument in Charleston, and American Jews were battling on both sides of the Civil War and then the civil rights movement in this quintessentially Southern city.[36] Charleston's outdoor Holocaust Memorial, showcasing a forlorn prayer shawl with fringes cut off as if for burial, is a short walk from the Mother Emanuel AME Church, where Dylann Roof had opened fire, murdering nine Bible study members less than a year before this study trip.

The visitors from Charlotte sat in the church basement where the tragedy had unfolded. One of the victims of this senseless violence was Cynthia Graham Hurd, a beloved Charleston librarian and sister of former North Carolina state senator Malcolm Graham. Senator Graham spoke to the visitors in the sanctuary upstairs, followed by Emanuel AME's new pastor, Rev. Dr. Betty Deas Clarke, who was hired to bring healing to a deeply wounded congregation and community. Several of the Jewish women had tears rolling down their cheeks during these remarks. Pastor Clarke asked them the source of their tears. A twenty-one-year-old remarked, "I thought I was born into a world beyond this, but I wasn't."

And the pastor consoled them, "Out of pain, love can arise."[37]

When we leave the shelter of our sanctuaries and travel as a minyan on the move, we encounter the personal stories of others that can move us to tears. Out of tears, prayers can be answered. Out of tears, justice can arise.

## Communicating Petitions with Proximity

As a minyan on the move, we gather to support social justice causes outside our synagogues, petitioning as a Jewish community. According to Rabbi Elazar, the person who cries before God is heard by the Divine, but how do we ensure that our petitions are also heard by those who are making decisions on earth? Proximity as the basis for creating change is a concept taught in the Torah and in the work of racial justice today in our country.

In the Book of Numbers, the five daughters of Zelophehad saw themselves as victims of unjust inheritance laws. In challenging the status quo, the first Hebrew word used to describe their case is *vatikravnah*, which means "and they drew near." The sisters were undoubtedly bereft from their father's death and likely distressed that they were soon to lose their land, yet they appealed to Moses, Eleazar, the princes, and all the congregation in a respectful but firm manner:

> The names of the daughters were Mahlah, Noah, Hoglah, Milcah, and Tirzah. . . . They said, "Our father died in the wilderness. He was not one of the faction, Korah's faction, which banded together against the Eternal, but died for his own sin; and he has left no sons. Let not our father's name be lost to his clan just because he had no son! Give us a holding among our father's kinsmen!" (Numbers 27:1–4)

Moses heard their story, saw their pain, and brought their case before God. The laws of inheritance were changed to allow women to receive a legacy of land. The story of the daughters of Zelophehad shows us how proximity matters for those who seek to create change. When we draw close enough to tell our stories and to listen to the stories of others, we begin to understand where justice is lacking and how systemic change is required. Torah is a book both of legend and of law (*aggadah v'halachah*), each influencing the other. We learn from Torah and Talmud, and from case law today, that legal statutes necessarily evolve as stories of injustice are redressed. When we communicate our petitions effectively by drawing near, we can create a more equitable world.

Attorney Bryan Stevenson teaches the concept of proximity in his work to reform America's justice system and seek racial reconciliation in this country. A professor at New York University School of Law, Stevenson is the author of *Just Mercy: A Story of Justice and Redemption* and the founder and executive director of the Equal Justice Initiative in Montgomery, Alabama. His Christian faith and his passion for his calling require him to draw near to those in need in order to achieve justice:

> Proximity is power. It's powerful because you can learn things that you need to know to be a better problem solver. It's powerful because your proximity is a witness to those who feel abandoned and alone. It's powerful because you learn things about what you can do that you did not understand before.[38]

Stevenson relies on proximity to see and hear firsthand the plight of those who are suffering, understand the injustice they are experiencing, share their story, and illuminate a path to reform.

Sometimes proximity is more convincing than intellectual appeals for justice. The Freedom to Marry movement realized that telling personal stories of shared values was more powerful than a message about equal rights, a strategy that the movement credits with changing the hearts and minds of voters toward same-sex marriage. Initially, the Civil Marriage Collaborative—an alliance of funders seeking to advance marriage equality with a national strategy—had focused their campaign message on equal rights for lesbians and gays wanting to marry. In contrast, opponents were making an emotional argument that same-sex marriage would harm children.

Prior to the 2012 Maine referendum for same-sex marriage, the alliance realized the power of telling personal stories of shared values. Amy Mello, field director for Freedom to Marry, explained:

> We weren't telling the story that gay couples valued marriage for
> the same reasons [as straight couples]: love and commitment.
> . . . When we made an emotional connection around shared
> values, we gave conflicted Maine residents a way to override
> the negative reaction to the attack ads claiming kids would be
> harmed by "gay marriage" and come back to their better selves.[39]

The organization used happily married parents and grandparents
of gay and lesbian couples as their spokespeople. These family
members reflected on their journey to accepting these same-sex
partners, achieved through seeing in those relationships the love
and commitment that mirrored their own. These "journey" ads
brought straight allies of the LGBTQ (lesbian, gay, bisexual, transgender, queer) community into proximity with Maine voters—into
their kitchens, living rooms, and dens—effectively persuading more
people to support marriage equality. Maine became one of the first
four states to authorize marriage equality with a voter referendum.
The shift in messaging was particularly meaningful because Maine
voters had vetoed legislation in favor of marriage equality three years
previously.[40]

We create the opportunity for proximity with those who are suffering through our travels as a minyan on the move. Sometimes
change is only possible through drawing near to others and hearing
their personal stories and their pain; intellectual arguments for
equal rights may fail to convince those whose support is needed for
justice. The narratives that we hear become the fuel and the tool for
the work of social justice in our communities and in our country.
Just as the Torah is a book of law and the narrative that transforms
law, so too the narratives that we hear outside our synagogues can
transform the laws of our country.

## Building Memories with a Minyan
Memory is essential to who we are as a people. It binds us to one
another and helps us to know to whom we belong. And in Judaism,
memory is not passive; it is active. It is a commandment. The word
*zachor* (remember) appears 197 times in the Torah. "Remember!"

our Torah tells us. "Remember Shabbat. Remember you were slaves in Egypt. Remember Amalek—our archenemy."

Rabbi Jonathan Sacks discusses this contrast between memory and history:

> History is his story—an event that happened sometime else to someone else. Memory is my story—something that happened to me and is part of who I am. History is information. Memory, by contrast, is part of identity. I can study the history of other peoples, cultures and civilizations. They deepen my knowledge and broaden my horizons. But they do not make a claim on me. They are the past as past. Memory is the past as present, as it lives on in me. Without memory there can be no identity.[41]

Our identity as a Jewish people stems from our historic journey to freedom. Shortly following our redemption from slavery in Egypt, we stood at Sinai and made a commitment to one another and to the ethic that would guide our future. We annually reenact this ancient journey to freedom through our Passover seder—ritual stories, foods, and songs that remind us that we were slaves and now we are free. Even those Jews who say they have no religious ties often feel called to the seder table—and to contemporary fights for justice that evoke its message. Indeed, it is these memories of oppression from the slavery of Exodus, and more recently, from the fires of the Holocaust, that call many of us to act. This commitment to achieving liberation is so fundamental to our faith that some Jews recall this moment of freedom not just once a year at Passover, but twice daily. Morning and evening through a prayer called the *Mi Chamochah* ("Who is like You, Eternal One"), the daily worshiper sings from the song that the Israelites sang on the shores of freedom (Exodus 15:11).

Judaism is about transmitting memories from one generation to the next—memories that move us to action. Using a teaching from the Mishnah, the Passover Haggadah instructs us: *B'chol dor vador, chayav adam lirot et atzmo k'ilu hu yatza miMitzrayim*, "In every generation, a person must regard himself or herself as though he or she personally had gone out of Egypt" (*Mishnah P'sachim* 10:5).

A minyan on the move creates and re-creates these Jewish memories as we work to fulfill the imperative of redeeming those who are oppressed. As Jews, we have known and lived journeys for justice. Congregants interviewed for this book proudly shared their congregations' involvement in the civil rights movement. "Our rabbi once marched in the South," so many of them said.

When asked which text was most inspirational to their own social justice work, congregants often cited Rabbi Abraham Joshua Heschel's famous quote from marching in Selma. For more than twenty-five years, Heschel was a professor at the Jewish Theological Seminary, the ordaining institution for most Conservative rabbis. He took temporary leave from his role as professor of Jewish ethics and mysticism to march in Alabama with Dr. Martin Luther King Jr. in March 1965 (see figure 2).

Heschel wrote, "For many of us the march from Selma to Montgomery was both protest and prayer. Legs are not lips, and walking is not kneeling. And yet our legs uttered songs. Even without words, our march was worship."[42] Dr. Susannah Heschel, Heschel's daughter and a scholar herself, added that after that march he said, "I felt my legs were praying."[43] Many of our interviewees echoed Heschel's message, remarking that their social justice work was their way of "praying with their feet."

Perhaps that is what was so appealing about the NAACP Journey for Justice in 2015, which inspired nearly two hundred rabbis and many of their congregants to walk for racial justice at the busiest time of the rabbinical year—just prior to the High Holy Days. Rabbi Seth Limmer, senior rabbi of Chicago Sinai Congregation, posted on the RAC blog why he recruited rabbis for the journey:

> My mind immediately made associations: 40 days of walking towards the promise of a better America were so perfectly parallel with the Jewish people's saga of walking 40 years towards our own Land of Promise. I knew the Jewish community needed to be on this march, from beginning to end. Inspired by the image of Dr. King and Rabbi Abraham Joshua Heschel on the bridge [in Selma], I wanted to find a way to make sure

**Figure 2.** Third Selma March. African-American civil rights activist Dr. Martin Luther King Jr. (1929–68, center) in the front line of the third march from Selma to Montgomery, Alabama, to campaign for proper registration of black voters, March 23, 1965. Starting third from left: Ralph Abernathy (1926–90), King, Ralph Bunche (1903–71), and Rabbi Abraham Joshua Heschel (1907–72). (Photo by Popperfoto/Getty Images.)

the Reform Jewish community shared the entire distance of this journey. Compelled by the legacy of our Rabbi Eisendrath [carrying the Torah while marching with Heschel and King at a separate rally[44]], I thought it would be powerful if our Torah scroll didn't just appear in DC for the final rally, but accompanied us the entire 860-mile journey. I knew I could no longer be inspired by pictures and stories of the past if I wasn't willing to walk the walk in the present. I cannot wait to see how I, how we, are changed by the experience. And how this shared experience of a Journey for Justice can change America.[45]

It was the memory of these marches that moved so many American rabbis to set aside their most pressing task of writing High Holy Day sermons to do the holy work of walking for racial justice—40 days, 860 miles, from Selma, Alabama, to Washington, DC. After a summer of racial tensions including church burnings in the South, murders in Charleston, and headlines alleging excessive police force, rabbis responded from all over the nation, each committing to march a one-day leg of the journey with members of the NAACP. Each state confronted a different issue with a rally: economic equality in Alabama, education reform in Georgia, criminal justice in South Carolina, voting rights in North Carolina, and justice and equality in Washington, DC. The rabbis carried a Torah scroll in their arms or in a backpack the entire journey, physically holding the values of equality and justice that they yearned to bring to these Southern states and to our United States.

Rabbi Peter Stein of Temple B'rith Kodesh in Rochester, New York, walked across the Alabama-Georgia state line just before Shabbat. He blogged after the march about our responsibility for one another as Jews and Americans:

> That particular day, moving from state to state, gave us the opportunity to reflect on the significance and meaning of what the name "United States of America" stands for. Is there equal opportunity throughout our country? Are we united in ending racism and discrimination? . . . This journey from Selma to Washington is sacred, and God is present in every step down those country highways. We answered hateful cries with songs of peace. We met ignorance and bigotry with love and dignity. We shared stories of vulnerability and fear and we shared hopes and dreams. And we did it all carrying a Torah scroll, proudly, alongside the American flag. Torah, which begins with the story of creation, because we are all responsible for one another.[46]

On Shabbat Zachor (the Shabbat of Remembrance), occurring just before the holiday of Purim, we are called to remember the cruelty of Amalek, an enemy of our people whose attacks were more brutal than any other in the Bible. According to Deuteronomy 25:17–19, Amalek surprised us on our journey through the wilderness. When we were famished and weary, the Amalekites attacked us from the rear—killing those members of our community who had fallen behind, most likely women caring for their children, as well as the elderly and the ill.

Our tradition tells us to remember the evil of Amalek. Indeed,

Amalek, as a nation, became the archetype of subsequent persecutors of Jews. A Chasidic commentary expands on the commandment that bids us to remember Amalek:

> If the community of Israel had not forgotten these stragglers, but rather, had brought them close under the wings of God's presence in order to return them underneath the clouds of glory so that they would be together with the whole house of Israel, then Amalek would not have overcome them. But because these stragglers were left behind, Amalek was successful. This is a sign for generations: When the entire community is supported and together, then Amalek cannot gain control.[47] (*Iturei Torah*, Deuteronomy 25:17)

The commandment to remember Amalek requires us not only to remember the evil of Amalek, the nation, but also to remember our failure to support those who had fallen behind. By taking physical journeys to hard places, we remind ourselves of our responsibilities to the most vulnerable among us in our country. As Jews and as Americans, we remember the powerful march from Selma when Heschel prayed with his legs alongside Dr. Martin Luther King Jr. In drawing near to see and know the plight of others, we create indelible memories that command us to act and to free the oppressed because we were once oppressed. The minyan on the move literally moves us and challenges us to work toward a liberation that will redeem us all.

## In Conclusion

Rabbi Alexander Schindler, president of the now Union for Reform Judaism from 1973 to 1995, and teacher, mentor, and father of Rabbi Judith Schindler, often told the following story illustrating the power of a minyan:

> Abba Kovner, a great poet and Warsaw ghetto fighter, wrote about his initial alienation when he made *aliyah* (immigrated) to Israel. For months he longed to feel that sense of connection that the sages and prophets before him had felt, but all he experienced were pangs of emptiness. It wasn't until someone asked him, "Would you join us for a minyan? We need a tenth," and he joined the worshipers, that for the first time he felt that he was truly a part of a community.

Years later, when Kovner conceived his idea of the Diaspora Museum in Tel Aviv, he designed a corner called "The Minyan." It is an exhibit of wax figures representative of various Jewish communities throughout the world.

But in this grouping of sculptures there are only nine and not the required ten figures because, explained Kovner, he wanted to call out to museum visitors, as others had called out to him: "Come and join us . . . be counted. We cannot do without you. We need you as you need us."

As we march in the Martin Luther King Day parade, journey for justice through Georgia, and fly overseas to stand with our sisters at the Kotel in prayer, we realize that we do need others as they need us. Our tradition teaches that ten souls can save the world, but now we must recruit others in new ways, or we may end up shouting alone like the one Just Man of Sodom, hoping simply to save ourselves. Petitions for justice are more readily heard when we draw near, as did the daughters of Zelophehad, and more Americans are likely to become receptive to societal change when these petitions draw nearer to them, as we saw in Maine.

Like the traditional minyan of prayer, the minyan on the move provides healing and community. In addition, relationships are built outside the synagogue through these minyans, strengthening ties to our congregational community. The memories that we keep of these transformative experiences bind us together as Jews, for as Rabbi Sacks said, "Without memory there can be no identity."[48] When we recruit a minyan outside our synagogue walls through the work of civic engagement, the potent combination of communal prayer and collective protest builds waves of change toward justice.

## Why Ten Constitutes a Minyan
## and the Pertinence of Prayer

The Talmud states that *"kol d'var sheb'k'dushah*, any expression of sanctity, may not be recited in a quorum of fewer than ten" (Babylonian Talmud, *M'gilah* 23b). Among these "expressions of sanctity" are reciting the Mourner's *Kaddish* (a prayer sanctifying God's name recited after the death of a close relative), reading of the Torah, singing the initial portion of *Birkat Ha-Mazon* (Blessing after Meals), and chanting the *Sheva B'rachot* (seven wedding blessings). From mourning a loved one to chanting from Torah to celebrating a couple joined in marriage under the chuppah (wedding canopy), life's sacred moments should not be marked without a minyan.

Judaism acknowledges that holiness is heightened through community. On a ritual level, certain prayers and acts are deemed especially sacred and compel us to gather as a community, a minyan of ten. Through the Jerusalem Talmud's interpretation of a central line of the Holiness Code—"Speak to the whole Israelite community and say to them: You shall be holy, for I, the Eternal your God, am holy" (Leviticus 19:2)—one can also deduce that a communal response is required for an array of ethical actions, ranging from alleviating poverty to protecting immigrant rights.

The two explanations below of why ten souls are essential for community prayer teach us the importance of both creating holiness inside our sanctuaries and creating holiness through our actions in our world. The Jerusalem Talmud (*M'gilah* 4:4) uses a principle of biblical interpretation that compares a pair of verses sharing identical terminology. One explanation focuses on sanctifying God's name in the *Mishkan* (ancient Tabernacle), using the word *toch* (in the midst of) and the phrase *B'nei Yisrael* (Children of Israel). The other explanation—using the word *eidah* (community)—enjoins us to sanctify God's name in the world.

### Community Is Created in the Midst of the Children of Israel
In one explanation, both the word *toch* (in the midst of) and the phrase "Children of Israel" (*B'nei Yisrael*) are used in the following verses:

> The *Children of Israel* came to buy provisions *in the midst* of those who came, for the famine prevailed over the [whole] land of Canaan. (Genesis 42:5)

> You shall not profane My holy name, that I may be sanctified *in the midst* of the *Children of Israel.* (Leviticus 22:32)

The words "in the midst of" and the "Children of Israel" in the Genesis text refer to the ten sons of Jacob (also known as Israel), who came to Egypt during a famine to buy grain from their brother Joseph. Since these terms in Genesis refer to ten individuals, the Rabbis conclude that ten is the number needed in the Leviticus instructions to sanctify God's name.

### We Experience the Divine in Community

The Mourner's *Kaddish* is recited for thirty days after the burial of a sibling, spouse, or child, and for eleven months after the burial of a parent, and then again on the anniversary of the relative's passing (*yahrzeit*). As we join a circle of at least ten Jewish souls, we are meant to praise God at a time when we might otherwise be inclined to challenge or question divine existence. In the face of tragedy and loss, the bereft may ask the question, "Where is God?" The minyan—the congregation surrounding the mourner—becomes the answer. Holiness and healing happen when we gather with others.

Because it is written in Aramaic, the vernacular of its day, the meaning of the Mourner's *Kaddish* may elude some who feel called to recite it in the minyan. Yet the prayer has a power that transcends reason, summoning even nonobservant Jews in times of mourning. The modern Jew who is mourning may be drawn to say the Mourner's *Kaddish* for any of a multitude of reasons: community, healing, tradition, or taking time to honor the life loved so deeply.

Many American Jews who struggle to connect to the Divine through liturgy more readily acknowledge sensing God's presence in community. As Rabbi Harold M. Schulweis, a prominent Conservative rabbi, eloquently explained in the first stanzas of his poem "Between":

God is not in me
nor in you
but between us.
God is not me or mine
nor you or yours
but ours.
God is known
not alone
but in relationship.
Not as a separate, lonely power
but through our kinship, our
friendship
through our healing and binding
and raising up of each other.[49]

Rabbi Schulweis's poetry was no doubt inspired by the theologian Martin Buber, who, in his famous treatise *I and Thou*, taught that God is present in the authentic encounter between two individuals.[50]

This sense of the Divine that is experienced in community— whether inside or outside the sanctuary—is the basis of this next explanation of why ten people constitute a minyan.

### Ten Constitutes "Community"

The other explanation from the Jerusalem Talmud of why ten constitutes a minyan is based on the word "community." Shortly after liberation from slavery in Egypt, twelve scouts—one from each tribe—were dispatched to survey the Promised Land. Ten of them brought a pessimistic report back to Moses, moving God to call out in distress, "How much longer shall that wicked community [*eidah*] keep muttering against Me?" (Numbers 14:27).

The example of the ten scouts reminds us that a community has the power to lead us astray and make dysfunctional decisions. Rabbi Thomas Alpert, of Temple Etz Chaim in Franklin, Massachusetts, notes that this text also teaches that "community is so important that even when it is disappointing God, it still gets the honor of being named a community. How much more so when it is engaged in holy actions!"

A verse in Leviticus uses *adat*—a form of *eidah*, the same Hebrew word for "community"—when instructing the people how to reflect God's holiness in the world: "Speak to the whole Israelite community [*adat*], and say to them: You shall be holy, for I, the Eternal your God, am holy" (Leviticus 19:2). Since the Numbers text referred to ten scouts as a community, the Rabbis again deduce that ten constitutes the minimum needed for worship as a community. Yet this second proof text speaks not to the holiness of the Israelites inside the *Mishkan*, but rather to their ethical acts in the world around them.

The sacred work of Jewish community prescribed through the text in Leviticus is particularly powerful, as it enumerates holy acts that necessitate our civic engagement: alleviating poverty, combating hunger, treating workers fairly, employing ethical business practices, accommodating those affected by disabilities, dispensing justice irrespective of wealth, responding to threats to others' lives, honoring the elderly, and preserving immigrant rights. It is this Holiness Code that stands in the physical center of the Torah and as the centerpiece of the Yom Kippur afternoon service in Reform congregations.

These explanations from the Jerusalem Talmud quantifying a minyan teach about the necessity of community: a minyan is needed for sanctifying God's name inside the sanctuary for prayer and healing, and a minyan is needed for honoring God outside the sanctuary through acts of civic engagement specified in the Holiness Code. Whether one is facing a personal loss or a community crisis, when one cries out "Where is God?" the Jewish community that we create in a minyan offers healing, evoking for many a sense of the Divine Presence among us.

### Connecting Prayer to Civic Engagement

Today, many liberal Jews have an ambivalent relationship with liturgy, and even with the premise of prayer, that is, their relationship with God. The newest Reform prayer book reflects the lack of conformity in how these Jews choose to pray. Prayers in *Mishkan T'filah*, first published in 2007, are frequently offered in four or five versions on the spread of two facing pages—Hebrew, transliterated Hebrew, a faithful translation, and one or two choices of contemporary interpretations.

Even for those whose primary Jewish passion is the pursuit of justice, prayer can provide powerful lessons. First, praying is an active process. The Book of Samuel tells how Hannah struggled with infertility and wept at the House of God while praying passionately for a child. Though the priest Eli at first mistook her for a drunk, the solemnity with which she undertook her task inspired a Rabbinic model for prayer. Based on the misunderstanding stemming from Hannah's lips moving silently in prayer, the Rabbis of the Talmud taught, "One who prays must enunciate the words with one's lips, not only contemplate them in one's heart" (Babylonian Talmud, *B'rachot* 31a).

According to traditional Judaism, in order to fulfill the obligation of worship, specific prayers need to be uttered aloud. The same holds true with the work of civic engagement. Thinking about the social ills of our times is not enough to create change. Literally articulating one's passion for a cause helps to move it forward. To fulfill one's commitment to heal a neighbor's pain, thought must be transformed into words and then into action.

Second, the Rabbis of the Talmud teach that our central prayers of worship (the *Amidah*) must be said while standing, if one is able, and while in a solemn state (Babylonian Talmud, *B'rachot* 30b). Hannah returned to Eli with Samuel, the son she conceived, saying, "I am the woman who stood here beside you and prayed to the Eternal" (I Samuel 1:26). From this comes the requirement for us to stand when we are in the presence of others reciting the *Amidah*, even if we are not praying ourselves (Babylonian Talmud, *B'rachot* 31b). Both prayer and the pursuit of justice require us to stand up for—and with—others.

A third lesson of liturgy that can inspire the Jew who has a passion for justice is that petition is a central component of both prayer and civic engagement. In Judaism, there are three forms of prayer: praise, gratitude, and petition. One praises God for divine strengths, expresses gratitude for what one sees and knows, and lastly, makes requests of God. These are also three compelling paths for speaking truth to power; as we make our requests for change, we praise, we petition, and we thank.

These three forms of prayer are often expressed through a formula called a blessing (a *b'rachah*) that begins with the words "Blessed are

You, Eternal our God." In addition to the blessings uttered in formal worship, there are blessings that are said before enjoying material pleasures, performing a commandment, and celebrating special moments. The Talmud teaches that a person should say one hundred blessings each day (Babylonian Talmud, *M'nachot* 43b). While the majority of liberal and secular Jews do not feel obligated to offer this litany of blessings on a daily basis, words of praise, gratitude, and petition often stream through our minds: praise for the goodness that we do see, gratitude for all that we have, and petitions for a better, safer, and healthier world.

Lastly, Jewish worship is meant to be reflective, motivational, and a source of strength. Rather than God answering our prayers, Jewish prayer emphasizes that God gives us the tools to find the answer ourselves. As the fourth blessing of the *Amidah* states, "You grace humans with knowledge and teach mortals understanding. Graciously share with us Your wisdom, insight, and knowledge."[51]

The power of Jewish prayer lies in the words that are spoken aloud, as Hannah did with solemnity, sincerity, and sobriety. The solace of prayer is found in the ways in which one stands with others. The prayer structure of praise, petition, and thanksgiving broadens our perspective. The strength of prayer lies in tapping a wellspring of resources that starts within oneself and connects to insights and wisdom from the centuries of Jews who have struggled before us.

The path to civic engagement through our synagogues is paved with the rich teachings of Torah. Words, concepts, and teachings surrounding Jewish worship ground our calls for change, even if we are uncomfortable articulating these prayers in their traditional form. When our synagogues embrace civic engagement and we pray as a minyan on the move, our eyes can open to the rich array of Jewish resources that may fortify us on our journey.

## Notes to Chapter 2

31. Paysach J. Krohn, *In the Spirit of the Maggid* (Brooklyn, NY: Mesorah, 2008), 133–35.

32. Elie Wiesel, *One Generation After* (New York: Schocken Books, 1965, 1967, 1970, 2011, paperback edition, 1982), 77.

33. Lesley Sachs, pers. comm.

34. Elise Mikus, as quoted in Connie Dufner, "Temple Members Respond to the News of Egalitarian Prayer at the Kotel," Temple Emanu-El, February 2, 2016, http://www.tedallas.org/blog/temple-members-respond-to-the-news-of-egalitarian-prayer-at-the-kotel.

35. Betsy Kleinman, as quoted in Dufner, "Temple Members Respond," http://www.tedallas.org/blog/temple-members-respond-to-the-news-of-egalitarian-prayer-at-the-kotel.

36. Samuel D. Gruber, "USA: Monuments to Francis Salvador, (Jewish) Hero of the American Revolution," Samuel Gruber's Jewish Art and Monuments, July 6, 2009, http://samgrubersjewishartmonuments.blogspot.com/2009/07/usa-monuments-to-francis-salvador.html.

37. Rev. Dr. Betty Deas Clarke, pers. comm.

38. Bryan Stevenson: Faith Forum interview at Christ Church by Rev. Chip Edens, rector, Charlotte, NC, February 21, 2016, video, 39:50, http://www.christchurchcharlotte.org/sermon/bryan-stevenson/.

39. Amy Mello, quoted in David Lewis, *Hearts and Minds: The Untold Story of How Philanthropy and the Civil Marriage Collaborative Helped America Embrace Marriage Equality* (Amherst, MA: Proteus Fund, 2015), 12, http://www.proteusfund.org/sites/default/files/upload/inline/29/files/CMC%20Case%20Study%20FIN3_pages.pdf.

40. Lewis, *Hearts and Minds*, 9, 13.

41. Jonathan Sacks, *Rabbi Jonathan Sacks's Haggadah* (New York: Continuum International, 2006), 29.

42. Abraham Joshua Heschel, *Moral Grandeur and Spiritual Audacity*, ed. Susannah Heschel (New York: Farrar, Straus and Giroux, 1996), 293.

43. Heschel, *Moral Grandeur and Spiritual Audacity*, vii.

44. As pictured on the cover of this book, Rabbi Maurice Eisendrath, president of the Union of American Hebrew Congregations, is carrying a Torah alongside Dr. Martin Luther King Jr. and Rabbi Abraham Joshua Heschel as part of a Vietnam War protest at Arlington National Cemetary on February 6, 1968.

45. Rabbi Seth Limmer, quoted in "The Journey for Justice," Religious Action Center of Reform Judaism, accessed February 26, 2017, http://www.rac.org/journey-justice.

46. Rabbi Peter Stein, "Marching toward a World of Justice," Religious Action Center of Reform Judaism, August 24, 2015, http://www.rac.org/blog/2015/08/24/marching-toward-world-justice.

47. Translation by American Jewish World Service, On1Foot: Jewish Texts for Social Justice, http://on1foot.org/text/itturei-torah-deuteronomy-2517.

48. Sacks, *Haggadah*, 29.

49. Rabbi Harold M. Schulweis, "Between," in *Hearing the Call Across Traditions: Readings on Faith and Service*, ed. Adam Davis (Woodstock, VT: SkyLight Paths, 2009), 107.

50. Martin Buber, *I and Thou* (New York: Charles Scribner's Sons, 1970).

51. Elyse D. Frishman, ed., *Mishkan T'filah: A Reform Siddur* (New York: CCAR Press, 2007), 84.

# CHAPTER 3

# Responding to Complaints
# on the Journey
## The Teachings and the Realities

A S OUR CONGREGATIONS seek to expand from volunteerism to civic engagement, we face many of the same barriers encountered by the ancient Israelites traveling from slavery in Egypt to the Promised Land. The journey is long and hard, the destination seems elusive, and the people are fearful of new paths. Though we beheld God's presence—in the vision of a pillar of cloud by day and a pillar of fire by night—we questioned and challenged our leadership throughout our wilderness wanderings. Despite exceptional prophets who spoke for us and for God, we doubted whether the path on which we were walking would indeed lead us to a place of promise.

If the Israelites newly freed from the oppressions of slavery were this skeptical of the leadership of Moses in the presence of God, what reactions should clergy and lay leadership expect from today's congregations, comfortably settled inside their synagogue buildings? Four common complaints illustrate the challenges of leading Jewish congregants outside the walls of their synagogue on the journey to civic engagement:

1. Political issues don't belong in the synagogue.
2. Advocating for others doesn't help Jews.
3. We don't have enough money or volunteers to spare.
4. Civic engagement will divide the congregation.

Both Jewish teachings and examples from congregations already engaged in this work offer ways to address these complaints and overcome the challenges of this journey.

COMPLAINT 1: **Political Issues Don't Belong in the Synagogue**

> "I come to synagogue for prayer and comfort,
>     not to be reminded of injustice."
> "Synagogues should focus on Jews, not the
>     larger community."
> "We might lose our nonprofit status."[52]

Congregants who are resistant to their synagogue working for change in their community often claim that political issues don't belong in the synagogue. They maintain that synagogues are there to help Jews, not the larger community. Board members raise the possibility of the synagogue losing its nonprofit status. Others who protest focus on their own needs; they come to the synagogue to find the shelter of peace, prayer, and comfort in a chaotic and painful world. They seek to be insulated, even insular—celebrating the sanctity of what they have rather than being shaken and sobered by the justice that society lacks. But the teachings of our faith and the realities of synagogue life today offer an alternative perspective.

**Political Issues Don't Belong in the Synagogue—The Teachings**
Congregants who rationalize that praying in a synagogue is the most essential religious act fail to recognize that synagogues have windows for a reason—to move their prayers to action. Windows draw us to connect with our community and remind us that our prayers are not divorced from the world around us. Rabbi Chiya bar Abba teaches in the name of Rabbi Yochanan, "One may pray only in a house with windows" (Babylonian Talmud, *B'rachot* 34b). The *Shulchan Aruch* (*Orach Chayim*, 90:4), the core text of Jewish mysticism, recommends that sanctuaries have twelve windows, symbolic of the twelve tribes of Israel.

In ancient Babylon, Daniel prayed in his room with the windows opened toward Jerusalem despite a royal decree forbidding worship directed to anyone other than the king (Daniel 6:8–17). Daniel's commitment to openly praying to God three times a day teaches that Jewish prayer must not be disconnected from the world around us.

The consequences to Daniel—landing in the lion's den—teach that bringing our faith to action and our prayers into practice is not without challenges.

The lion's den of social justice can be a fearful place. Away from the comfort of the sanctuary and thrust up close to poverty, homelessness, human trafficking, and other painful realities of social injustice today, we might wish to be praying safely back in our pews. But like Daniel, we must courageously connect to the world in order to heal it.

Rabbi Abraham Joshua Heschel, one of the most influential Jewish philosophers of the twentieth century, understood the inextricable link between prayer and the earthly struggle for justice. As one of eleven refugee scholars imperiled by the Nazis in Germany and brought to the United States by the Hebrew Union College,[53] Heschel personally knew the horrors that happen when moral voices speak only inside a sanctuary.

Eloquently articulating a theology of a mysterious yet knowable God with whom we can connect in the world, Heschel taught that the goal of prayer is to actualize God's vision for justice. He wrote:

> Prayer is meaningless unless it is subversive, unless it seeks to overthrow and to ruin the pyramids of callousness, hatred, opportunism, falsehoods. The liturgical movement must become a revolutionary movement, seeking to overthrow the forces that continue to destroy the promise, the hope, the vision.[54]

Like the biblical prophets, Heschel believed that prayer in isolation is ineffectual and empty. The sanctity of our utterances inside the sanctuary is dependent on our actions outside. He saw his work in the civil rights movement as a means of honoring God in human beings, specifically in the African-American community, which had long endured humiliation and oppression. Prior to attending a White House meeting on racism, Rabbi Heschel sent a telegram to President John F. Kennedy asking the president to make tangible demands at the meeting:

> We forfeit right to worship God as long as we continue to humiliate negroes. Churches [and] synagogues have failed....Ask

of religious leaders to call for national repentance and personal sacrifice. Let religious leaders donate one month's salary toward fund for negro housing and education. . . . The hour calls for moral grandeur and spiritual audacity.[55]

Heschel saw social justice as both an act of prayer and an obligation of prayer. Personal action must follow petitioning of the Divine.

### Political Issues Don't Belong in the Synagogue—The Realities

Some congregants who seek the solace of prayer in their synagogues may not wish to look outside of the sanctuary windows, but research reveals that the majority of Jews today define their Judaism in terms of social justice and attend synagogue at most a few times each year. Keeping synagogues relevant to all these Jews—providing both comfort and civic engagement—requires an understanding of these loosely affiliated Jews, secular Jews, and Jewish millennials.

The Pew Research Center quantified the profound relevance of social justice to American Jews in their 2013 study *A Portrait of Jewish Americans*. Pew asked nearly thirty-five hundred Jewish respondents across America, "What does it mean to be Jewish?"[56]

For about three-fourths of those surveyed, the top response was that "remembering the Holocaust is an essential part of what being Jewish means to them" (see table 2). Nearly seven out of ten said that leading an ethical and moral life was essential to being Jewish, and more than half cited working for justice and equality.[57]

**Table 2.** Responses to "What's Essential to Being Jewish?"

| | |
|---|---|
| Remembering Holocaust | 73% |
| Leading ethical/moral life | 69 |
| Working for justice/equality | 56 |
| Being intellectually curious | 49 |
| Caring about Israel | 43 |
| Having good sense of humor | 42 |
| Being part of a Jewish community | 28 |
| Observing Jewish law | 19 |
| Eating traditional Jewish foods | 14 |

**Source:** Pew Research Center's Religion and Public Life Project, "A Portrait of Jewish Americans: Findings from a Pew Research Center Survey of U.S. Jews" (Washington, DC: Pew Research Center, 2013), 14.

A common question activists ask one another is "What keeps you up at night?" There is no historical event that disturbs our Jewish sleep more than the Holocaust. One lesson of this tragedy is that we must continue to call out sins of complicity and silence when it comes to hatred and discrimination, teaching the wrongs of remaining a bystander while elevating the righteousness of those who courageously risk their lives or livelihoods to do what is right.

If we consider the category of "Remembering the Holocaust" as an aspect of this vigilance against injustice, then the top three Pew responses capturing expressions of Jewish identity all reflect an overwhelming commitment to social justice for the majority of American Jews today.

Contrast this to the modern Jew's less profound commitment to Jewish ritual and Jewish institutions. More than two-thirds of American Jews are not members of a synagogue;[58] 41 percent seldom or never attend religious services, and another 35 percent attend only a few times per year, combined equaling three-fourths of Jews with loose synagogue attachments at most (see figure 3).[59]

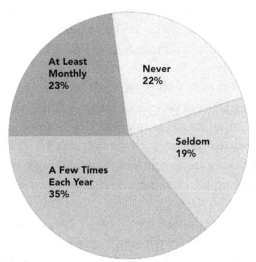

**Figure 3.** Frequency of Synagogue Attendance.

Data from Pew Research Center's Religion and Public Life Project,
A Portrait of Jewish Americans: Findings from a Pew Research Center
Survey of U.S. Jews" (Washington, DC: Pew Research Center, 2013), 75.

Included in the Jewish population are secular Jews, cultural Jews, and Jews of no religion—collectively identified as the "nones."[60] They consider themselves as part of the Jewish people and are proud to be Jewish, but do not consider themselves Jews by religion.[61] For about half of these "nones," social justice is essential to their Jewish identity, and both prayer and traditional synagogue programming are irrelevant to them.[62]

Synagogue leaders worrying about the sustainability of their institutions would be wise to expand the social justice gateways to engage these Jews, who represent 22 percent of the Jewish community.[63] The work of civic engagement is attractive to this demographic, but creative outreach and rebranding of the modern synagogue would be required to reach these "nones." They have already chosen not to participate in the traditional offerings of a synagogue, and their disengagement prevents them from seeing the diverse cultural and social justice offerings now common in synagogues.

Millennials, too, are more inclined to focus their energy and efforts outside the synagogue rather than inside. Millennials—the generation born after 1980 and coming of age at the time of the millennium—are digital natives who find community concerns compelling and yearn to make a difference in the world, yet are skeptical of organized religion.

Only 32 percent of Jewish millennials see themselves as Jews by religion, compared to 78 percent of the overall Jewish population.[64] We would be mistaken to assume that this is solely a reflection of their being in the earlier stages of the cycle of life; all American millennials are less religiously affiliated than their peers of the past four decades, according to a separate Pew study entitled *Millennials: A Portrait of Generation Next*.[65]

Despite their detachment from Jewish institutions, Jewish millennials are proud to be Jewish (96 percent), and they have a strong sense of belonging to the Jewish people (69 percent).[66] And, their definition of what is essential to being Jewish mirrors the average: remembering the Holocaust is top, at 68 percent; leading an ethical life is second, at 65 percent; and working for justice/equality is third, at 55 percent (see table 3).[67]

**Table 3.** Comparison of Millennials' to Total Responses to
"What's Essential to Being Jewish?" (top three responses)

|                          | All  | Millennials |
|--------------------------|------|-------------|
| Remembering Holocaust    | 73%  | 68%         |
| Leading ethical/moral life | 69 | 65          |
| Working for justice/equality | 56 | 55        |

Data from Pew Research Center's Religion and Public Life Project,
"A Portrait of Jewish Americans: Findings from a Pew Research Center
Survey of U.S. Jews" (Washington, DC: Pew Research Center, 2013), 14, 57.

Social justice offers a fertile opportunity to engage the "nones" and the millennials in Jewish life. The potential to reconnect these Jews to our institutions requires rethinking our outreach to address the meaning and sense of purpose that these Jews seek. If we are successful attracting them, the friendships and sense of community that will almost certainly follow will have the power to keep them engaged. Enabling these two demographics—the "nones" and the millennials—to experience a new way of expressing their Judaism in the world outside could inspire them to count themselves among the congregation. But this requires redefining the traditional functions of the synagogue, creating more opportunities to engage outside its walls.

Civic engagement adds a fourth leg to the synagogue's three traditional legs of prayer, Torah, and acts of loving-kindness. To those who challenge this premise fearing threats to a congregation's nonprofit status, it is highly unlikely that such a path would threaten your synagogue's nonprofit status with your state or the Internal Revenue Service. While your board's legal counsel undoubtedly will want to investigate the state and federal regulations themselves, the two key issues are ones that temples already manage tightly: not endorsing a candidate for political office and not devoting more than a specific percentage of the synagogue's budget to political activities. No synagogue that we interviewed came close to spending the amount of money on the specific activities of political advocacy that would jeopardize their nonprofit status, and President Trump's May 2017 Executive Order Promoting Free Speech and Religious Liberty specifically protects religious institutions against adverse action to their tax status.[68]

Stephen Phillips, of Temple Beth El in Charlotte, provides a model for redefining religiosity. Unlike his grandfather, who prayed three times each day, Phillips expresses his own Jewish commitment by developing a synagogue advocacy program on aging, serving on SPICE (the committee of seniors), and participating on the Tzedek Council (the social justice committee). These commitments bring him to synagogue almost daily, which his grandson perceives as religious devotion, paralleling how Phillips had viewed his own grandfather. Philips reflected, "My grandson (age eight) says I'm the most religious person he knows. My grandfather davened three times a day. Am I a faker that he thinks that?"

Just as religious devotion can mean worshiping three times daily, it can also mean serving the community to bring the values of Judaism into the world. In expanding our definition of being religious, both affiliated and unaffiliated Jews can grow to view civic engagement as a fulfillment of the values taught inside the synagogue; it is an obligation articulated in our liturgy and learning. Political issues belong in the synagogue so that our prayers for justice are meaningful and our synagogues remain relevant to more American Jews.

## Complaint 2: Advocating for Others Doesn't Help Jews

> "Time in the community takes away from nurturing
>    the congregation."
> "We cannot afford to divert our attention from
>    the Jewish community."
> "Antisemitism is rising. If we advocate for others,
>    who worries about us?"

Some congregants fear that their synagogue advocating for others is not good for the Jewish community. They worry that time spent on civic engagement cannibalizes time nurturing the congregation.

Some respond to antisemitism with a defensive stance: since others don't defend us, we are not obligated to defend others. But the teachings of our faith and the realities of advocating for others defuse these complaints.

## Advocating for Others Doesn't Help Jews—The Teachings

The ancient Rabbis command us to help non-Jews "for the sake of peace," recognizing that these acts build goodwill for us in the larger community: "One sustains poor gentiles along with poor Jews, and one visits sick gentiles along with sick Jews, and one buries dead gentiles along with dead Jews. All this is done on account of the ways of peace" (Babylonian Talmud, *Gittin* 61a).

Building strong bridges of support across lines of difference through civic engagement strengthens the Jewish threads in the multicultural fabric of our country. We know well what can happen when any minority group suffers from inequality; it can easily lead to dehumanization and demonization of the "other."

Pastor Martin Niemöller, the Lutheran conscientious objector who was imprisoned in a concentration camp during the Holocaust, famously said:

> First they came for the Socialists, and I did not speak out—
>   Because I was not a Socialist.
> Then they came for the Trade Unionists, and I did not speak out—
>   Because I was not a Trade Unionist.
> Then they came for the Jews, and I did not speak out—
>   Because I was not a Jew.
> Then they came for me—
>   and there was no one left to speak for me.[69]

In 2017, Rabbi Michael Adam Latz, of Congregation Shir Tikvah in Minneapolis, Minnesota, wrote an updated version of Pastor Niemöller's message:

> In response to Martin Niemoller (*z"l*) [of blessed memory]:
> First they came for the African Americans and I spoke up—
>   Because I am my sisters' and my brothers' keeper.

And then they came for the women and I spoke up—
  Because women hold up half the sky.
And then they came for the immigrants and I spoke up—
  Because I remember the ideals of our democracy.
And then they came for the Muslims and I spoke up—
  Because they are my cousins and we are one human family.
And then they came for the Native Americans and Mother
Earth and I spoke up—
  Because the blood-soaked land cries and the mountains weep.
They keep coming.
We keep rising up.
Because we Jews know the cost of silence.
We remember where we came from.
And we will link arms, because when you come for our
neighbors, you come for us—
  And THAT just won't stand.[70]

Maintaining a democracy requires that no voice is stifled and no minority is relegated to second-class status. In supporting the voices and protecting the rights of other marginalized communities— whether Muslims, African-Americans, refugees, LGBTQ individuals, Native Americans, the disabled, among so many more—we are working to protect our own rights.

### Advocating for Others Doesn't Help Jews—The Realities
The diversity of American Jews today is far different than in previous generations when the stereotypical congregant was married to another white Jew, of Eastern European (Ashkenazi) descent, and heterosexual. Today, 44 percent of all married Jews are currently with a non-Jewish spouse. The number goes up to 58 percent of those married since 2000.[71] Six percent of American Jews are people of color.[72] Non-Orthodox American seminaries ordain LGBTQ Jews as clergy, and even some Orthodox congregations now welcome LGBTQ Jews into their communities.

While fears of the "other" can sometimes cause people to resist engaging with those who are different, this increasing diversity means that those "others" include members of our Jewish family—Jews of color, LGBTQ Jews, and non-Jews married to Jews. Outreach to people of color, or to people of different sexual orientation or gender expression, or to those who are in some other way different from ourselves, sends a message that our communities are welcoming. Although it may be far easier or more comfortable to create a congregation with people of similar backgrounds, our experiences at Temple Beth El in Charlotte are that outreach to those "others" makes the Jewish community stronger. This approach helps us see that those "others" whom we sometimes avoid are, in fact, much like ourselves.

Consider the story of Margie and Jo Anne (last names intentionally omitted). Margie was originally introduced to Judaism when she was raising Jewish children with her Jewish husband. More than a decade after her divorce from him, she and her partner, Jo Anne, came to Temple Beth El to learn more about Judaism, attracted by the temple's open and affirming policy toward LGBTQ Jews. They were moved to join the temple in 2010, and both converted to Judaism after a yearlong course of study and engagement in Jewish life. In 2011, they were among the seven couples who traveled to Washington, DC, with Rabbi Schindler and other clergy to be legally married. For years, they have rarely missed a Shabbat evening service. In 2014, Margie's wife Jo Anne assumed the leadership of the *chevrah kadisha*, the holy society organization within the congregation that prepares the dead for burial. In 2015, Jo Anne studied Hebrew and celebrated an adult bat mitzvah, and Margie served on the temple finance committee. Margie and Jo Anne are an example of how working to ensure an inclusive community has attracted a flow of diverse Jews into the synagogue and inspired them to share their time, talent, and sacred gifts with the congregation.

When the skeptics claim that our role as a synagogue is to help Jews, they are closing their eyes to the modern-day reality that we have many non-Jews in our congregational communities. Temple Beth El has learned the value of a warm and welcoming embrace of non-Jews. For example, the temple's clergy officiates at interfaith marriages for couples committed to keeping Jewish homes. In these families, the non-Jewish partners who choose to join the temple are accorded full membership, with the exceptions of serving on the board and voting on the ritual committee. Recognizing the important role that non-Jewish parents serve in raising Jewish children, the temple routinely honors and expresses gratitude to non-Jewish parents who enroll their children in Hebrew School and who support their sons and daughters on the journey to bar and bat mitzvah.

This respect and acceptance contributed to so many non-Jewish spouses converting after years of marriage—realizing they were already living a Jewish life—that a second conversion class was established for them called MOJO, Making Our Judaism Official. (For both practical and philosophical reasons, the class was later combined with the main conversion class.) Regardless of their path to Judaism, these Jews-by-choice have emerged as committed Jews and often temple leaders, giving endless hours to lifting up the Jewish community.

Conversely, our silence on issues of diversity alienates those in our congregation who represent today's heterogeneous Jewish community. In the wake of the 2014 acquittal of the Ferguson (Missouri) police officer and subsequent racial violence, clergy at one Reform congregation (name and city intentionally omitted) decided not to speak from the pulpit on the conflict, deeming it outside the Jewish sphere of concern. On the following Shabbat, services were conducted by the temple youth group on the theme of social justice, and a black Jewish teen said sadly before his portion of the service, "I would like to say some things about the current situation in our country, but I'm not sure everyone would agree, so I'll just not say them."[73] Now that the diversity of our congregations has been enriched—no longer exclusively white, Ashkenazi, heterosexual Jews—the definition of what constitutes the Jewish perspective requires expansion.

A synagogue presence in the broader community inspires the unaffiliated to rethink their assumptions about the relevance of synagogue life. It sends a message to interfaith couples, to LGBTQ people, to those with special needs, to ethnically and racially diverse Jewish families, and to so many others that the congregation is not insular—focusing only on itself—but open to the growth that can emerge from education, dialogue, and collaboration. Advocacy on behalf of those considered to be the "other" communicates that the synagogue is a place where the Jewish family of today—in all its rich diversity—would be welcomed.

Supporting the non-Jewish community for the sake of peace has been the practice of Jews from Talmudic times through today. The ambiguity of whether our goal is serving the broader community or our own self-interest is both irrelevant and instructive. Our work in the non-Jewish community models an inclusive society that values each citizen. We use our power to amplify others' voices, sending the message that we value the "other" and thereby opening the door for many Jewish "others" to join us.

## COMPLAINT 3: We Don't Have Enough Money or Volunteers to Spare

"We don't have enough money."
"We don't have enough volunteers."
"Money and volunteers will be diverted
from Jewish causes for this."

Some congregants worry that extending ourselves outside the synagogue walls will strain our resources. They are concerned that we don't have enough money or volunteers to sustain involvement in community causes or that these precious resources will be diverted from Jewish causes.

### We Don't Have Enough to Spare—The Teachings

Consider the lesson of two seas in Israel. The Sea of Galilee is filled with fresh water, and its lushness contributes to its popularity as a vacation destination for Israelis and tourists. In an odd sequence of events, the spring waters of the Jordan River that feed into the Sea of Galilee then flow south into the Dead Sea, augmented along the way by thermal springs. But instead of continuing on their southern path, the waters of the Jordan River are hoarded in the Dead Sea. There, the water evaporates into the atmosphere, leaving salts and minerals behind to inhibit any life in the Dead Sea and along its shores.

The metaphor is that the Sea of Galilee thrives because a drop flows out for every drop that enters from the River Jordan. Like the Sea of Galilee, human beings who give are the ones who thrive. The same can be said for synagogues. Giving generously of time and treasure creates positive energy and an elevated image that attract still more resources to fulfill greater needs.

This lesson of giving versus hoarding is emphasized by Rabbi Nachman of Breslov, who taught that *tzedakah* should be given "with both hands" (Reb Nachman, *Sefer HaMidot*, "T'filah" I, 45; "Tzedakah" I, 27). We should not give halfheartedly, thinking about ourselves as we give to others, but wholly.

An experienced and talented fundraiser, Lynne Twist echoes the lesson of the Sea of Galilee and Rabbi Nachman with the story of a fundraising event in the basement of a church in Harlem, where Gertrude, an elderly woman of modest means, was eager to give what little she had to the Hunger Project. Gertrude donated fifty dollars that she had earned from washing clothes, saying:

> To me, money is a lot like water. For some folks it rushes through their life like a raging river. Money comes through my life like a little trickle. But I want to pass it on in a way that does the most good for the most folks. I see that as my right and as my responsibility. It's also my joy.[74]

Whether money is abundant or trickles in, receiving and giving as part of the divine flow becomes life-sustaining. Both the Sea of Galilee and the elderly donor to the Hunger Project thrive because they give freely. Giving with one hand or closing one's wallet and one's heart to hoard is life-limiting to people, just as hoarding water inhibits life in the Dead Sea.

The Book of Proverbs tells us that "righteous giving [*tzedakah*] saves from death" (Proverbs 10:2). *Tzedakah* saves the recipient from death—from hunger, from freezing, from sweltering, and from despair. But *tzedakah* also saves the *giver*—from spiritual death. Observing the pain of others without responding hardens hearts and leads to spiritual flatlining.

The same holds true on a congregational level. Congregations can thrive sharing a portion of what they have with others, or they can hoard their own resources for themselves, remaining insular, stagnant, and stifled. Truly, there is enough.

### We Don't Have Enough to Spare—The Realities

Shalom Park is a fifty-four-acre campus in Charlotte, hosting both a Reform and a Conservative synagogue, a Jewish community center, the local Jewish Federation, and many other Jewish agencies. In 2011, eight of these agencies collaborated to sponsor and host a Freedom School site, a summer literacy program created by the Children's Defense Fund (CDF) for children living in poverty.

Even in the wilderness where the Israelites focused only on the immediate challenges of the sand beneath their feet, there were those who could see more clearly the potential of arriving to a more promised place. Such was the case in starting the Shalom Park Freedom School site, where some were worried about draining donors and volunteers from existing programs. But others, like Sue Worrel, executive director of the Jewish Federation of Greater Charlotte, saw the possibilities of attracting more people and resources. Worrel explained:

> The Shalom Park Freedom School can open doors to members of our community who have otherwise not been engaged. As with all Jewish communities, there are people in Charlotte for whom the conventional Jewish community model holds no appeal. The Shalom Park Freedom School can enable these community members to create a connection between their passion for social justice and their previously unengaged Judaism, while at the same time offering an opportunity for all of us to put our Jewish values to work.

The Jewish Federation bears the greatest burden of fundraising for the Charlotte Jewish community. Raising funds for the Freedom

School's initial year was unwittingly started during Federation "blackout"—when all participating agencies stop their own fund-raising so that Federation can reach its goals. Yet Worrel, the leader of the agency for whom a new fundraising project could arguably be construed as the greatest risk, recognized the potential gains and collaborated with the project fundraisers during the blackout so that both the Jewish Federation and the Shalom Park Freedom School site could meet their financial goals.

Since that first year, the Jewish Federation has consistently supported the Shalom Park Freedom School site, allocating funds along with other resources every year. Contrary to the worst fears of some, the Jewish Federation has actually gained new donors—and seen increased contributions from some existing donors—as a result of its support of this project.

Fears of diverting existing volunteers were similarly groundless. Consider the story of Deidre (last name withheld), the first co-chair of the Shalom Park Freedom School site. Deidre had recently re-tired from volunteering for many years at Habitat for Humanity, a Christian-led agency, when Rabbi Schindler recruited her to lead the Shalom Park Freedom School. A "High Holy Day Jew" who paid dues to Temple Beth El but rarely attended, Deidre became far more connected to the Jewish community as a consequence of this new involvement. She became a Jewish Federation donor, consulted with Jewish Family Services, and even was called upon to complete a weekday minyan at the Conservative temple. In an interfaith mar-riage, she and her husband made their first trip to Israel a few years later with their children, and subsequently their daughter chose to become a bat mitzvah. By the time the Shalom Park Freedom School site was in its fourth summer, Deidre had joined the board of Temple Beth El.

Deidre's journey to wholehearted engagement is not unique. Many interviews revealed how Jewish institutional investment in the broader community connected uninvolved Jews, expanding the volunteer base rather than cannibalizing it.

Dr. Nick Morse, at Temple Israel in Boston, Massachusetts, was one of many lay leaders interviewed who cited his civic engagement work as the gateway to deepening his synagogue involvement. When Temple Israel took on Massachusetts health care reform with the Greater Boston Interfaith Organization, Dr. Morse was energized and inspired to work on his temple's behalf, mostly outside the synagogue walls. After the bill passed, his new connection to the temple led him to work on an internal project on aging and join a leadership committee.

> This [health care advocacy work outside the temple walls] changed my relationship with the temple. . . . I was not really present at temple. [The aging initiative] was my first visible temple leadership. As a result, I was invited to join the Leadership Council at temple. . . . Now I am at temple every other week at some meeting or function.

When we stop to reflect, or perhaps even to map our assets, we realize that we have seats in our sanctuary, space in our social halls, relationships with organizations in the community, and skills that can support the work we need to do.[75] The examples from the Shalom Park Freedom School and Temple Israel illustrate how there is enough—enough money for fundraising and enough volunteers for all the worthwhile projects. Like the Sea of Galilee and the church worker in Harlem, the more we give, the more we are enriched. Rather than being afraid, we should have faith in the continuity of both the divine flow of blessings and the human flow of time, talent, and treasures when our community shares what we have with others.

### COMPLAINT 4: Civic Engagement Will Divide the Congregation

"Taking a public stand will antagonize some congregants."
"Some in our congregation disagree on these issues."
"We cannot run the risk of losing members over this issue."

Some congregations worry that taking a public stand on issues will antagonize those congregants who disagree with the synagogue's position. Board members especially are often concerned about the risk of losing synagogue members. But establishing a framework for advocacy and creating a process for intentionally and reflectively selecting issues help congregations manage these fears.

## Civic Engagement Will Divide the Congregation—
## The Teachings

Judaism is built on dialogue and debate—from Abraham's first argument with God in Genesis to the thousands of pages of the Talmud to today's synagogue board meetings and study groups.

In Genesis, God considers hiding the plans to destroy Sodom and Gomorrah but instead shares them with Abraham, using debate as an educational tool. "Should I hide from Abraham what I am doing? . . . For I have selected him, so that he may teach his children and those who come after him to keep the way of the Eternal, doing what is right and just" (Genesis 18:17–19).

Abraham successfully bargains with God, altering the original plan. If there are but ten righteous individuals in Sodom and Gomorrah (the same number composing a minyan), God's wrathful retribution will be assuaged. While Abraham ultimately loses his quest to save Sodom and Gomorrah from destruction, he learns from his debate that God yearns for human beings to challenge the inequities and iniquities that they see.

The Talmud—the foundational document of ancient, medieval, and modern rabbinic thought and teaching—consists almost entirely of arguments, with the debates of the Rabbis brilliantly woven together across centuries. Theories are proposed, explored, contradicted, and clarified as laws, ethics, values, and their limits are ultimately explained and transmitted from one generation to the next. The Mishnah teaches us to distinguish between worthy and unworthy arguments:

> Every argument that is for the sake of heaven's name, it is destined to endure. But if it is not for the sake of heaven's name—it is not destined to endure. What is an example of an argument for the sake of heaven's name? The argument of Hillel and Shammai. What is an example of an argument not for the sake of heaven's name? The argument of Korach and all of his congregation. (Pirkei Avot 5:17)

What was Korach's failing? Korach revolted against Moses, together with 250 leaders of the community, saying to him in anger, "You have gone too far! . . . Why then do you [Moses and Aaron] raise yourselves above the Eternal's congregation?" (Numbers 16:3).

Korach's sin was not his rebellion, but that he was a rebel without a cause. He did not care to improve the lives of those in his community nor broaden their understanding of what God wants; he simply sought power and the priesthood for himself. Korach compounded his wrongdoing with his confrontational approach and his desire to sow the seeds of disharmony and conflict. In the Book of Numbers, the ground opened up and swallowed Korach and his family alive, while a fire consumed the 250 chieftains he brought with him. From this event, a negative commandment is derived: "Anyone who is unyielding in a dispute violates a negative command, as it is written, 'And let him not be as Korach, and as his company' (Numbers 17:5)"[76] (Babylonian Talmud, *Sanhedrin* 110a).

By contrast, the Rabbis elevate the debates between the Houses of Hillel and Shammai (Beit Hillel and Beit Shammai). The Talmud records no fewer than three hundred arguments between the two schools. In the vast majority of cases, Jewish law was based upon the logic of Hillel, which leads the Rabbis of the Talmud to pose the following question:

> Since [a divine voice declared] both these and those are the words of the living God, why were Beit Hillel privileged to have the halachah established in accordance with their opinion? The reason is that they were agreeable and forbearing, showing restraint when affronted, and when they taught the halachah they would teach both their own statements and the statements of Beit Shammai. Moreover, when they formulated their teachings and cited a dispute, they prioritized the statements of Beit Shammai to their own statements, in deference to Beit Shammai. (Babylonian Talmud, *Eiruvin* 13b)

The structure and lessons of the Talmud teach that healthy debate entails allowing both sides of an issue to be heard, honored, and recorded, whether it is a ritual issue or a matter of justice. The esteemed Hillel-Shammai debates acknowledge the truth contained in contradictory perspectives and avoid belittling those who stand on the opposing side of an issue. The United States Supreme Court embraces this same process of valuing and preserving both the majority and the minority opinions.

The challenges in our country today are too formidable for many Jews to ignore. Synagogues eager to avoid divisiveness would be wise to consider that the greater risk is that these debates will erupt at inappropriate times or without ground rules of respect and foundations of facts. Worthy and enduring debates are those that are for "the sake of heaven's name," serving a higher purpose. We can maintain a vibrant congregation when our arguments are not about a single person's issues of power, but about trying to understand the holiest path we can collectively take.

## Civic Engagement Will Divide the Congregation— The Realities

The risk of dividing the congregation by venturing into civic engagement frightens many temple leaders. Yet, clergy and lay leaders whose temples have already stepped out into the public space consistently debunk these fears. How have experienced congregations avoided divisiveness? How can congregations contemplating this journey overcome the barriers that they perceive?

In part 3 of this book, entitled "Your Guide to Plugging into Civic Engagement," we provide a framework to alleviate these fears and avoid these pitfalls, illustrating a path with real examples from synagogues across our country. The three chapters that comprise the guide are intended to assist congregations as they institutionalize civic engagement alongside the traditional synagogue offerings of worship services, Torah study, and acts of loving-kindness.

The journey of civic engagement is impossible without effective leadership. In chapter 7, "Rabbis, Lay Leaders, and Congregations: A Threefold Cord Is Not Readily Broken," we discuss the respective leadership roles of clergy and laypeople. This chapter includes ten steps for rabbis to forestall controversy and a strategy (the Five $P$'s) for developing successful lay leadership. The role of the congregation is illustrated in terms of the covenantal relationship that calls us to stand with the Jewish community.

Detailed blueprints are critical to guiding your congregation. In chapter 8, "Blueprints of the Tabernacle: God Is in the Details," we share four models successfully used by synagogues to guide their civic engagement work. A series of questions helps you select among the Resolution Model, Agenda Model, Coalition Model, or Traction Model, based on the dynamics of your congregation.

Choosing the issue with which to engage is perhaps the most complicated part of this journey. In chapter 9, "The Cycle of Civic Engagement: The Work That Fills the *Mishkan*," we offer guidelines for wisely selecting your issues. The cycle of listening, educating, strategizing, acting, and reflecting provides a thoughtful framework for making meaningful change as a synagogue.

Engaging in each step with deliberation enables the congregation to understand where its members stand and sensitively address their differences. Rabbi Asher Knight reflected on how this process worked at Temple Emanu-El in Dallas:

> We created ample opportunities for members to express their values and beliefs. The two listening campaigns calmed down differences of opinion and created opportunities for people to be heard. Members with dissimilar worldviews also saw the numbers of people who took another side. They heard their stories of pain, suffering, and desire to make a change. This is the Jewish way. The Talmud respects the diversity of voices and values them by recording multiple arguments and the minority opinions. But the Talmud also takes the side of a majority opinion. Congregations can, too, if they create opportunities for people to feel heard and valued for their opinions.

These same challenges of divisiveness arise around the issue of advocating for Israel. Since the Pew Study tells us that 43 percent of Jews identify "caring about Israel" as essential to their Jewish identity,[77] some might erroneously assume that because Israel is important to so many and because Israel advocacy is helping not the "other,"

but our fellow Jews, that less controversy would be created by embarking on this path. The reality is that in most congregations today,
addressing Israel advocacy does not mitigate but rather intensifies
passionate debate and divisiveness. Any advocacy, whether focused
on Israel or America, would benefit from the approach outlined in
this book.

While many worry that civic engagement will be divisive, congregations who have overcome their fears have found it to be an overwhelming source of pride. Lay leaders and clergy commented on the
gratification congregants feel from this work—even those who are
on the sidelines:

> People take an enormous amount of pride in the work the tem-
> ple congregants have done, even if they are not involved. Many
> go out of their way to tell me how they appreciate and value
> the work, what an enormous sense of pride they have in our
> temple. (Janet Goldenberg, Temple Beth Elohim, Wellesley,
> Massachusetts)

> Social justice work is a source of huge pride at Temple Israel
> [Boston, Massachusetts]. It doesn't mean that all people who
> take pride in it are actively engaged. They take pride in knowing
> that their community is committed to making a righteous im-
> pact beyond its walls. They celebrate that. (Rabbi Matt Soffer)

> People feel better about Temple Israel [Tallahassee, Florida]
> because we were involved. We reported it in the temple bulletin,
> there was a general feel-good nature for the congregants who
> were not involved. (Barry Moline)

Like Abraham, we have been called to pursue the path of justice and
righteousness in partnership with God. We cannot remain passive;
we must wrestle with the tough issues of our day. Rather than sowing
divisiveness, civic engagement can become a unifying force, creating
both pride in our institutions and positive change in our communities and our country.

## In Conclusion
We are Jews. We complain. Throughout our wilderness wanderings, we challenged Moses. Today, some congregants email board

members when their synagogue takes action, and other congregants contact clergy when their synagogue fails to take action. But ultimately our leadership strives to respond with strength and understanding in order to guide us forward.

The complaints delineated in this chapter are about our fears, not about the core teachings of our faith, nor about the realities of leading our synagogues on a path of civic engagement. Social justice is work that is deeply rooted in Judaism—commanded by our faith and an essential expression of Judaism for the majority of Jews today. Fighting for equality for others offers additional benefits, creating a welcoming congregational environment for the increasingly diverse Jewish population. Those who embark on this journey of civic engagement ultimately learn that we do have enough human and financial resources to share, as giving leads to a greater flow of energy and funds.

Civic engagement has become a source of pride for synagogues that have overcome these fears and ventured thoughtfully on this journey, ultimately recharging synagogue life. Making time and space to hear debates for the sake of heaven enables us to fulfill our religious mandate and embrace the rich legacy bequeathed to us by Abraham of challenging, questioning, and instructing our children and those who come after us to do what is right and just.

## Notes to Chapter 3

52. These comments—and the ones that follow each of the other three complaints—are illustrative of the resistance we hear to changing the historical focus of American synagogues.

53. Michael Meyer, *Judaism Within Modernity: Essays on Jewish History and Religion* (Detroit: Wayne State University Press, 2001), 345.

54. Abraham Joshua Heschel, *Moral Grandeur and Spiritual Audacity*, 262–63.

55. Abraham Joshua Heschel, *Abraham Joshua Heschel: Essential Writings*, ed. Susannah Heschel, Modern Spiritual Masters Series (Maryknoll, NY: Orbis Books, 2011), 64–65.

56. *A Portrait of Jewish Americans: Findings from a Pew Research Center Survey of U.S. Jews* (Washington, D.C.: Pew Research Center Religion and Public

Life Project, 2013), 119, http://www.pewforum.org/2013/jewish-american-beliefs-attitudes-culture-survey/.

57. *A Portrait of Jewish Americans*, 14.

58. *A Portrait of Jewish Americans*, 60.

59. *A Portrait of Jewish Americans*, 75.

60.*A Portrait of Jewish Americans*, 7–8, 18.

61. *A Portrait of Jewish Americans*, 52.

62.*A Portrait of Jewish Americans*, 55, 60.

63. *A Portrait of Jewish Americans*, 32.

64.*A Portrait of Jewish Americans*, 7.

65. *Millennials: A Portrait of Generation Next* (Washington, DC: Pew Research Center, 2010), 89), http://www.pewsocialtrends.org/files/2010/10/millennials-confident-connected-open-to-change.pdf.

66.*A Portrait of Jewish Americans*, 52.

67. *A Portrait of Jewish Americans*, 57.

68. Donald J. Trump, "Presidential Executive Order Promoting Free Speech and Religious Liberty," May 4, 2017, The White House, https://www.whitehouse.gov/the-press-office/2017/05/04/presidential-executive-order-promoting-free-speech-and-religious-liberty.

69. United States Holocaust Memorial Museum, "Martin Niemöller: 'First They Came for the Socialists . . . ,'" Holocaust Encyclopedia, accessed February 27, 2017, https://www.ushmm.org/wlc/en/article.php?ModuleId=10007392.

70. Jonathan Kligler, "Remembering the Words of Rev. Martin Niemoller," Lev Shalem Institute of the Woodstock Jewish Congregation, January 5, 2017, http://lsi-wjc.org/remembering-the-words-of-rev-martin-niemoller/.

71. *A Portrait of Jewish Americans*, 9.

72.*A Portrait of Jewish Americans*, 46.

73. The source of this quote, not the teen himself, has asked to remain anonymous.

74. Lynne Twist, *The Soul of Money: Reclaiming the Wealth of Our Inner Resources* (New York: Norton, 2003), 100.

75. Luther K. Snow, "The Quick and Simple Congregational Asset-Mapping Experience," in *The Power of Asset Mapping: How Your Congregation Can Act on Its Gifts* (Herndon, VA: Alban Institute, 2004), https://alban.org/uploadedFiles/Alban/Bookstore/pdf/resources/Asset_Mapping/resource2.pdf.

76. Translation from *The Soncino Babylonian Talmud, Seder Nezikin*, vol. 3 (London: Soncino Press, 1935), 755.

77. *A Portrait of Jewish Americans*, 14.

# How Civic Engagement Recharges the Synagogue

Rabbi Jonah Dov Pesner
*Religious Action Center of Reform Judaism*

Picture this scene: A sixth-grade pre–bat mitzvah student named Hannah is a featured speaker at her temple in a meeting organized by the Greater Boston Interfaith Organization, a coalition of fifty institutions working for social justice. In the sanctuary, hundreds of people have gathered—Jews along with allies across lines of difference. Jewish texts on social justice are studied, prayers are offered, and songs are sung. Seated on the stage are several state representatives and senators. Various speakers discuss the problems of homelessness and the lack of affordable housing that are challenging the community. Hannah explains that as part of her bat mitzvah celebration, she and her peers organized social action projects; hers was to visit homebound senior citizens. She then tells the story of asking one senior why she couldn't come to temple anymore. The woman told her that she couldn't navigate her stairs anymore and couldn't afford to move houses. Hannah asks those assembled the following simple, agitational question:

> How could it be that a member of her temple could no longer participate in Jewish life because she cannot afford to move houses?

After a long pause, she asks each representative and senator to commit to voting for the $200 million Affordable Housing Trust Fund. Each of them does so on the spot.

Hannah Yarmolinsky's experience, and those of her classmates and fellow congregants, is not unique. It is an example of the transformative power of synagogue social justice. It demonstrates how civic engagement gives meaning and purpose to individuals and families as they engage in study and ritual related to important Jewish life-cycle moments. It also demonstrates that pursuing justice as a congregation strengthens the very institution itself while improving the community at the same time.

There are several powerful lessons in Hannah's story. First, the pursuit of social justice empowers congregations to act on enduring Jewish values and live the teachings of Torah—to "practice what they preach." Second, when individuals and families participate in serious civic engagement, the ancient rituals and values of Jewish texts come alive and become relevant in their real lives. Third, the commitment to congregational social justice builds community within the temple and beyond, as members come together to act collectively to improve the community; social action initiatives engage more members more broadly and inspire new leaders to become more deeply involved.

Synagogues must act for social justice in order to be authentic houses of Jewish learning. This principle is affirmed in the Talmudic debate between Rabbi Akiva and Rabbi Tarfon on the question "Is study greater or is action greater?" Rabbi Tarfon answered that action is greater. Rabbi Akiva asserted that study was greater, and the Sages agree, because study leads to action (Babylonian Talmud, *Kiddushin* 40b). In the daily liturgy recited in synagogues, we read, *Eilu d'varim she-ein lahem shiur, she-adam ocheil peiroteihem*, "These are things that are limitless, of which a person enjoys the fruit of this world, while the principal remains in the world to come."[78] This prayer describes many beautiful and meaningful mitzvot (commandments) that are sacred acts of justice and mercy; and the prayer concludes, "But the study of Torah encompasses them all."

I witnessed another example of the intersection of Jewish study, ritual, and action when my congregation, Temple Israel in Boston, welcomed janitors to join us for Sukkot, the joyful harvest holiday during which we give thanks for the earth's bounty. A local service workers' union had asked us to support these low-wage custodians, who were underpaid, overworked, and had no health care benefits— the very opposite of a bountiful existence. The workers were in the midst of a "Justice for Janitors" campaign to improve their working conditions and compensation. On Sukkot, the janitors dwelt in our sukkah and told their painful stories. Together we studied Jewish sources on fair treatment of workers; we also shook the *lulav* and the *etrog* (symbols of the harvest). For the many people present that night, the texts were never more relevant nor the ritual of *ushpizin* (welcoming guests into the sukkah) more meaningful.

Because social justice brings Judaism to life and makes it relevant in people's real lives, it often engages more members. More people participate, and their participation deepens as they take on leadership roles. Many congregations organize "listening campaigns" to engage dozens, if not hundreds of people in social justice work by probing their concerns, passions, and common values. People are asked to discuss what role they think their congregation should play in addressing the real problems they experience in the world and what Jewish values animate their passions. In one such campaign at Temple Emanu-El in Dallas, many members expressed their frustration with an unjust health-care system. There was widespread concern that lower-income people didn't have the same access to quality care as the more privileged did. In response, joining together with churches through Dallas Area Interfaith,[79] many members of the congregation worked with the city to set up a medical device exchange to make sure medical equipment was repurposed and reached people who needed it. The medical exchange was but one of many initiatives Temple Emanu-El launched that brought hundreds of members to participate, and congregations across North America similarly engage their membership through civic engagement. The leader of the effort in Dallas ultimately became the temple president, as do many members who become passionate about their temple when it becomes a force for justice in the community.

Chicago Sinai Congregation, the oldest Reform Jewish temple

in the city, engaged hundreds of members in various campaigns to improve the local public schools, increase health-care access, and reduce gun violence. One member, Alec Harris, organized members of Sinai to join with members of churches through United Power (an IAF affiliate) to close down a significant gun dealer, who was responsible for many of the weapons used in Chicagoland murders. Alec also went on to become the temple's president.

Ultimately, congregation-based civic engagement builds stronger community even beyond the walls of the synagogue. Many congregations have organized efforts to stand with local Muslim communities, whose members have faced harassment and whose mosques have been vandalized and construction opposed. Others have worked with predominantly black churches to hold law enforcement accountable to principles of equality and racial justice. Still others have partnered with local churches and immigrant rights groups to become "sanctuary" congregations for undocumented immigrants. In all these cases, congregations and their members become more deeply interconnected and relevant in their own communities.

The call to Jews to act for justice is expressed most clearly by the prophet Isaiah. Picture this scene: Thousands have gathered on Yom Kippur, the holiest day of the year in the Temple in Jerusalem, the holiest space on earth. Amid the praying and fasting, the prophet barges in and cries out:

> Because on your fast day
> You see to your business
> And oppress all your laborers!
> Because you fast in strife and contention,
> And you strike with a wicked fist!
> Your fasting today is not such
> As to make your voice heard on high.
> Is such the fast I desire,
> A day for people to starve their bodies?
> Is it bowing the head like a bulrush
> And lying in sackcloth and ashes?
> Do you call that a fast,

A day when the Eternal is favorable?
No, this is the fast I desire:
To unlock fetters of wickedness,
And untie the cords of the yoke
To let the oppressed go free;
To break off every yoke.
It is to share your bread with the hungry,
And to take the wretched poor into your home;
When you see the naked, to clothe them,
And not to ignore your own kin.

(Isaiah 58:3–7)

Franz Kafka portrayed the scene as if a leopard entered the sanctuary. Isaiah succeeded in utterly disrupting the ancient Jews in their sanctuary and holding them accountable to their higher purpose. Like Hannah's plea, Isaiah's outcry too still has a powerful impact, thousands of years after it was first articulated. They were both challenging their congregations: Will you act for the vision of justice demanded by God and recorded in Scripture?

## Notes

78. Elyse D. Frishman, ed., *Mishkan T'filah: A Reform Siddur* (New York: CCAR Press, 2007), 44 (based on *Mishnah Pei-ah* 1:1).
79. An affiliate of IAF, Temple Emanu-El's CBCO at that time.

PART II

*Recharging Ourselves as Jews*

# CHAPTER 4

# Listening to the Call

## Sh'ma

WE ARE BOMBARDED with emails, online petitions, phone solicitations, mass mailings, and personal requests to join in the fight for one social justice cause or another. But each of us individually has finite resources of time, energy, and money. Even if we sympathize with a cause, we have limited capacity to understand its complexity, explore its history and context, consider the local realities, hear multiple perspectives, empathize with those most deeply affected, determine appropriate courses of action, and find the most effective community partners to accomplish meaningful change. It is far easier to hit delete, ignore the phone, or file the unopened solicitations in our recycling bins.

Yet some appeals manage to make their way past the sensory barriers that numb our reactions. Some pleas touch our hearts. Some requests rouse our weary souls. And, so often, the ones that compel us to respond are those that speak to our own experiences or awaken our generational memories.

One issue that resonates strongly for many American Jews is the contemporary controversy over admitting refugees to the United States. We cannot bear the idea of our country closing its doors to children fleeing persecution in Central America—or deporting them as they become young adults—because we remember when Jewish children were refused refuge here.[80] We cannot support meager immigration quotas for Syrian refugees—or halting their entry altogether—because we remember when severe restrictions limited entry to Jews desperate for safe havens.[81] We cannot be silent when immigrants are demonized, because so many of us have parents and grandparents who were themselves immigrants.

Personal connections to issues such as the plight of Syrian refugees or the unaccompanied minors from Central America arriving at our borders motivate us to engage in the political process to change our communities and our country. The feminist rallying cry in the 1960s and 1970s was "The personal is political," telling us as women that our lower paychecks and limited reproductive rights were not just our own problems, but issues worthy of political change.

Today's civic engagement slogan could be "The political is personal." When political injustices resonate with our own personal experiences, we are moved to heed that call. Because of our collective Jewish experience, rhetoric that diminishes the dignity of our neighbor—or worse yet, incites fear and hatred—forces us to respond.

When someone's story of pain speaks to us and we can see clearly the humanity of a person struggling before our eyes, our sense of discomfort can become too great to ignore. The soul of another has spoken to our soul, inaction is no longer viable, and we are moved to take the first step. As we tell our own stories of the anxiety or pain that we feel, and as we listen to the stories of others, we gain clarity around the issues that compel us to act.

The mandate of Leviticus to love our neighbor (Leviticus 19:18) is not specific enough. To love our neighbors, we need to discover how we are alike and appreciate how we differ. In today's America, with its diversity of religious beliefs, loving our neighbors means that we become familiar with the basics of their religious beliefs and that we share with them the basics of our own. When we truly love our neighbor, we understand each other's pain and source of solace, and we use our collective voices to create greater justice.

It was the capacity of personal stories to move people to action that inspired a collaboration between Temple Beth El and Charlotte community agencies to produce a series of social justice videos. These award-winning documentaries—*Souls of Our Students, Souls of Our Teachers*, and *Souls of Our Neighbors*—communicate the stories of students coping with discrimination, teachers struggling to succeed in inner city schools, and families moving from homelessness to housing.

Listen to the pain of three high school students who speak on camera in 2008 in *Souls of Our Students*:

> Being a minority right now as a Hispanic is actually dangerous for me. It's not . . . , "Oh you're different, so let's get to know each other." It's more like, "You're different, you're Hispanic, go away."

> If the media tells you that illegal aliens are bad and uses words like "illegal aliens" . . . it's going to affect you in a way where, not so directly but more indirectly . . . people look down on you, versus looking up at you or . . . just kind of respecting you.

> My middle name is Ahmed and they're like, "Oh, you know, you must be a terrorist." . . . They were really kind of harsh about it. But to me I kind of spoke out and said, "No, not every Muslim is a terrorist. Do you think every German is a Nazi? No."[82]

These *Souls* documentaries allow us to listen to the stories of neighbors we might not otherwise meet and to awaken our own souls, inspiring us to action.

It is no coincidence that the name of the central prayer of our faith, the *Sh'ma*, means "listen." In turning the principles of community organizing inward, Temple Emanu-El in Dallas, Texas, formed dozens of small groups of congregants that build relationships by listening to one another as they discuss meaningful questions. These groups are called "Sh'ma Emanu-El."

The single line of the *Sh'ma*, both in Deuteronomy 6:4 and in Jewish prayer books spanning the denominations, is immediately followed by the *V'ahavta*, meaning "And you shall love." We are instructed not only to listen, but then also to act, in the morning and the evening, in our homes and along our way. Being Jewish is not a passive experience. It is active.

Reinterpreting many segments of Jewish liturgy, poet and scholar Dr. Marcia Falk concludes the *V'ahavta* prayer with an acknowledgment of the symbiotic relationship between prayer and action:

> I will teach this to our children
> throughout the passage of the day—
> as I dwell in my home
> and as I go on my journey,
> from the time I rise
> until I fall asleep.
> And may my actions
> be faithful to my words
> that our children's children
> may live to know:
> Truth and kindness
> have embraced,
> peace and justice have kissed
> and are one.[83]

Judaism's ethical monotheism teaches that belief in the oneness of God necessitates both a belief in the oneness of humanity and action on those beliefs. We are obligated to see and support that divine source of every soul and to ensure the dignity and humanity of all. Only when we take the time to truly listen to others do we affirm the divine connection that links us all.

## Responding with Jewish Community

What happens once we hear the call for justice that resonates with our beliefs and then we are moved to action? We quickly realize that the steps from acknowledging an injustice to actively working toward its eradication are overwhelming. The path is uncharted, and the course requires a constant recalculation of the route. The process of organizing can feel like a metaphoric wilderness. Yet, a prayer by Michael Walzer from *Mishkan T'filah*, the Reform prayer book, calls us to take this journey together:

> Standing on the parted shores of history
> we still believe what we were taught
> before ever we stood at Sinai's foot;
> That wherever we go, it is eternally Egypt
> That there is a better place, a promised land;

That the winding way to that promise
Passes through the wilderness.
That there is no way to get from here to there
Except by joining hands, marching together.[84]

Finding our path through the wilderness of injustice is easier with the help of our synagogues. Jews from all streams of Judaism see their synagogue as a *beit t'filah* (a house of prayer), a *beit midrash* (a house of study), and a *beit k'neset* (a house of gathering). For some Jews, the synagogue helps them to faithfully live the laws of Torah and Rabbinic tradition and celebrate Jewish ritual, time, and life in the midst of community.

For Jews unsettled by the inequities and injustices of our world, the synagogue can also provide a path to actualizing our Jewish values. When we hear a call that compels us to act, we can mobilize our congregation to act with us, thus increasing the impact of our actions. Instead of shouting alone like the one Just Man of Sodom, we can join our minyan on the move to make real change. We can accomplish this work of civic engagement as Jews, in Jewish community, and guided by Jewish teachings.

Rabbi Arnold Jacob Wolf (z"l), of Congregation Solel in Highland Park, Illinois, wrote in 1966 about how he wrestled with his personal Jewish path:

> I try to walk the road of Judaism. Embedded in that road there are many jewels. One is marked "Sabbath" and one "Civil Rights" and one "Kashruth" [Jewish dietary laws] and one "Honor Your Parents" and one "Study of Torah" and one "You Shall Be Holy." There are at least 613 of them and they are of different shapes and sizes and weights. . . . I believe that God expects me to keep on walking Judaism Street and to carry away whatever I can of its commandments. I do not believe that He expects me to lift what I cannot, nor may I condemn my fellow Jew who may not be able to pick up even as much as I can.[85]

Each person has his or her own Jewish path. Some are spiritually fulfilled in the sanctuary; others find the wholeness they seek through their service in the outside world. And some of us incorporate elements of both along our way. But all would do well to embrace the nonjudgmental stance of Rabbi Wolf, recognizing that each of us picks up different jewels among those that Judaism offers us.

The congregants we interviewed were passionate about their synagogue's role in fulfilling their personal commitment to social justice. Lara Ettenson, at Congregation Emanu-El in San Francisco, California, commented, "Some of our congregants are really into the Torah; some are not. [The sentiment is] we could volunteer anywhere, but congregants choose to volunteer through the temple, as it brings our Jewish values to the forefront of our lives and builds community." This recognition that their work was grounded in Jewish values was repeatedly voiced by lay leaders, whether or not a specific Jewish text had inspired their work.

For many lay leaders, this belief that social justice was an authentic expression of their Judaism led them more deeply into synagogue life. As they became more active in their synagogue's civic engagement work, they built relationships with their rabbi and fellow congregants and participated in more synagogue activities. Most notably, Mike Sims, one of Dallas's Temple Emanu-El lay leaders noted, "Members cease being consumers and become active participants in their Judaism."

For some Jews, their path is paved with ritual, prayer, and study. For others, the Jewish path is paved by congregational events and life-cycle celebrations. Yet for still others, the Jewish path is paved by civic engagement. For many, it is a combination. For those responding to the call to pursue justice, civic engagement through their synagogue can become their connection to Jewish community.

## Fulfilling Our Faith versus Self-Fulfillment
The mistreatment of any person affects not only the victim but also the bystander and the oppressor. It stains our souls, constrains our spirituality, and destroys our sense of peace. Rabbi Abraham Joshua Heschel articulated the redemptive power of social justice not just for the oppressed, but also for the privileged: "The tragedy of Pharaoh was the failure to realize that the exodus from slavery could

have spelled redemption for both Israel and Egypt. Would that Pharaoh and the Egyptians had joined the Israelites in the desert, and together stood at the foot of Sinai!"[86]

More recent history reveals how some non-Jews fulfilled the tenets of their faith through their actions during the Holocaust. In the 1930s, the German Lutheran theologian and pastor Dietrich Bonhoeffer started the Confessing Church with Pastor Martin Niemöller, in defiance of the German Christians who had allowed their institutions to be permeated by Nazi ideology. Bonhoeffer could have found sanctuary in the church and survived, but he chose to live the values of his faith, and he died for them. He recognized that the goal of religion is not to achieve peace solely for oneself, but work to achieve it for the "other." In his last writings from prison before execution by the Nazis, Bonhoeffer wrote:

> Here and there people flee from public altercation into the sanctuary of private virtuousness. But anyone who does this must shut his mouth and eyes to the injustice around him. Only at the cost of self-deception can he keep himself pure from the contamination arising from responsible action.[87]

In another compelling story of acting on one's faith to help others during this tragic time, non-Jews in a small French village called Le Chambon-sur-Lignon saved as many as five thousand Jews. Risking their own lives, these Protestants—who as a minority in Catholic-dominated France had known persecution themselves—quietly acted under the leadership of their pastor, André di Trocmé, to provide homes, education, and passage to Switzerland for Jewish refugees.[88] The pastor's wife, Magda Trocmé, found homes for families and residential schools for children, remarking years later, "Sometimes people ask me, 'How did you make the decision?' There was no decision to make. The issue was: Do you think we are all brothers or not?"[89]

While many non-Jews actively or passively collaborated with the Nazis during the Holocaust, some righteous non-Jews like those of Le Chambon-sur-Lignon risked their lives to save Jews without ulterior motives or benefits. Along the Avenue of the Righteous among the Nations outside Israel's Holocaust History Museum, trees are planted for righteous gentiles. This garden at Yad Vashem, the World's Holocaust Remembrance Center in Israel, is a living testament to the power of finding common ground in our shared sense of humanity and morality.

Bonhoeffer, Niemöller, and those righteous gentiles honored outside Israel's Holocaust Museum, including the Trocmés, understood that their faith required them to resist the evils of Nazi Germany. Dr. Martin Luther King Jr. eloquently spoke to the universality of defending all the oppressed in his now-famous words from the Birmingham jail: "Injustice anywhere is a threat to justice everywhere."[90]

There is an important distinction between fulfilling the values of one's faith when it comes to justice and finding personal fulfillment. Many American volunteers find the work of social service and social justice personally fulfilling. Yet we must remain wary that the satisfaction we feel from helping others does not distract us from our greater goal. Remember the parable from chapter 1 about the villagers who rescued strangers from drowning in the river, investing more and more resources until someone suggested traveling upstream? Undoubtedly, these villagers found fulfillment in being hailed as local heroes for their lifesaving work. Caught up in their success, they needed someone to remind them that exploring *why* people were falling in the river was important work, too. The gratification one feels from helping others reinforces one's desire to continue the work, but we are obligated to consider first the long-term well-being of those we seek to help.

A fundamental organizing principle is that we do this work with others and not for others. Anything less than a partnership runs the risk of a detrimental result. Robert D. Lupton, author of *Toxic Charity: How Churches and Charities Hurt Those They Help (And How to Reverse It)*, lambasts the mission work of many churches that focus more on spiritually fulfilling the volunteer than sustainably lifting up the recipient—a message also applicable to synagogues. In "The Oath for Compassionate Service," Lupton warns against one-way efforts (except in emergency crises), noting that the gratification that volunteers feel can create an unhealthy dependency:

> Give once and you elicit appreciation;
> give twice and you create anticipation;
> give three times and you create expectation;
> give four times and it becomes entitlement;
> give five times and you establish dependency.[91]

Soul work is supplanted by the ego when our work is driven by self-fulfillment. Even worse, our labor may yield less than productive results. Only when our task of healing is grounded in the hard work of meeting the other and finding a common path for bettering us all does our civic engagement also become soul work. The wholeness we seek is found through our work of sustainable repair.

The journey from that first step to achieving systemic change can take decades. The battle for equal rights on any front can be long, presenting both entrenched opposition and unexpected resistance along the way. Discrimination, the politics of exclusion, oppression of minorities, and abuses of power have challenged us from the time of the Israelites' slavery, as recounted in the Book of Exodus, until today. Consider the following American examples:

- Women were granted the right to vote by the Nineteenth Amendment in 1920, yet a century later, women remain underrepresented in American politics and are still fighting for equal pay and reproductive rights.
- The Emancipation Proclamation was signed in 1863 abolishing slavery, and the Fifteenth Amendment in 1870 granted blacks the right to vote. More than fifty years after the 1965 Voting Rights Act, barriers to the ballot box are still being created, and racial equality is far from achieved.
- Although faster progress was made between the Stonewall protest of 1969 and the 2015 U.S. Supreme Court decision in favor of marriage equality, this path from the start of the gay rights movement to same-sex marriage still required forty-six

years to journey. Yet even with the relative speed of this milestone achievement, we will be fighting for LGBTQ equality in classrooms, courtrooms, bathrooms, and boardrooms for decades to come.

Many quote Dr. Martin Luther King Jr. as having said, "Faith is taking the first step, even when you don't see the whole staircase."[92] While we do not know the precise path, we know that we must move forward. We recognize that we cannot create change alone and that our power is increased as we partner with others. The journey will be long, and potentially as harsh as the Sinai desert, but together we can bring our society closer to a place of promise. Journeying on this path with our synagogues helps us fulfill the obligation to pursue justice, as our faith demands.

### Sh'ma Yisrael

The premise of organizing is listening to the stories of others that connect us and lead us to collective action for change. The watchword of our faith, the *Sh'ma*, is brought to life through this work. Jews say the *Sh'ma* in the morning and before bedtime, proclaiming our faith to ourselves and to God. A story about this prayer illustrates the power of listening to achieve redemption for ourselves and for others:

> After Germany's surrender in May 1945, Rabbi Eliezer Silver of the United States and Dayan Grunfeld of England served as army chaplains, rescuing Jewish survivors remaining in the concentration camps. Upon hearing that a monastery had been concealing Jewish children as Christian orphans during the war, Silver and Grunfeld traveled to Alsace-Lorraine, seeking to reunite these children with the Jewish community. However, the priest running the monastery refused to release any children without proper papers, and asked the visitors to leave if they could not prove which children were Jewish. Faced with an impossible task in the chaos of post-war Europe, Rabbi Silver asked permission to return for five minutes at bedtime that evening.

That night, the chaplains walked through the aisles of the dormitory where the children were going to sleep. They called out *"Sh'ma Yisrael"* causing the Jewish children to weep and call for their mothers in French, German, or Russian—the languages of their parents. These children, many of whom had been in the monastery for six years, had held onto their early memories of their parents putting them to bed with these words on their lips, and their responses led them on the path back to the Jewish people.[93]

After the tragedy of the Holocaust, Rabbi Silver and Dayan Grunfeld were committed to pursuing justice. The Jewish children they rescued were unlikely to be reunited with the parents who had sent them to the monastery in desperation and, absent Silver and Grunfeld's persistence, likely to remain in the world of Catholicism. The chaplains' commitment to listening brought these children out of the monastery and back into Jewish community.

*Sh'ma* is the first prayer many Jewish parents teach to their toddlers. *Sh'ma* means "hear." *Sh'ma* means listen to God's voice amid the cacophony of our multimedia world. *Sh'ma* means listen to the calls for justice and heed them for our children, for all children, and for all human beings as children of God.

## The Refugee Crisis through a Jewish Lens

The photo of the three-year-old Syrian boy Aylan Kurdi, who drowned off the shores of Turkey in 2015, struck not only a humanitarian chord, but also a Jewish chord. His family was en route to Greece, seeking ultimate refuge in Canada, when their boat capsized in high waves. This toddler could have been the innocent son of any one of us today or the orphan son of a Holocaust victim of a previous generation.

Many Americans, Jew and non-Jew alike, may recall the story of the SS *St. Louis*, which in May 1939 set sail for Cuba from Hamburg, Germany. The *St. Louis* was carrying over nine hundred passengers, of whom the vast majority were Jews seeking safety from the Nazi regime. Outside the port of Havana, the passengers' hopes for liberation were crushed when they became victims of Cuba's corrupt visa system and anti-immigration sentiment.

Though the ship was visible from the beaches of Miami as it sailed away from Havana, pleas for American sanctuary went unanswered. Accounts differ as to whether the American Coast Guard ships viewed from the deck of the *St. Louis* were simply tracking the ship as part of their duties or actively preventing it from docking on the U.S. coast. Nevertheless, the anti-immigration sentiment of the country was demonstrated around this same time with the defeat in the House Immigration Committee of the Wagner-Rogers Bill, which would have enabled twenty thousand German Jewish children to enter our country.[94]

As the *St. Louis* passengers faced a return trip to Europe, the Joint Distribution Committee (the "Joint") was successful in steering them away from German ports and finding safe harbor for one-third of them in Great Britain. Sadly, the remainder landed in vulnerable countries—France, Belgium, and Holland—only a few months before the start of World War II, and 254 of them were murdered in the Holocaust.[95]

Just imagine being in the New York City conference room with the leadership of the Joint, trying to save nearly a thousand refugees in a boat off the shores of Cuba—strategizing, brainstorming, raising funds, and wondering whether your civic engagement efforts could save lives. Historians say that Germany released the *St. Louis* (and other ships) to demonstrate that other countries did not want Jewish refugees. Finding even temporary oases for these German Jews required hundreds of thousands of dollars in financial support to their host countries.

Many of us are similarly in conference rooms today, discussing the plight of the millions of Syrian refugees who are fleeing their civil war. The tensions remain as high now as they did then, with meager numbers successfully finding refuge here. The United States admitted only 2,500 Syrian refugees cumulatively from 2011 to 2015[96] and 12,587 more in 2016.[97] While the Obama administration intended for the numbers for all refugees to increase by 29% in 2017 to respond to the spike in global refugees,[98] President Donald Trump's subsequent executive orders on immigration (originally signed January 2017 and revised two months later) restricted the number of refugees who would be allowed to enter and imposed temporary bans on individuals entering from Syria and five other countries, in order to review vetting procedures.[99]

Echoes of conversations from more than seventy years ago reverberate throughout the modern debates about Syrian refugees. The xenophobia and antisemitism of the 1930s is not dissimilar from the xenophobia and Islamophobia of today. The fears of security threats—or of refugees competing for jobs or requiring public assistance—mirror the public sentiment against German Jewish immigrants in the final years of the Great Depression.

Indeed, many waves of immigrants to America have found themselves landing on inhospitable shores. The Irish workers in post–Civil War America faced business signs saying "No Irish Need Apply." Asian émigrés were barred by the Chinese Exclusion Act of 1882. Italian immigrants of the late nineteenth and early twentieth centuries were feared as strikebreakers. The bias against the stranger resurfaces with each new ethnic group seeking better lives for themselves and their families.

From 1860 to 1920, at least 13 percent of Americans were immigrants in any single year, swelling the population of second- and third-generation Americans in the twentieth century.[100]

Yet so many were willing to close the door behind themselves. In a poll published in 1939 by *Fortune* magazine, more than 80 percent of Americans opposed opening the gates of immigration wider, though many of them likely had immigrant parents or grandparents.[101]

In another modern humanitarian crisis, thousands of families in El Salvador, Guatemala, and Honduras are desperately sending their children illegally into the United States to escape gang violence and drug wars. These families take this risk despite the expenses and dangers of the journey and the uncertainties after arrival. From 2013 to 2016, over two hundred thousand unaccompanied children were apprehended crossing into the southern United States and subject to deportation proceedings.[102]

As we struggle to respond to those fleeing unimaginable violence

in their home countries, it is affirming to note that the images of the
*St. Louis* being turned away have become part of the American story,
not just the story of the Jews. Both Massachusetts governor Deval
Patrick and California senator Dianne Feinstein, when responding to
proposals to send back to Central America unaccompanied children
who had crossed our border, referenced the failure of the United
States to offer sanctuary. When a reporter asked how he viewed the
border crisis, Governor Patrick said:

> My inclination is to remember what happened when a ship full
> of Jewish children tried to come to the United States in 1939 and
> the United States turned them away, and many of them went
> to their deaths in Nazi concentration camps. I think we are a
> bigger-hearted people than that as Americans, and certainly as
> residents of Massachusetts.[103]

Likewise, Senator Feinstein "likened the situation to the 'boatloads
of Jewish immigrants trying to come to this country during Nazi
Germany and getting turned back. That's not what this country is all
about,' she said. 'This, in my view, has to be handled in a way which is
compassionate.'"[104]

In an open letter to the U.S. Congress, more than one thousand
American rabbis also referenced the *St. Louis* as "a stain on the history
of our country—a tragic decision made in a political climate of deep
fear, suspicion and antisemitism." In their petition to elected officials
to support refugee resettlement, they wrote, "In 1939, our country
could not tell the difference between an actual enemy and the victims
of an enemy. In 2015, let us not make the same mistake."[105]

The personal call to action that so many Jews feel in responding
to the plight of refugees is illustrated in the transformation of HIAS
(formerly known as the Hebrew Immigrant Aid Society). In its first 120
years, the organization rescued and resettled 4.5 million Jews. As the
number of Jews needing a safe haven markedly dwindled, the organization was at a crossroads; it could either close or refocus its mission.
HIAS chose the latter path and today helps refugees of all religious
and ethnic backgrounds through resettlement, advocacy, and support
internationally. Rabbi Jennie Rosenn, vice president of community
engagement at HIAS, explains: "We used to help refugees because

they were Jewish. Now we help refugees because we are Jewish."[106]

Because we are Jews and have known exile, we hear more clearly the call of refugees seeking safety on our shores. Because we are Jews and have known oppression, we respond more readily to those fleeing oppressive regimes. Because we are Jews, we feel moved—if not commanded—to answer the call, respond to the cry, and work to expand our country's embrace of those seeking refuge.

## Notes to Chapter 4

80. During World War II, the Wagner-Rogers Bill to admit twenty thousand German Jewish children into this country was defeated in the United States House Immigration Committee.

81. The quotas established by the immigration laws of 1921 and 1924—combined with the bureaucracy intentionally established by the State Department during the Holocaust—created insurmountable barriers for most Jews seeking refuge in the United States from Nazi-occupied countries; "Jewish Refugees from the German Reich, 1933–1939," United States Holocaust Memorial Museum, https://www.ushmm.org/exhibition/st-louis/teach/supread2.htm. For an example of the devastating impact of this policy, see "The Refugee Crisis through a Jewish Lens" in this chapter.

82. *Souls of Our Students: Appreciating Differences* (Charlotte, NC: Professional Communications, 2008), DVD.

83. Marcia Falk, *The Book of Blessings: New Jewish Prayers for Daily Life, the Sabbath, and the New Moon Festival* (New York: CCAR Press, 2017), 24, 26.

84. Michael Walzer, adapted in *Mishkan T'filah: A Reform Siddur*, 17.

85. *The Condition of Jewish Belief: A Symposium Compiled by the Editors of "Commentary" Magazine* (Northvale, NJ: Jason Aronson, 1989), 268.

86. Abraham J. Heschel, *The Insecurity of Freedom: Essays on Human Existence* (Philadelphia: Jewish Publication Society of America, 1966), 103.

87. Dietrich Bonhoeffer, *Letters and Papers from Prison*, ed. Eberhard Bethge (New York: Macmillan, 1971), 5.

88. "André and Magda Trocmé, Daniel Trocmé," The Righteous Among the Nations, Yad Vashem, http://www.yadvashem.org/righteous/stories/trocme.

89. Carol Rittner and Sondra Myers, *The Courage to Care: Rescuers of Jews During the Holocaust* (New York: New York University Press, 1986), 102.

90. Dr. Martin Luther King Jr., "Letter from Birmingham Jail," April 16, 1963.

91. Robert D. Lupton, *Toxic Charity: How Churches and Charities Hurt Those They Help (And How to Reverse It)* (New York: HarperCollins, 2011), 130.

92. "MLK Quote of the Week: Faith Is Taking the First Step," The King Center, accessed February 28, 2017, http://www.thekingcenter.org/blog/mlk-quote-week-faith-taking-first-step.

93. Adapted from the story by Miriam Swerdlov in Lisa Aiken, *The Hidden Beauty of the Shema* (Brooklyn, NY: Judaica Press, 1997), 17–19.

94. United States Holocaust Memorial Museum, "Voyage of the St. Louis," Holocaust Encyclopedia, accessed February 28, 2017, https://www.ushmm.org/wlc/en/article.php?ModuleId=10005267; and for name of committee: David S. Wyman Institute of Holocaust Studies, "Wagner-Rogers Bill," Encyclopedia of America's Response to the Holocaust, accessed February 28, 2017, http://enc.wymaninstitute.org/?p=523.

95. United States Holocaust Memorial Museum, "Voyage of the St. Louis."

96. "Who We Really Are: A Conversation with Syrian Refugees in America," Brookings Institution, Washington, DC, February 19, 2016, http://www.brookings.edu/events/2016/02/19-syrian-refugees-america.

97. Philip Connor and Jens Manuel Krogstad. "U.S. on Track to Reach Obama Administration's Goal of Resettling 110,000 Refugees This Year." Pew Research Center Fact Tank, January 20, 2017. http://www.pewresearch.org/fact-tank/2017/01/20/u-s-on-track-to-reach-obama-administrations-goal-of-resettling-110000-refugees-this-year/.

98. The ceiling of 85,000 refugees from all countries in 2016 was intended to rise to 110,000 in 2017, an increase of 25,000 or 29%. Refugee counts are from the Connor and Krogstad article cited above. http://www.pewresearch.org/fact-tank/2017/01/20/u-s-on-track-to-reach-obama-administrations-goal-of-resettling-110000-refugees-this-year/.

99. Donald J. Trump, "Executive Order Protecting the Nation from Foreign Terrorist Entry United States," The White House, January 27, 2017, -ro-evitucexe/72/10/7102/ecffio-sserp-eht/vog.esuohetihw.www//:sptth setats-detinu-yrtne-tsirorret-ngierof-noitan-gnitcetorp-red; and Donald J. Trump, "Executive Order Protecting the Nation from Foreign Terrorist Entry United States," March 6, 2017,-eht/vog.esuohetihw.www//:sptth -ret-ngierof-noitan-gnitcetorp-redro-evitucexe/60/30/7102/ecffio-sserp .setats-detinu-yrtne-tsiror

100. Migration Policy Institute; see chart of U.S. Census Bureau data "U.S. Immigrant Population and Share over Time, 1850-Present," http://www.migrationpolicy.org/programs/data-hub/charts/immigrant-population-over-time?width=1000&height=850&iframe=true.

101. "Poll Reveals Majority Here Would Bar Doors to Refugees; View on Jews Held Static," Jewish Telegraphic Agency, March 27, 1939, http://www.jta.org/1939/03/27/archive/poll-reveals-majority-here-would-bar-doors-to-refugees-view-on-jews-held-static.

102. "United States Border Patrol Southwest Family Unit Subject and Unaccompanied Alien Children Apprehensions Fiscal Year 2016: Statement by Secretary Johnson on Southwest Border Security," U.S. Customs and Border Protection, October 18, 2016, https:/www.cbp.gov/newsroom/stats/southwest-border-unaccompanied-children/fy-2016.

103. Jim O'Sullivan and Maria Sacchetti, "Patrick Wants Mass. to Host Immigrant Children: Says Immigrants Detained in Southwest Deserve a Safe Haven," *Boston Globe*, July 17, 2014, https://www.bostonglobe.com/metro/2014/07/16/patrick-says-will-try-find-ways-for-mass-host-immigrant-children/ivsfotVmqJKYHDAGtQ5oFP/story.html.

104. Jackie Calmes and Ashley Parker, "Obama Challenges Perry to Rally GOP Around Border Plan," *New York Times*, July 9, 2014, https://www.nytimes.com/2014/07/10/us/politics/immigration.html?_r=0.

105. "1,000+ Rabbis Sign Letter in Support of Welcoming Refugees," HIAS, December 3, 2015, https://www.hias.org/1000-rabbis-sign-letter-support-welcoming-refugees.

106. Rabbi Jennie Rosenn, "Syria & Beyond: A Jewish Response to Today's Refugees" (lecture, Temple Beth El, Charlotte, NC, May 5, 2016).

CHAPTER 5

# Finding Our Jewish Voice
## Alone I Cannot Sing

INSECURITIES plague most of us when we contemplate speaking out on controversial issues. Our minds race as we silently ask ourselves: What gives me the authority to say this? Do I have the facts to serve as a strong foundation? Do I have convincing arguments that will withstand a challenge? Am I transgressing the rule of etiquette to not discuss politics and religion in polite company? Do I want to risk turning a pleasant situation into one that might become uncomfortable or even confrontational?

Discussing an issue of social justice can be intimidating. We may be comfortable listening to someone else's story; yet, when the opportunity arises to share our own narrative of vulnerability or pain, or to articulate what it is about another's struggle that moves us, the task becomes more challenging. A passive role is far easier than voicing our own opinions and feelings. Asking a congregant to speak in a public forum magnifies those anxieties exponentially. Congregants (and perhaps some clergy) are understandably concerned about stepping outside their comfort zone.

Singing in a choir provides a fitting metaphor for finding our voices in civic engagement. When people join a choir, they are placed in a section that fits their vocal range. It is within that group that individuals learn the music while relying on other voices to guide their own. Only after training and experience is someone called upon to sing a solo. There is a Chasidic teaching from the eighteenth century that speaks to this issue: "When one is singing and cannot lift his voice, and another comes and sings with him, another who can lift her voice, the first will be able to lift his voice too."[107] This same teaching applies to Jews who are fearful of speaking out on social justice issues. If we say, "I don't know the tune" (I am not educated on a given issue), or "I am afraid to be off-key" (I don't want create conflict), or "I don't want to embarrass myself" (I don't feel sufficiently articulate), we can find comfort in knowing that others' voices will lift our own.

The beauty of civic engagement as part of the organized Jewish community is that not everyone has to speak. There is power in numbers, and each person can rely on the strength of another congregant. For example, a well-organized lobbying trip usually means that a handful of people deliver the message to the elected representative, and the others communicate support solely with their physical presence. The meeting is carefully planned so that speakers present only the points with which they are comfortable and familiar.

When we join the choir of civic engagement in our synagogues, we give voice to the voiceless so that they will one day have the freedom to sing their own songs. We find the words to articulate the issues that stir our souls, and we learn to express why these issues matter to us, not only as human beings, but as Jews. We feel the strength of Jewish prayer, whether we express our Judaism through song, liturgy, or the pursuit of justice, and we build relationships with other congregants who stand with us.

### Bringing Voice to the Voiceless

The sacred work of the synagogue is found not only in voicing our prayers, but also in responding to the unspoken prayers of others. Tears are often shed silently and alone in situations of domestic abuse—a pattern of coercive behavior aimed at gaining and then maintaining power and control over an intimate partner. Domestic abuse steals childhoods, kills self-esteem, and ends lives.

"The Sages taught: One who loves his wife as he loves himself, and who honors her more than himself . . . about him the verse states: 'And you shall know that your tent is in peace' (Job 5:24). As a result of his actions, there will be peace in his home, as it will be devoid of quarrel and sin" (Babylonian Talmud, *Y'vamot* 62b). Our homes are meant to be our greatest source of holiness and peace, yet for many, their homes are devastated by domestic abuse.

Marsha Stickler was volunteering her communications skills at a transitional home for victims of domestic abuse in Charlotte when she was appalled to learn that this societal tragedy was not acknowledged by the Jewish community. Many Jews dismiss domestic abuse as a problem not found in Jewish homes, yet abuse happens in Jewish relationships at about the same rate as in other families (one in four), across all socioeconomic levels.[108] Stickler enlisted her synagogue, Temple Beth El, to bring voice to this issue, leading to the passage of the temple's first board resolution on a social justice issue.

The 2007 Temple Beth El Board Resolution on Domestic Abuse inspired other Charlotte Jewish institutions to partner in this life-saving work, compelling clergy and the community to talk about this previously undiscussed topic. Subsequently, nineteen Jewish organizations signed on to support the work, community clergy were trained to recognize and refer victims, and domestic abuse became a formal component of the work of Jewish Family Services.

Although domestic abuse continues to be endured largely in silence in Charlotte—as in many Jewish communities across the country—the impact of this advocacy continues to be felt. Most bathroom stalls in the fifty-four-acre Shalom Park stock sticky notes offering a hotline for those suffering harm inflicted by someone they love. Every year since the 2007 resolution passed, sermons, stories, and prayers are shared, workshops are offered, and lessons about healthy relationships are taught to high school youth.

In summing up the legacy of her decade of work, Stickler noted, "And we go forward. I don't have to be there personally. It's not just one person anymore." Joining the choir of social justice enables voice to be given to the voiceless, addressing critical issues in our communities. Sharing responsibility for initiatives with others in the choir also amplifies a solo voice, expanding the impact an individual can have.

Nationally, many synagogues and churches address abuse not only within the home but also on their own city's blocks as they fight sex trafficking and work to free those who may be enslaved. Rabbi John Linder, at Temple Solel in Phoenix, mobilized his congregation as part of the local organizing movement to pass Arizona legislation protecting sex-trafficking victims instead of criminalizing them. He commented on how this work is part of living one's Judaism: "At its core, this is one way to realize your Jewish identity. I am not sure how we can exist in the world without Jewish values pushing us to be engaged in the greater community."

As part of Jewish prayer, one of the morning blessings woven into the liturgy called the *Nisim B'chol Yom*, "For Daily Miracles," states, "Praise to You, Adonai our God, Sovereign of the universe, who frees the captive." While originally said in the home, these blessings are now said in the synagogue to reflect our gratitude for the acts of stretching our bodies and sitting up in our beds after awakening. Yet, each morning as we celebrate our personal liberation, thousands in our country have no freedom over their own bodies.

The Jewish morning prayer for daily miracles includes two additional blessings relevant to this issue: praising God for giving us the ability to distinguish day from night and praising God for opening the eyes of the blind. When we can distinguish light from darkness and open our eyes to tragedy, we become aware of the deeply disturbing human rights travesty of human and sex trafficking that exists for tens of thousands in our country. This abuse, oppression, and slavery occurs among boys as young as eleven years old and girls as young as twelve. Sex trafficking disproportionately impacts undocumented migrants, runaways, and homeless youth, as well as other marginalized and vulnerable populations in many of our own cities.[109]

A double injustice afflicts many children who are supposedly served by the American child welfare system. Six out of ten underage sex-trafficking victims found in 2013 as part of a national FBI operation across seventy cities were children from foster care or group homes.[110] These children were not only born into homes with parents who failed to keep them safe, but we, as a society, failed them a second time when we did not provide them with the protections we promised when we removed them from their homes.

The National Council of Jewish Women (NCJW), which makes sex trafficking a primary focus of its social justice work, describes yet another disturbing element of this abuse. In our flawed system, underage victims are often prosecuted as criminals rather than protected as victims. As a result, NCJW is promoting federal legislation requiring states to adopt "Safe Harbor" legislation prohibiting minors under the age of eighteen from being prosecuted for prostitution.[111]

Rabbi Julie Schonfeld, executive vice president of the Rabbinical Assembly of Conservative Judaism, speaks to the responsibility we all have to identify the voiceless victims of slavery in our communities. She says, "Part of what we really need is for all Americans to have their eyes and ears [open] and recognize what are the signs of slavery, not only for sex but also for labor."[112]

One of the 613 commandments of Judaism is to free the captive. The great medieval commentator Moses Maimonides highlights its pressing nature:

> [The mitzvah, the commandment of] redeeming captives takes precedence over feeding and clothing the poor. And there is no commandment as great as redeeming captives, for a captive is among the hungry, thirsty, naked, and is in mortal danger. And one who averts one's eyes from redeeming him or her violates: "You shall not harden your heart, nor shut your hand [from your needy brother]" (Deuteronomy 15:7). (*Mishneh Torah, Hilchot Matnot Aniyim* 8:10)

Giving voice to the voiceless who are victims of sex trafficking is religiously fulfilling to individual Jews, even if they are unaware of the texts and traditions that inspire this work. Jean Wolman is a lay leader at Congregation Beth Am in Los Altos Hills, California. Wolman worked for two years raising awareness in her congregation, partnering with Bay Area organizations, and advocating for the victims of sex trafficking. Like many lay leaders interviewed for this book, she did not have a specific Jewish text that inspired her work: "I'm not so knowledgeable about that [Jewish texts]. . . . But I have awareness of the links to Judaism and that's what drives me. It's not our monopoly, but it's very Jewish. It's much more meaningful to me as a Jew than prayers or rituals."

The *G'vurot*, the second prayer of the center segment of Jewish worship called the *Amidah*, praises God, "who supports the fallen, heals the sick, and releases the captive." Yet we know that we cannot solely rely on God to right our country's wrongs, clear our society's sins, heal those who are sick, or free those who are held captive. It is up to us as Jews to do this divine work, giving voice to the voiceless, supporting victims of domestic abuse who are afraid to come forward, and working to free those who are enslaved in our own American cities.

## Finding the Words

Music has power. Words have power. Congregants have power. Social justice work in the context of congregational life harnesses our transformative power.

Elie Wiesel, Holocaust survivor and renowned author, lived the lesson of the power of words through his life's work and legacy. When Wiesel met with twenty local religious leaders in Charlotte in 2007, they asked him, "How can we respond to the enormity of the world's problems?" And he said to the assembled clergy, "All of you, because of who you are, know how to use words."[113]

Judaism teaches us that with words, worlds are created. The Torah opens by telling us it was God's speech that sparked Creation. "God said, 'Let there be light!'—and there was light" (Genesis 1:3). Judaism also teaches us that with words, worlds can be destroyed. Tradition ascribes to King Solomon the teaching that "death and life are in the power of the tongue" (Proverbs 18:21).

Choosing words wisely on issues of justice can be challenging. There will be times when we do not have the perfect words to respond to ignorance or to clearly articulate the fitting counterargument. There will be times when we will be perplexed because issues are complex and a clear path may not be apparent. Whether we have the eloquence of a clergyperson or thrive only in the world of numbers, the obligation remains to use our voices. Health, safety, equality, human rights, and even lives themselves are often at stake. Our technologically advanced world eliminates our excuses for not speaking.

Indeed, social media offers us impactful ways to protest an injustice with a simple click of a button. In 2016 the Stanford University student who was sexually assaulted while unconscious read a powerful and personal statement to her assaulter Brock Turner, also a Stanford student. The letter closed with a message of support to other rape victims: "And finally, to girls everywhere, I am with you. On nights when you feel alone, I am with you. When people doubt you or dismiss you, I am with you. I fought every day for you. So never stop fighting, I believe you."[114]

The then vice president Joe Biden sent an open letter to the Stanford victim, which earned over two million hits, reading in part:

> Your story has already changed lives.
> You have helped change the culture.
> You have shaken untold thousands out of the torpor and
>     indifference towards sexual violence that allows this
>     problem to continue.
> Your words will help people you have never met and never will.
> You have given them the strength they need to fight.
> And so, I believe, you will save lives.[115]

Both letters went viral, contributing to the voluntary reassignment of the judge presiding over the case, changes in California legislation on sentencing rapists, and widespread reexamination by many colleges of their responses to campus rape. Using others' words by sharing a Facebook post of someone who holds an opinion similar to our own or by re-posting a YouTube video enables us to take a stand on a critical human rights issue of our day. It is also incumbent on each of us to ensure that the message we are sharing is based on factual data.

Self-identification is another simple way to lift our voices. Gail Baron, a Temple Beth El congregant, sent an email asking her Charlotte friends to donate to help the residents of Flint, Michigan, who were facing dangerously polluted water. She prefaced her message by saying that Flint was her hometown and concluded by saying, "I got out but almost 100,000 others were not so lucky."

Self-identification does not require you to have lived in the town that was affected. It requires that you empathize in an effort to elicit a response from others. What if I were trapped in a marriage in which I was abused by my spouse? What if the professional sporting events in my city were leading to increased sex trafficking? We are more inclined to care when we realize that human rights abuses afflict not some stranger in some far-off place, but oppress and dehumanize those in our very midst or those who are similar to ourselves.

Using an "I-statement" about one's own beliefs rather than challenging someone else's beliefs is another path to more comfortably and effectively sharing our social justice passions:

- "I believe that all human beings are created in the image of God, so every person should be treated with dignity and equality."
- "I believe that the earth belongs not to individuals but to God, and it is our responsibility to be good stewards for future generations."
- "I believe that Judaism requires us to care for those in need— no one should suffer from hunger, homelessness, or lack of health care."

Finding the right words requires a measure of reflection and learning—from personal stories, from professionals, from pastors and professors, and from the texts of our faith. It is in educating ourselves that we expand our vocabulary and strengthen our arguments. The economic argument, the compassionate argument, and the religious argument each have their time and place.

Clergy naturally espouse the religious argument when advocating for change. Social justice advocates would do well to expand their repertoire of reasoning. Too often, they rely solely on arguments of compassion to convince others to act. Economic and political arguments, when applicable, can be powerful tools as well.

Traditional appeals on the basis of faith had inspired Charlotte congregations to fund homeless shelters for years, but advocating for the upstream issues of affordable housing and support services were harder sells. An endowment to subsidize rent to move families out of shelters into housing was envisioned, and that concept required a different conversation. A Way Home, a $20 million public/private partnership, became a reality once philanthropists understood the more advantageous economics of an endowment versus mixed-income housing, and the city council embraced the less disruptive neighborhood impact of scattered site housing.

Listening to the other voices in the choir and in the community teaches us which words will communicate our positions most effectively. Being intentional rather than reactive, creating dialogue rather than debate, and learning from disharmony enable us to effectively speak and sing on our own.

Eliezer Schindler, the grandfather of Rabbi Judith Schindler, respected the power of words. A writer and published poet in Germany in the 1920s and early 1930s, Eliezer Schindler not only spent his life crafting his own words; he also read the words of others—even those that were hateful. After reading Adolph Hitler's *Mein Kampf*, Eliezer was alarmed by Hitler's menacing demonization of the Jews and his incendiary plot to scapegoat them for Germany's economic woes. Eliezer used his words to warn the Jewish community of Hitler's danger to democracy and humanity in an underground Yiddish newspaper. As part of the first round of arrests, the Nazis arrived at Eliezer's front door on the evening of March 4, 1933. Yet, because he had listened to the words of others, he found refuge that night at the Jewish hospital and the next morning fled Germany forever. His wife and children would be reunited with him prior to *Kristallnacht* five years later.

Two generations later, Rabbi Judith Schindler was so shy as a child that her mother sought counsel from a psychologist to provide her daughter with assertiveness training. In the early years of rabbinical school, Schindler's great anxiety with public speaking placed her at the bottom of her class for leading worship and preaching. After decades of speech coaching, she has overcome her fears and speaks before audiences numbering in the thousands. Reflecting on the legacy her grandfather left her, she shared:

My grandfather's voice calls to me, saying, "Never be compla-
cent. Be vigilant about hatred. Speak out against injustice, no
matter what the cost." When I hear of rhetoric or legislation
built upon racism, antisemitism, homophobia, Islamophobia,
xenophobia, or any other bigotry, I cannot be silent. Even in the
face of those who seek to intimidate and threaten me, my past
enjoins me to act. My grandfather's voice does not allow me to
look the other way when inequities permeate our society and
prejudiced voices echo in the air.[116]

Ecclesiastes teaches that there is a time to be silent and there is a time
to speak (Ecclesiastes 3:7). Even those with emotional or physical
speech impediments can find a way to express themselves. Joining
the social justice choir of others who have experience in this realm is
an empowering step.

### Finding Our Personal Jewish Voice

When it comes to articulating the call of one's faith to fulfill a mission, many Christians, particularly evangelicals, are far more comfortable using religious language than are most Jews. When others
ask us about our church affiliation, when public prayer is overtly
Christian, or when someone uses the phrase "good Christian" to
praise someone for doing civic work, we are relegated to the place of
the "other."

Many Jews choose not to address the exclusion implicit in someone else's choice of language. As a part of a minority whose difference can be concealed, we have the option of remaining silent in
order to avoid awkward conversations or even confrontations. We
may feel less vulnerable ducking these issues rather than correcting
misconceptions or explaining how language is creating barriers. In
some instances, we may not feel confident enough in our knowledge
of Judaism to launch such a discussion. Yet, in the first century,
Rabbi Hillel urged us to acknowledge our identity, saying, "Do not
separate yourself from the community" (Pirkei Avot 2:4).

When we identify ourselves as Jews, we learn and grow. We are
forced to find the words to articulate who we are and why we are

choosing this particular path of civic engagement. In doing so, we open ourselves to both asking questions about others' faith and having questions posed to us in return.

When Ari Goldman was a religion correspondent for the *New York Times*, he took a year's sabbatical to study at Harvard Divinity School. In reflecting on his education there, he wrote a book entitled *The Search for God at Harvard*, and in it shared one of the most important lessons he learned from Professor Diana Eck: "If you know one religion . . . you don't know any."[117]

The choice to share our identity can be difficult, depending on the situation. Rabbi Allen Bennett, now retired from Temple Israel in Alameda, California, once said wryly, "Every day I come out to someone. Some days I come out as gay, some days I come out as Jewish, some days I come out as fat. Some of these are easier than others."

Sharing who we are in the course of our social justice work enables us to model the inclusive community that we are striving to create. For example, Judy Seldin-Cohen was asked by a group of Charlotte agencies to help conceptualize how "church volunteers" could participate in moving a set of clients from homelessness into rental housing. Sensitive to the Christian language in the room and experienced in the sometimes complicated volunteer world, Seldin-Cohen asked in a private conversation with one of the organizers, who affiliated with an evangelical Christian church, whether a Jewish team would be welcomed.

The resulting discussion led to the use of more inclusive language, such as describing participating groups as "congregations" as opposed to "churches." With a more welcoming mandate, Seldin-Cohen was empowered to recruit Temple Beth El volunteers to join in the project while deepening her personal relationship with the evangelical Christian organizer. The door was opened to future dialogue, respecting differences in faith, and enlisting additional volunteers.

The issue of prayer can also confront and confound the Jew engaged in interfaith and multicultural community work. Someone starting a meal or meeting with the words ~~~~ ~~~~ diately create a sense of discomfort and exclusion. Addressing these differences in how we pray can be critical to achieving harmony in our civic engagement efforts.

Linda Glazner is her temple's representative to NAOMI, an interfaith coalition of congregations in Wausau, Wisconsin. Glazner grew up in New Jersey, where her public schools were closed on Jewish holidays, a model of religious inclusion. By contrast, she is often the only Jew at NAOMI meetings, and it is a personal challenge that all the meetings open and close with a prayer. Her discomfort is deepened when the group prays in the name of Jesus. After five years, she marks it as a personal victory that she was able to help the group understand why this practice excludes her, and she is proud that a more inclusive prayer is now used.

Barry Moline, in Tallahassee, Florida, faced a similar challenge in his work with his synagogue's CBCO, Tallahassee Equality Action Ministry (TEAM). TEAM's meetings had also started and ended with a prayer, which created objections among the representatives from thirty diverse houses of worship, including Jews, Muslims, Baptists, and many other Christian denominations. Moline described how they resolved the ill feelings:

> Finally, we said this is about spirituality and maybe people should pray the way they wanted to pray. We rotated and would say before the prayer, "This is how we pray." It tipped us off to be ready to hear "Jesus." When I did the prayer, I would do the *Shehecheyanu* [blessing of gratitude for special moments and first occasions] in Hebrew and translate it, even embellish it in giving thanks for the food and fellowship before us. They fell over; they loved hearing the Hebrew and understanding the prayer. So that was fascinating, and it got us talking about the diversity of our prayers.

Glazner and Moline found different solutions to the challenges of prayer. In Glazner's case, peace was achieved by finding common ground. For Moline, intentionally celebrating differences deepened connections and understanding among the members of the group.

Another disconcerting moment of dissonance is hearing someone called a "good Christian" in recognition of their civic engagement. Seldin-Cohen has been called "a good Christian" by strangers on more than one occasion in the course of her volunteer work in Charlotte. She usually explains that she is Jewish, risking discomfort to affirm that this work is a tenet of her faith, too.

Contrast that term to the use of the phrase "good Jew," which is often considered a reflection of attendance at worship services or one's food choices. Far too many Jews assume that the "good" measuring rod is the traditional standard of being *shomeir Shabbes* (keeping the laws of Shabbat) or observing kashrut (following the Jewish dietary laws). A Chabad rabbi in San Mateo, California, Rabbi Yossi Marcus, labels the need of many Jews to confess to him their lack of ritual observance as "low Jewish self-esteem." He affirms that good Jews are, indeed, defined by their actions outside the synagogue. Rabbi Marcus writes:

> Because being a good person is fundamental to being a good Jew—to bring G-d[118] and G-dly notions such as justice, righteousness and kindness, into the world. Being a good Jew does not just mean going to the synagogue. Yes, a Jew has to go to the synagogue, but most of Judaism takes place outside it—how we behave outside the synagogue.[119]

Civic engagement is intimidating because there may be two new languages to learn: the jargon of the causes we embrace and the declarations of our faith. Becoming comfortable with Jewish teachings helps us understand why civic engagement is Jewish and how to articulate the teachings of our faith to others. When we encounter church volunteers using Christian language to describe their own religious call to civic engagement, we have an opportunity for ourselves as Jews to educate non-Jews about our faith, to find our points of commonality, and to move forward with more mutual respect for each other's traditions. And, as we reach out in partnership to different faith communities, we learn valuable lessons about others and about ourselves. As we find our own voices in the comfort of the synagogue, we feel empowered to step out into the larger community, where we may also rise to the challenge of finding our own religious language.

### Building Relationships in the Choir

Marsha Stickler, the Temple Beth El lay leader on domestic abuse issues, also sings in the synagogue's High Holy Day choir. She explains how the music connects her to Judaism far more meaningfully than simply speaking the words of the liturgy. She says:

> For me, the High Holy Days are not about the prayers; they are about the music. That's what resonates with me. When I sing, I am making an offering to my congregation and to my Divine in my way. I don't read the prayer book; I concentrate on the music. The music and the songs are my prayers.

Like singing in the synagogue choir, civic engagement can provide a powerful Jewish connection. Perhaps that is why Rabbi Abraham Joshua Heschel's remark that he was "praying with his legs" in the 1965 Selma to Montgomery march seems to resonate so strongly with many Jews. When we sing with the metaphoric choir of social justice, we find like-minded people who share our passions and concerns, and they become our congregation. They often become the friends who change not just our communities and our world, but also the friends who change our own lives in the process.

Stickler talks about the relationships she has built in the choir, saying, "The more often we sing or rehearse, the more we build relationships." In this same way, deep connections are created as we work on social justice initiatives with our fellow congregants. Whether it's strategizing, organizing, or lobbying to create systemic change, we find ourselves bonding with those who choose, as we do, to give their time to civic engagement. Success in the social justice realm is dependent on the relationships within our congregation, through which we can find our common passions and determine a collective path.

In his seminal book *Relational Judaism: Using the Power of Relationships to Transform the Jewish Community*, Dr. Ron Wolfson articulates transformational goals for synagogues, inspiring leaders to focus on building relationships instead of simply offering programs. In this model, measures for success are based on the connections created, rather than on headcounts of those in attendance.[120]

Congregations engaging with civic initiatives start by finding common ground as they uncover the issues for which congregants feel the greatest passion. A "listening campaign" is a tool of community organizing in which shared concerns emerge from face-to-face discussions and leaders for the ensuing work are identified. These listening campaigns—whether one-on-one conversations, parlor meetings, or facilitated discussions—are all based on sharing personal stories and building relationships. It is through this foundational and relational work that individual voices create chords and harmonies in the social justice choir. Just as we may not feel we can sing alone, we may not successfully make social change alone, but with others our voices are amplified and the relationships we create give us the shelter of peace for which we pray.

Joining the High Holy Day choir is not a casual commitment. Long and arduous rehearsals are required through the summer and early fall. Likewise, joining the civic engagement choir can become exhausting through long campaigns that require years of commitment. But joining these choirs can help us move from alienation to belonging and from marginalization to inclusion.

### *Hineini*: Moses, Jeremiah, Esther, and Me

Using our voices to create change can make us feel vulnerable—to criticism, complaints, counterarguments, and even personal attacks. It is easy to find reasons to remain silent. If that is your first response, you may find comfort in knowing that you are indeed following in the footsteps of our ancestors.

When called to free the Israelites from slavery, Moses said, "I have never been a man of words, either in times past or now that You have spoken to Your servant; I am slow of speech and slow of tongue" (Exodus 4:10). Filled with a sense of inadequacy, he begged to be relieved of the enormous burden of confronting Pharaoh.

Likewise, Jeremiah asked God to choose someone else when he was called to rebuke the Israelites for their errant ways and prophesize the painful consequences of their actions. He said, "I don't know how to speak, for I am still a boy" (Jeremiah 1:6). Jeremiah understood that the Israelites of his day would not welcome God's warning of the destruction of Jerusalem and the prospect of their exile.

And, when begged by Mordecai to speak to King Ahasuerus to save her people, Queen Esther feared for her own life, saying, "If any person, man or woman, enters the king's presence in the inner court without having been summoned, there is but one law for him—that he be put to death. Only if the king extends the golden scepter to him may he live. Now I have not been summoned to visit the king for the last thirty days" (Esther 4:11). Queen Esther invited the king to two consecutive banquets before finding the courage to reveal her Jewish identity and ask him to reverse the genocidal decree.

In the face of fear and with a sense of inadequacy, each generation of biblical leaders found the strength to fulfill the mission of a historic moment. Recognizing the potentially transformative power of their positions, each ultimately found his or her own voice to say, "Here I am—*hineini*."

Despite our own limitations and even our own reluctance, we nevertheless are links in the chain of our prophetic tradition that instructs us to pursue justice. When we likewise listen to the call and respond with the words "Here I am—*hineini*," we soon realize that in the process of healing our world, we ourselves find healing. In the process of helping others achieve liberation, we find liberation, too. In the process of heeding the Jewish values supporting civic engagement, we ourselves become more engaged with our Judaism.

The ongoing cycle of repairing the world requires our voices. Even if we sing off-key and lack a vision of the finale, the choir of civic engagement needs our voices. When we collaborate, we lift each others' voices to move our country toward justice, even as we recharge ourselves as Jews.

## *Is a Blessing Appropriate for Civic Engagement?*

While all streams of Judaism connect our service to God with our acts of justice, the question of whether these acts require a blessing is answered differently by leaders and teachers across the denominations. Debate in Judaism is encouraged, and hearing multiple points of view deepens our understanding of the relationship between words of prayer and acts of justice. The Talmud lays out the arguments of rabbis from different times and places; we apply the construct of Talmudic debate to weave together opinions from different streams of Judaism as though they were conferring together.

Imagine these denominational voices debating the issue of saying a blessing over acts of social justice:

> **Imaginary Tractate *Tikkun Olam* 18a**
> Rabbi Saperstein says there is a blessing over social action
>    and social justice.
> Rabbi Sacks says there is no blessing.
> Rabbi Groner says the morning text *Eilu D'varim*, "These are
>    the precepts," applies;
> Do we not say *g'milut chasadim*, "deeds of kindness"?

The leaders of the Religious Action Center of Reform Judaism, formerly headed by Rabbi David Saperstein, wanted to concretize the link between Judaism and social justice work for Reform Jews. To do so, they created a blessing for participating in an act of social justice:

> Blessed are You, Adonai our God, Ruler of the universe, who
> hallows us with Your mitzvot and commands us to pursue justice.
>
> *Baruch atah Adonai, Eloheinu Melech haolam, asher kid'shanu
> b'mitzvotav v'tzivanu lirdof tzedek.*[121]

Believing in the evolutionary nature of Jewish expression, the Reform Movement developed this prayer to infuse acts of justice with spiritual meaning and a sense of holiness. Such civic engagement activities as lobbying on Capitol Hill for immigration reform, organizing at local fast food restaurants on behalf of Immokalee farm workers, and visiting an assisted living community are the contemporary corollaries to the obligations cited in the central text of the Holiness Code of Leviticus of loving the stranger, treating workers fairly, and honoring the elderly (Leviticus 19:33–34, 19:13, 19:32). Reciting a prayer is intended to heighten awareness that these actions are sacred.

Espousing a more traditional approach, in the above fictional debate Orthodox rabbi Jonathan Sacks would hold up an interpretation of the *Kesef Mishneh* on Maimonides's *Mishneh Torah, Hilchot B'rachot* 11:2, saying, "Commands between us and God [*mitzvot bein adam LaMakom*] require a blessing; commands between us and our fellow human beings [*mitzvot bein adam lachaveiro*] do not."[122]

Ritual acts between ourselves and God require words to express our intention. When we say a blessing before lighting the Shabbat or Chanukah candles, we acknowledge that we are not lighting the candles for ambience, but rather as a connection to our past and an expression of our values of faith and freedom. Conversely, in traditional Judaism, ethical acts between one human being and another do not require a blessing. Rabbi Sacks would teach further, "Far from needing a blessing, the act itself is the blessing."[123]

Meir Lakein, an Orthodox Jew whose professional life and passion is training Jews in the work of community organizing, also teaches that there is no blessing for acts of righteous giving (*tzedakah*). The first reason he offers is that the intended recipient of *tzedakah* may decline it, and thus, it becomes a blessing said in vain, meaning one has inappropriately used God's name with a purposeless promise (Babylonian Talmud, *B'rachot* 33a). Lakein's second reason speaks to our shared humanity:

> We say *b'rachot* on the object of the mitzvah we are about to perform—on food we are about eat, on the *lulav* [four species of plants] we are about to shake. We do not say a blessing before giving or doing an act of *tzedakah* because people must never be objectified as our means to an end.

As part of traditional morning worship, a prayer is recited for the study of Torah. A text from the Mishnah, *Eilu D'varim* (*Mishnah Pei-ah* 1:1), immediately follows to ensure that the prayer is not said in vain.

Rabbi Yossi Groner, a leader in the Chabad-Lubavitch movement, teaches that this Mishnaic text provides the context and the intention for all deeds of kindness that we perform during the day, including acts of justice:

> These are precepts
> the fruits of which a person enjoys in this world,
> [while] the principal [reward] is preserved for him in the
>     World-to-Come.
> They are: honoring father and mother,
> [performing] deeds of kindness,
> early attendance in the House of Study morning
>     and evening,
> providing hospitality to guests, visiting the sick,
> participating in making a wedding,
> accompanying the dead [to the grave],
> concentrating on the meaning of prayers,
> making peace between fellow men
> —and the study of Torah is equal to them all.[124]

Rabbi Groner adds further that we do not introduce new blessings on mitzvot that were not affirmed by our Sages.

Let us imagine the voice of Rabbi Abraham Joshua Heschel providing commentary to this Mishnah. This renowned activist and professor at the Conservative Movement's Jewish Theological Seminary might say in this imaginary debate, "I can see why and how Rabbi Saperstein would teach that one should say a blessing. For far too long, activism has been isolated from Torah. What I wrote in my diary in 1965 upon my return from Selma is applicable today":

> Jewish religious institutions have again missed a great opportunity, namely, to interpret a civil-rights movement in terms of Judaism. The vast majority of Jews participating actively in it are totally unaware of what the movement means in terms of the prophetic traditions.[125]

Whether or not we say a specific blessing over our acts of social justice, there is agreement across the denominations that these acts are an expression of our Jewish obligation. Individual clergy may wish to add their own voices to this fictional debate as they evolve or explain their own practices. Yet, when we compartmentalize our fight for justice into the secular realm, we fail to fully receive and transmit the teachings of Torah that Moses, the first freedom fighter, bequeathed to us. Saying a blessing over these acts reminds Jews—and other Americans present at these moments—that our civic engagement is grounded in our Jewish values.

## Notes to Chapter 5

107. Adapted from Martin Buber, *Ten Rungs: Collected Hasidic Sayings*, trans. Olga Marx (London and New York: Routledge, 2002), 65.
108. "Domestic Violence within the Jewish Community," Criminal Justice, http://criminal-justice.iresearchnet.com/crime/domestic-violence/jewish-community/.
109. "Sex Trafficking: What You Need to Know," National Council of Jewish Women, August 2014, http://f.cl.ly/items/1J22003f240dojoF1yoj/talking-points_sex-trafficking_final.pdf.
110. "Sex Trafficking: What You Need to Know."
111. "State Advocacy Fact Sheet: Safe Harbor Laws," National Council of Jewish Women, September 2016, https://act.ncjw.org/wp-content/uploads/dlm_uploads/2016/09/Fact-Sheet_Safe-Harbor_Updated-2016.pdf.
112. Josh Lipowsky, "Jewish Groups Ramping Up Response to Sex Trafficking," Jewish Telegraphic Agency, August 12, 2013, http://www.jta.org/2013/08/12/news-opinion/united-states/a-painful-memory-sex-trafficking-and-the-jewish-community.
113. Tim Funk, "Elie Wiesel Encourages Global Activism," McClatchy Newspapers, March 28, 2007, http://www.popmatters.com/article/elie-wiesel-encourages-global-activism/.
114. Katie J.M. Baker, "Here Is the Powerful Letter the Stanford Victim Read Aloud to Her Attacker," BuzzFeed News, June 3, 2016, https://www.buzzfeed.com/katiejmbaker/heres-the-powerful-letter-the-stanford-victim-read-to-her-ra?utm_term=.tgnpmRr3v#.ju8A2xVY9.
115. Joe Biden, "An Open Letter to a Courageous Young Woman," as quoted by Tom Namako, "Joe Biden Writes an Open Letter to Stanford Survivor," BuzzFeed News, June 9, 2016. https://www.buzzfeed.com/tomnamako/

joe-biden-writes-an-open-letter-to-stanford-survivor?bftwnews&utm_
term=.jcl4bv7bK#.comp5Oe5K.

116. Rabbi Judith Schindler, originally published in *God, Faith and Identity
from the Ashes: Reflections of Children and Grandchildren of Holocaust Survivors*
(Woodstock, VT: Jewish Lights, 2015), 250.

117. Ari L. Goldman, *The Search for God at Harvard* (New York: Ballantine
Books, 2008), 33.

118. Rabbi Marcus uses the spelling "G-d" as a means of adhering to the prohibition against erasing or destroying G-d's name (Rashi on Deuteronomy
12:4) as a precaution in the event that the paper upon which it is written
will one day be irreverently discarded. Other legal authorities understand
this prohibition as applying to only when God's name is written in Hebrew. This practice is not followed by the Reform Movement, but it appears here out of respect for Rabbi Marcus.

119. Rabbi Yossi Marcus, "'Rabbi, I'm a Bad Jew!,'" Chabad of the North Peninsula, accessed March 1, 2017, http://www.chabadnp.com/templates/
articlecco_cdo/aid/1025039/jewish/Rabbi-Im-a-Bad-Jew.

120. Ron Wolfson, *Relational Judaism: Using the Power of Relationships to Transform the Jewish Community* (Woodstock, VT: Jewish Lights, 2013).

121. "Social Action Blessing Cards," Religious Action Center of Reform
Judaism, http://www.rac.org/sites/default/files/social_action_blessing_
cards_2012_-_front.pdf.

122. Jonathan Sacks, *To Heal a Fractured World: The Ethics of Responsibility* (New
York: Schocken Books, 2005), 104.

123. Sacks, *To Heal a Fractured World*, 105.

124. *The Complete Metsudah Siddur* (Brooklyn, NY: Metsudah Publications,
1990), 15–16.

125. Abraham Joshua Heschel, *Moral Grandeur and Spiritual Audacity*, xxiii–
xxiv.

CHAPTER 6

# Living Our Values

## Protecting the Earth That Sustains Us

HEARING A CLEAR CALL amid the noise of competing and countless cries for justice, finding the voice with which to speak in a
way that is comfortable and compelling, and then making the choice
to have our actions mirror our words so that we are not only talking
the talk, but also walking the walk—these are the tasks of the Jew
committed to creating positive change in the world. Being Jewish is
not just about belonging to community; being Jewish is also about
living the values of our faith.

Despite the idyllic image of the Garden of Eden as a place of lei-
sure and abundance, the first human was given the responsibility to
work the land and to protect it (Genesis 2:15). A midrash (an inter-
pretive commentary on Torah encompassing both legend and law)
on Ecclesiastes, written at least twelve hundred years ago, states:

> When the Blessed Holy One created the first human beings,
> God took them and led them round all the trees of the Garden
> of Eden and said: "Look at My works, how beautiful and praise-
> worthy they are! And all that I have created, it was for you that I
> created it. Pay attention that you do not corrupt and destroy My
> world: if you corrupt it, there is no one to repair it after you."
> (Kohelet Rabbah 7:13)

We are required to fulfill our obligation to protect the earth, even
while we use its resources to sustain ourselves. A vision for the agricultural life we will live in the Promised Land permeates the Torah.
The lessons we are taught and the laws we are given acknowledge
that working our land, sharing our harvest, and eating our food are

not independent of God. These activities—necessary for our own survival—all fall within the framework of our faith. The Torah defines our relationship with the land, from establishing three pilgrimage festivals tied to the agricultural cycle, to reserving the gleanings for those in need, to prescribing laws that restrict the foods we eat.

The prayer recited before meals, *HaMotzi*, is a declaration of gratitude to God for bringing forth bread from the earth. Yet even the Jewish preschoolers who sing this blessing can see that God alone does not bring bread to our tables. The Talmud and midrash are replete with stories and teachings that make it clear that partnership with God is required for humans to eat bread. This lesson is expanded to instruct the Jewish people that human partnership is needed to sustain and complete all creation, for as the midrash above says, truly there is no one else to repair this earth if we spoil and destroy it.

### Evolving Kashrut: What Is Fit to Eat?

Jewish life is centered not only in the synagogue but in the home—especially when it comes to food. After the destruction of our Temple and exile from our land, our tables were meant to become an altar (*mizbei-ach*), and each of our homes was meant to become a small sanctuary (*mikdash m'at*). In Judaism, sharing food at these home altars is an essential element of hospitality, holy times, and justice. Culinary observance and additional prayers around the table are required to make certain religious celebrations complete. For example, Passover requires the retelling of the story of the Exodus through an elaborate meal and the eating of matzah (unleavened bread) and other ritual foods. Both these foods and the liturgical framework serve to strengthen our living memory of the journey from oppression to liberation, our foundational Jewish narrative.

For many Jews, food is an intrinsic component of their observance. They bring their faith to the table through kashrut (dietary laws). Orthodox and Conservative Judaism call for strict adherence to the literal laws of Torah through the lens of Rabbinic Judaism guiding the slaughtering of animals, enumerating prohibited foods, and governing meal preparation. Some Jews add sanctity to meals through a ritual washing of hands before eating, reflecting the heightened holiness of the ancient priests, who washed their hands before offering sacrifices. The Jew who recites blessings before and after meals lifts up the primal act of eating by first acknowledging God as the source of food and then expressing gratitude for the gift of sustenance that has been enjoyed.

In the earliest stages of Reform Judaism in America, kashrut was regarded as irrelevant. The CCAR Pittsburgh Platform of 1885 cited these rituals as obstructing rather than elevating a sense of spirituality. The Reform Movement, living up to its name, has evolved since the nineteenth century in its relationship with traditional kashrut. The CCAR's Centenary Perspective of 1976 urged Reform Jews to "exercise their individual autonomy, choosing and creating on the basis of commitment and knowledge."[126]

Had we been writing this book fifty years ago, the Reform Movement might still have stood as an exception to the Jewish concern with eating in a holy manner. However, in more recent years, Reform Jews also are viewing their food choices as a reflection of the Divine or an element of Jewish values. In the anthology *The Sacred Table: Creating a Jewish Food Ethic*, historian and rabbi Carole Balin writes:

> For nearly two centuries, Reform Jews have rejected, adopted, resuscitated, embraced, and even invented Jewish dietary law. Their changing view of kashrut results from an understanding of and belief in the elasticity of Judaism and its traditions, and the inevitable and necessary influence of historical circumstances upon them.[127]

Rabbi Balin notes, "No longer an oxymoron, 'Reform Kashrut' has entered the Jewish lexicon, though there is no consensus on what this means exactly."[128] The Hebrew word *kosher* may be translated as "fit" or "proper," and the Torah identifies the various foods that are appropriate for eating and the rules for their preparation. The laws of kashrut inform the food choices made by Jews who adhere to these religious values, creating for many a daily sense of separateness, holiness, and being in relationship with God. Today, many Reform Jews create a broader interpretation of what is fit or proper to eat.

Food choices create the "sacred apartness" articulated by Rabbi Sid Schwarz in chapter 1: one can maintain "the integrity of the Jewish idea, of the covenant of Sinai" by being "a little bit apart from the rest of the world."[129] Both a Jew who observes traditional kashrut and a Jew inspired by values of social justice may find a heightened sense of sacred apartness by living Jewish ethics with their daily food choices. In an effort to bring *k'dushah* (holiness) into our lives and *tzedek* (righteousness) to the world, a modern-day food ethic may include the Jewish values of avoiding unnecessary destruction, showing compassion for animals, not oppressing workers, and protecting the earth.

## *Bal Tashchit*: Avoiding Unnecessary Destruction

The Torah teaches the concept of *bal tashchit* (do not destroy), which has far-reaching implications for today's society. As part of the ethics guiding the reality of wartime, cutting down fruit trees to assist in a siege is prohibited (Deuteronomy 20:19–20). Trees not bearing fruit may be destroyed for building military structures and weaponry, but not to deprive the enemy of their use, neither during the battle nor in the future. Even during wartime, we are supposed to respect the gifts of the earth.

The Talmud captures a discussion between two fourth-century sages, Rav Papa and Rav Chisda, about the unnecessary squandering of resources through our food choices. These rabbis discuss whether one should eat bread made from barley rather than from the more desirable wheat, or drink beer rather than the less readily available wine (Babylonian Talmud, *Shabbat* 140b). Summing up their conclusion, Rabbi Kevin M. Kleinman writes:

> According to Rav Chisda, when given a choice, one is religiously and ethically obligated to consume foodstuffs that require fewer resources to produce and are less expensive. Rav Chisda and Rav Papa expand *bal tashchit* to consider social, environmental, and economic factors when determining what type of food to

eat and beverage to drink. They deem it inappropriately wasteful to eat a product that is superfluously expensive and requires more resources to produce.[130]

The statement from Ecclesiastes that there is nothing new under the sun is proved true yet again (Ecclesiastes 1:9). Buying local has emerged as a modern food movement to avoid using transportation resources unnecessarily, but Rav Chisda and Rav Papa urged us to consider this ethic seventeen centuries ago.

### *Tzaar Baalei Chayim*: Compassion for Animals

The Torah is clear that the suffering of animals is prohibited. In Exodus we learn, "When you see the ass of your enemy lying under its burden and would refrain from raising it, you must nevertheless help raise it" (Exodus 23:5). The traditional laws of kashrut address how to alleviate suffering at the moment of slaughter, but the modern realities of livestock operations and slaughterhouses require us to broaden the timeline over which we evaluate the ethical treatment of animals. How these animals lived merits our attention, not just how they died.

In a watershed moment, the Jewish community was appalled and embarrassed when a *glatt* kosher meat-packing company in Iowa was in the news in 2004–5 for mistreating cattle, along with polluting the environment and violating labor laws. While the designation "*glatt*" reflects a higher level of scrutiny in determining the kashrut of the animal and hence, in some eyes, a heightened level of ritual observance, this company transgressed many ethical precepts. A few years later, the company filed for bankruptcy, and multiple executives were convicted and imprisoned, leading many in the Jewish community to question whether ethical misconduct should impact the certification of kashrut.

Founded in 2010, Brooklyn-based Grow and Behold Foods processes and sells *glatt* kosher, pasture-raised meats. Ethical treatment of animals is incorporated into its standards for sourcing and processing. Co-owner Anna Hanau explains, "We care about traditional kashrut, and we also care about the animals being outdoors and roaming around. We are fortunate to work with small process-ing plants where the pace is slow enough that we can work with the animals in a dignified way."

Hanau acknowledges that this smaller scale, more humane ap-proach affects prices. She says, "We are part of a bigger shift where many farmers, ranchers, and food producers are encouraging folks to consider the kind of world we create with our financial choices."

### *Bal Talin*: Paying Wages on Time

The morality implicit in our food choices extends to buying our food from businesses that treat their workers fairly. We learn in Deuter-onomy: "You shall not abuse a needy and destitute laborer, whether a fellow Israelite or a stranger in one of the communities of your land. You must pay out the wages due on the same day, before the sun sets, for the worker is needy and urgently depends on it" (Deu-teronomy 24:14–15).

Rabbi Dr. Shmuly Yanklowitz, an Orthodox rabbi who became a vegan in response to the realities of industrial slaughterhouses, cre-ated an ethical certificate for kosher restaurants called Tav HaYosher to protect service industry workers.[131] When a kosher restaurant went out of business without paying its workers their final week of wages, Rav Yanklowitz made an appeal on the Tav HaYosher Face-book page, raising the few thousand dollars needed to satisfy the owner's obligation. He wrote:

1. By Torah law, these workers deserve to be paid.
2. Jews not paying workers is a *chillul Hashem* ([and] reflects poorly on the Jewish community) —we must hold ourselves to the highest standard.
3. This is not just a Jewish-owned business but one that was serving the Jewish community (extending the responsibility from the owner to consumers as well).

They are owed $2,900. I have already raised 1K. Will you contribute? Please email us at info@utzedek.org if you can support. Let's clean this up together & turn it into a *kiddush Hashem* [sanctification of God's name]![132]

Ethical business practices are of paramount importance in Judaism. Mistreatment of workers is *chilul HaShem* (a desecration of God's name), impacting all who benefit from the product of their labor. In contrast, when we adhere to high ethical conduct, it is a sanctification of God's name, *kiddush HaShem*. Yanklowitz's vision for the "TAV" certification addressing food justice is part of Uri L'Tzedek, an Orthodox social justice organization. This program challenges Jews to eat at certified restaurants and encourages Jewish institutions to engage certified caterers.

According to the fourth-century scholar Rava, the first question a person will be asked upon entering the heavenly court after death will be "Did you conduct business faithfully?" (Babylonian Talmud, *Shabbat* 31a). In both earthly and heavenly courts, Jews are accountable for how workers are treated, not only in our own places of business, but in the businesses that we support.

### *Shomrei Adamah*: Protecting the Earth

Judaism teaches that each person is born with two inclinations: *yetzer hatov*, the good inclination, and *yetzer hara*, the evil inclination. The first drives us to compassion and selflessness, and the second drives us to ambition and acquisition. But consequences of *yetzer hara*, the evil inclination, can include creating nice homes in which to raise our families and building businesses that enrich our communities. It is when the evil inclination is unrestrained by the good inclination that we find ourselves interested in acquiring wealth only for ourselves and not helping others or achieving our own success through exploiting others.

These principles hold true when it comes to working our land. As previously mentioned, the first human being was given the responsibility to work the land and to protect it (Genesis 2:15). The second directive to "protect" the land sets boundaries around the first directive to "work" it. The bottom line is that we need to protect the environment from ourselves, ensuring that our *yetzer hara* is held in check by our *yetzer hatov*. Sustainability starts with each one of us and extends outward.

The founder of the Jewish Renewal Movement, Reb Zalman Schachter-Shalomi, was ordained by Chabad but evolved early in his life to a more flexible understanding of halachah (Jewish law). One of his gifts to modern Jewish thought was to reinvigorate and reimagine traditional ritual. He wrote:

> Disposable dishes—a Styrofoam take-out container, say, or a nonrecyclable soft-drink bottle—are, from the perspective of classical halakhah, ideal. Since nobody has ever used them before, no suspicion exists that they've ever been touched by trafe [unkosher] food. From an ecological point of view, however— from the perspective of the human race and our overflowing landfills—they are disastrous. . . . I began thinking of a new kind of kashrut, one that would combine the ancient ways of thoughtful consumption and avoidance of cruelty and violence with the new awareness of the wider repercussions of some of our actions, a way of thinking that I called eco-kashrut.[133]

Eco-kashrut became another label for considering how the entire process of bringing food to your table impacts the environment. This enabled a new generation of Jews to find deep meaning in incorporating ethical practices into their daily lives and inspired them to live their Jewish values with each meal.

### Bringing Morals to Our Menu: We Are What We Eat

For a segment of the Jewish people today, the concept of kashrut— of what is Jewishly proper for eating—has broadened to include the working conditions of the employees who grew our food or worked with the animals that became our food, the treatment of the animals themselves, the chemicals employed in growing our food, the energy needed to create our food and bring it to our table, and the unnecessary waste created in packaging our food.

As a result of his contact with the scandal-ridden kosher meat processing plant previously mentioned, Rabbi Morris Allen realized that the ethical wrongdoings extended not only to the producers but to the purchasers as well. In his 2006 High Holy Day sermon at Beth Jacob Congregation in Mendota, Minnesota, he reflected on his confession: "I too had become complicit as a kosher consumer. If we could certify the ritual aspects of kashrut, we certainly could certify the ethical values of Jewish life." Rabbi Allen led the way for the creation of the Magen Tzedek Standard (shield of justice) as a collaboration of the United Synagogue of Conservative Judaism and the Rabbinical Assembly to address such issues. The Magen Tzedek Standard was intended to provide additional certification to food products already deemed to be kosher, evaluating animal treatment, labor practices, and environmental issues.[134]

When first conceived in 2008, it was named the Heksher Tzedek (rabbinic certification of justice) and also endorsed by the Central Conference of American Rabbis (CCAR), the rabbinic organization of the Reform Movement. The CCAR Resolution praised the Conservative Movement and its Rabbinic Assembly for instituting the Heksher Tzedek and encouraged Jews who might not otherwise observe the laws of kashrut to consider these ethical guidelines in their food choices.[135]

Faced with a lack of cooperation from kosher processing plants and their *shochtim* (ritual slaughterers), this initiative to broaden the ethical dimensions of kashrut certification remains an ideal. To move forward, Rabbi Allen envisions a digital app that provides consumers with information culled from the public domain on animal treatment, labor issues, and environmental impact. These sources could include OSHA violations, comparative wages, and the environmental impact of salt water runoff. (Salt and multiple rinsings are part of the plant's process of making meat and poultry kosher.) Rabbi Allen himself has been a vegetarian since 1974.

What is the purpose of Judaism? It is to live our lives by the highest human standards as derived from our holy texts, with which we are in an ongoing dialogue. Kashrut, however interpreted, applies to the personal food choices an individual makes. When we reinterpret traditional Jewish ethics for how we live our faith through the foods we choose, we also find the sacred apartness that defines us as Jews. The adage "you are what you eat" reflects not only the health of our bodies but also the ethics of our faith.

## "Walking the Walk" in Our Synagogues

Recognizing our obligation to protect the earth that sustains us, an increasing number of congregations are exploring the links between our faith and our food and between our ethics and our earth. Discussions about such issues as reducing energy footprints, eliminating Styrofoam, and serving fair trade coffee—along with their implications for synagogue budgets—are finding their way onto board agendas. Synagogue gardens are increasingly common, grounding a hands-on curriculum of Jewish values, providing fresh produce to supplement canned food collections, fostering community-building, and serving as a noncontroversial first step toward environmental advocacy.

Abundance Farm in Northampton, Massachusetts, is a collaboration among Congregation B'nai Israel (a Conservative synagogue), the Lander-Grinspoon Academy (a K–6 Jewish day school), and the Northampton Survival Center (a food pantry). The farmland is owned by the synagogue, and the vast majority of the produce is harvested and consumed by clients of the food pantry.

Since the establishment of Abundance Farm, lesson plans about Jewish agricultural traditions are incorporated into the curriculum of every grade at the Lander-Grinspoon Academy and at Congregation B'nai Israel's religious school and preschool. Rabbi Jacob Fine, director of Abundance Farm and director of Jewish Life at Congregation B'nai Israel, talks about his personal journey to Jewish farming as a synthesis of his passions for food politics and Judaism: "As an educator, I find farming to be a profoundly meaningful educational platform for teaching Judaics and building community. . . . When I first encountered the tradition of *Sh'mitah* in college, it blew me away."

Occurring every seventh year, the *Sh'mitah* is a Sabbatical year when land is intended to lie fallow in order to regenerate. During the *Sh'mitah* year, the produce of the land becomes ownerless (*hefkeir*), and everyone—neighbors, strangers, the poor, the wealthy, and the owners themselves—has equal rights to it. Anyone may eat what the earth yields, but no one may take more than what is needed for a few meals, and the produce may not be harvested and sold. The Torah additionally calls for a Jubilee year (*Yoveil*), which occurs in the fiftieth year, after seven cycles of Sabbatical years. At this time, ancestral land that had been sold would revert to its original owner (Leviticus 25:1–13).

Both *Sh'mitah* and *Yoveil* teach that the land is not ours; we are but tenants on the earth that ultimately belongs to God. These prescribed years protect the soil from depletion and the land from exploitation, and prohibit the selling of the land in perpetuity or from foreclosure beyond reclaim. While *Sh'mitah* and *Yoveil* are commanded to be fulfilled only in the Land of Israel—and the latter has likely not been practiced since First Temple times—their underlying values continue to inform our lives today.

Abundance Farm has been tremendously successful in its mission to connect the synagogue to its two partner organizations and to the neighborhood surrounding their contiguous properties. Rabbi Fine comments on the farm's community building impact:

> Before the farm there was no deep relationship with the Northampton Survival Center. . . . But it has brought the communities together. There is no other example of these three organizations working together on this scale. . . . We are visible in the neighborhood and highly accessible by foot, which enables us opportunities that other Jewish farms don't have. . . . We laid out the farm to be inviting from the street—by planting berries, for example.

A member of Congregation B'nai Israel built a "Help Yourself" farm cart that is parked near the sidewalk during the growing season. Originally intended for surplus produce from Abundance Farm, the cart has become a community resource, attracting donations of excess fruits and vegetables from backyard gardens and other area farms. This practice brings to life the ancient biblical commandment to leave for the poor and the stranger the produce from the edges of our fields and the gleanings (the leftover crops) (Leviticus 19:9).

Rabbi Fine emphasizes the importance of treating the land as a resource for the community, respecting the dignity of those struggling with poverty. To reinforce this communal concept, Abundance Farm invites the community to help with major projects such as putting in new irrigation lines and planting the orchard.

> We are trying to treat the farm as completely *hefkeir*, which translates to ownerless, or in a more modern sense as communal. Our commitment is to not relate to the farm as ours, but instead to think of ourselves as the stewards of a communal resource. In this way, hopefully, food-insecure people in our community won't feel like the food they are harvesting on the farm is charity or a handout.

In October 2015, the farm hosted an interfaith festival as a *Hakheil*, the assembly traditional for the end of the *Sh'mitah* year, as articulated in the Book of Deuteronomy (31:10–13). The program, entitled "Harvesting Hope," encouraged participants to "restore damaged ecosystems," "reverse climate change," and "save the bees," in addition to offering children's musical performances, crafts, and parades typical of community events.

Abundance Farm has led Congregation B'nai Israel outside of its synagogue walls—into the farm, into stronger relationships with its partner institutions, and into its neighborhood. Importantly, the farm has also inspired these institutions and the community to advocate for protecting the environment and for food justice issues more broadly.

Likewise, five institutions on the Shalom Park campus in Charlotte created a community garden to promote Jewish values and sustainable living, part of a project called Shalom Green. These agencies—the Reform and Conservative synagogues, the Levine Jewish Community Center, the Jewish Federation, and the Foundation of Shalom Park—had built stronger relationships among themselves while partnering to host the Children's Defense Fund Freedom Schools© program.

Yonatan Thull, a dedicated environmentalist who volunteered at Shalom Green in its creation, touts the benefits of experiential learning in afterschool programs for today's tech-savvy Jewish children who have already spent a full day in the classroom before arriving for Hebrew school. Two other organizations on the Shalom Park campus—Camp Mindy and the Charlotte Jewish Preschool—added a garden educator to their program budgets after participating in Shalom Green activities. Young Jews in Charlotte can now experience their faith outdoors in addition to learning about it in the classroom; the pomegranate and fig trees planted in the garden are sensory learning aids for the trees of Torah, as are Hebrew words painted on rocks and benches.

Shalom Green impacts healthy food choices for the community as well. Thull tells the story of a student's mother who called him with gratitude for introducing her son to the tastiness of the fresh tomatoes picked that week in the community garden. The garden's organic produce is cultivated by children of every age and donated to the onsite food pantry of Jewish Family Services, as well as to the local Meals on Wheels agency. While incorporating fresh produce into meals, these activities also teach and fulfill the values of feeding the hungry, honoring the elderly, and healing the sick.

When Thull was eleven years old, he wanted to save the monarch butterfly, but he laments now that he did not have enough support to make a difference. Twenty-four years later he assisted the Jewish community and the North Carolina Wildlife Federation in creating two pollinator gardens on Shalom Park—part of the Butterfly Highway—to attract butterflies and other pollinators that are essential to farming. Installing birdhouses in partnership with Audubon North Carolina and the North American Bluebird Society created another layer of pollination, further restoring the balance of nature necessary to bring food to our tables—a balance that has been weakened through urbanization, excessive pesticides, and diseases.

Synagogues creating community gardens help us become more thoughtful about how our food and our environment are connected to our faith. As we tend and protect the earth—growing vegetables to feed the hungry and repopulating pollinators essentials for the vegetables to grow—we become more aware of how food arrives at our table. As we study the Jewish agricultural tradition, we learn the ways in which Judaism commands us to protect the earth and share its bounty. Teaching the agricultural heritage of Judaism to our children through our synagogue farms and gardens connects the next generation to a Judaism that is lived outside the classroom and sanctuary and in our world.

## Environmental Advocacy

It is not enough for us to plant gardens for only ourselves, to green our synagogues yet not our homes, or to care about sustainable food solely at the restaurants and kitchen tables where we eat. Starting with our tables, gardens, and synagogues is only the first step for us to become energized and to expand our focus beyond ourselves. Making these initial choices educates us and inspires us to protect and sustain our environment more broadly.

Congregations on the civic engagement journey often start their environmental work by transforming their synagogue building and property to support a greener world. For example, the Green Team at Temple Beth Elohim in Wellesley, Massachusetts, has worked on temperature control for the synagogue building and more recently arranged for solar panels to reduce its electrical power needs. Congregant Neil Silverston of Temple Beth Elohim explains how the Power Purchase Agreement works: "The vendor buys the panels, puts them on your roof, and then you sign a long-term contract for the power. The vendor can take advantage of the tax credits, which the synagogue cannot use, and the synagogue gets the residual life of the panels after the contract ends." Asked about the motivation to use the solar power, Silverston responded:

> We are trying to do the right thing, to live our values. Absolutely we looked at the numbers, the insurance for our building, and we made a fiscally prudent decision. But all the people whose job it is to manage the building are partners in this effort. Never was it about "*Can* we afford to do this?" but [rather] "*How* do we afford to do this?"

Steve Fox has been a member of Temple Isaiah in Los Angeles,

California, for nearly fifty years, serving on the temple board for more than half of that time. He talks about how the temple's green programs have evolved from congregant education to transforming the synagogue building to community advocacy: "We started with education programs, changing congregants' personal behavior. Then we focused on greening the temple itself. Now we are focused on changing policy because we are running out of time."

But Fox acknowledges that advocacy can be difficult over the long haul, saying, "Our Green Team gets discouraged occasionally, not just because of global events, but because we have trouble convincing others to do what seems so obvious to us . . . like bringing reusable cups to meetings rather than using disposable."

Through his work with the Temple Isaiah Green Team, Fox has found the support to continue working on his mission. He jokes that the original environmental team founded thirteen years ago was *bashert* (part of God's plan) because their last names all evoked the environment: Fox, Ivy, Moss, and Greenspan. He strongly believes that his environmental work reinforces his connection to the synagogue, and his long-standing relationship with the synagogue inspires his environmental work, explaining, "The synagogue provides an effective infrastructure to pool people's energies and passions, and the spiritual drive to make the daunting achievable."

Environmental advocacy and food justice converge in the new Jewish Food Movement, which calls the Jewish community to ensure that ethical and environmental practices related to our food are applied on a larger scale. The Religious Action Center of Reform Judaism defines food justice as "a social justice issue at the intersections of environmental sustainability, public health, economic justice, and deals with ethical eating choices, agricultural and food policy, and more."[136]

Judith Belasco, then director of Food Programs at Hazon, commented in her keynote address to the 2011 Hazon Food Conference that "four years ago the expression 'New Jewish Food Movement' didn't even exist." Sasha Feldstein was working for the American Jewish World Service (AJWS) when she attended the conference and posted her own pithy definition of the Jewish Food Movement on the AJWS blog:

> Yes, the New Jewish Food Movement is about more than growing your own food and eating healthfully (although these things are very important as well). It's about ensuring that everyone has equal access to fresh food and control over their food systems. It's about understanding that food is a right—not a privilege—and that hunger today is not caused by a lack of resources or overpopulation but by policies that directly impact people's ability to feed themselves. It's about policies and systems that we have the power to change.[137]

Jewish values can be learned both inside the classroom and outside in the garden. Jewish prayers can be lifted up from both the pages of the prayer book and from the physical acts of planting in the soil. Jewish voices calling for change can be uttered through the liturgy and as we work our synagogue farms and gardens. Congregational platforms can be created so that each of us can awaken to the reality that the land is ours to work and to protect, but not to exploit.

## In Conclusion

The Blessing after Meals, *Birkat HaMazon*, includes an expression of gratitude to God for the abundance that we have received, as commanded in Deuteronomy: "When you have eaten your fill, give thanks to the Eternal your God for the good land given to you" (Deuteronomy 8:10).

The blessings we recite are a symbolic pause button, allowing us to acknowledge the environment and the chain of human beings that bring our food to our table. Our experience of plenty should not be achieved at the expense of others. Food justice is about acknowledging that there is enough—so long as we protect the earth even as we work it. God requires our partnership not only in making our food, but in ensuring that our appetites driven by our *yetzer hara* do not overtake the values of justice, generosity, and hospitality that our *yetzer hatov* and the Torah call us to fulfill.

When we make our daily food choices with righteous intent—avoiding unnecessary waste, showing compassion for animals, treating employees fairly, and protecting the earth—and when we fulfill our responsibility to work the land and protect it for future generations, then we create blessings not only for ourselves, but for those with whom we share the earth and those who will inherit it from us.

From food justice to human trafficking to refugees, the theme of oneness emerges. We are interconnected. Still, the overwhelming number of crises and calls for help can be numbing and cause people to disconnect. When our synagogues serve as the gateway to civic engagement, alienation is transformed to connection. When we share the wisdom of the ancient texts and liturgy as a means of casting light upon today's places of darkness, Judaism becomes relevant. Civic engagement can spiritually charge the disconnected Jew, the disaffected Jew, and the Jew who senses that there is more, providing comfort, purpose, and community.

## An Environmentalist Reinterpretation of the V'ahavta

Jewish values are transmitted through the blessings we say around our tables, the foods we choose to purchase and eat, our care of the earth that sustains us, the social justice causes we embrace, and the prayers we utter in the synagogue. The values of Reform Jews are further expressed in the prayers eliminated, altered, or reinterpreted in the Reform Movement's prayer books. Examining interpretations of the V'ahavta prayer illustrates this principle of reconciling our liturgy and our worldview.

The Torah teaches that our actions have consequences; adherence to its teachings will result in blessings, and failure to abide by its mandates will lead to curses. The actions required by the Torah entail the fulfillment of its ritual and ethical commandments (mitzvot). This theology is articulated in the V'ahavta, the prayer that follows the Sh'ma. The prayer traditionally includes a paragraph excerpted from

Deuteronomy that describes both the natural abundance that will result from obeying God's commandments and the agricultural havoc we will face as a result of straying from the prescribed path. However, this paragraph is generally omitted from Reform liturgy:

> If, then, you obey the commandments that I enjoin upon you this day, loving the Eternal your God and serving [God] with all your heart and soul, I will grant the rain for your land in season, the early rain and the late. You shall gather in your new grain and wine and oil—I will also provide grass in the fields for your cattle—and thus you shall eat your fill. Take care not to be lured away to serve other gods and bow to them. For the Eternal's anger will flare up against you, shutting up the skies so that there will be no rain and the ground will not yield its produce; and you will soon perish from the good land that the Eternal is assigning to you. (Deuteronomy 11:13–17)

Many liberal Jews question this theology of God's justice, because the reality we see in our daily lives does not reflect this religious teaching. In terms of individual consequences for actions, we witness pious people encountering poverty and pain, and morally corrupt people enjoying riches and good health. In terms of collective culpability, we do not believe that failing to perform religious rituals leads to drought and famine.

However, many Jewish environmentalists embrace the powerful teaching undergirding this text. For the consequences of the *V'ahavta* can be understood not in response to fulfillment of religious ritual, but in response to environmental stewardship. The sins of corporate greed, wasteful consumption, and exploitation of resources that endanger our earth do, in fact, contribute to the drought and famine prophesied in the text.

Melissa Carpenter, a professional Jewish storyteller and blogger, comments on *Eikev*, the weekly Torah portion that includes the Deuteronomy verses that are in the *V'ahavta*:

> Environmentalists, extending the if-then statements in this week's Torah portion to the whole human race, have pointed out that our wanton degradation of the world's air, water, soil, flora, and fauna result in poisoned food, sickness, and rising sea levels,

all of which can result in starvation, death, and exile. We can certainly argue that if society as a whole does not put the welfare of our planet first, then disasters will follow. And perhaps taking care of the earth is one way to love and serve God.[138]

Other modern commentators reject this reading of the *V'ahavta*. A prominent professor of theology at the American Jewish University in California, Rabbi Elliot Dorff acknowledges the challenge this text poses to many modern Jews, yet he disputes the environmentalist interpretation:

> Contemporary Jewish environmentalists answer the objection [to Deuteronomy's theology] by pointing out that when we sin against God's world, pollution results, with the result that clean water and safe food become scarce. This is undoubtedly true, but Deuteronomy connects reward and punishment to *all* the commandments, not just those connected to the environment.[139]

The struggle with this theology of reward and punishment for religious observance is not new. The American Reform Movement excluded this text from its prayer books from the mid-1800s until 2015, recently adding it back as a historical alternative within the High Holy Day liturgy.[140] The commentary notes:

> It is possible to interpret the passage more naturalistically, as a dire prediction of the consequences of human arrogance. . . . If we forget the sacredness of all things, exploit the earth for short-term profit, and make idols of human comfort and convenience, "the ground will not yield its produce," and both we and our world may perish.[141]

The Reconstructionist prayer book substitutes a more positive blessing, noting that the original text bases both reward and punishment on Israel's "collective" performance of the mitzvot and presents "a supernatural theology that many contemporary Jews find difficult."[142]

Encountering a theology in the prayer book that is inconsistent with one's personal belief system may lead to questioning the relevance of religion to the "real" world. Environmentalists offer an alternative explanation for the disturbing words of Deuteronomy. Whether we subscribe to this theology or not, this environmentalist interpretation reminds us that our actions have long-term consequences.

## Notes to Chapter 6

126. "Reform Judaism: A Centenary Perspective," adopted by the Central Conference of American Rabbis in San Francisco, 1976, http://ccarnet.org/rabbis-speak/platforms/reform-judaism-centenary-perspective.

127. Carole B. Balin, "Making Every Forkful Count: Reform Jews, Kashrut, and Mindful Eating, 1840–2010," in *The Sacred Table: Creating a Jewish Food Ethic*, ed. Mary L. Zamore (New York: CCAR Press, 2011), 6.

128. Balin, "Making Every Forkful Count," 12.

129. Schwarz, *Judaism and Justice*.

130. Kevin M. Kleinman, "Curb Your Consumerism: Developing a *Bal Tashchit* Food Ethic for Today," in Zamore, *The Sacred Table*, 168.

131. "Tav haYosher," Uri L'Tzedek, http://utzedek.org/tav-hayosher/.

132. Tav HaYosher Facebook page, https://www.facebook.com/Tav-HaYosher-The-Kosher-Ethical-Seal-63620204784/, June 5, 2016 post.

133. Zalman Schachter-Shalomi with Joel Segel, *Jewish with Feeling: A Guide to Meaningful Jewish Practice* (Woodstock, VT: Jewish Lights Publishing, 2013), Kindle location 2002–2012.

134. Magen Tzedek, http://www.magentzedek.org/.

135. "Kashrut & Hekhsher Tzedek," resolution adopted by the Board of Trustees, August 2008, Central Conference of American Rabbis, http://ccarnet.org/rabbis-speak/resolutions/2008/kashrut-hekhsher-tzedek.

136. "Food Justice," Religious Action Center, accessed March 2, 2017, http://www.rac.org/food-justice.

137. Sasha Feldstein, "So, What's the 'New Jewish Food Movement?' A Movement for Justice," *AJWS Blog*, August 24, 2011, https://ajws.org/blog/so-whats-the-new-jewish-food-movement/.

138. Melissa Carpenter, "Eikev: Reward and Punishment," *torahsparks* (blog), August 11, 2014, https://torahsparks.wordpress.com/2014/08/11/eikev-reward-and-punishment/.

139. Lawrence A. Hoffman, ed., *My People's Prayer Book: Traditional Prayers, Modern Commentary*, vol. 1, *The Sh'ma and Its Blessings* (Woodstock, VT: Jewish Lights, 1997), 107.

140. Edwin Goldberg, Janet Marder, Sheldon Marder, and Leon Morris, eds., *Mishkan Hanefesh: Machzor for the Days of Awe* (New York: CCAR Press, 2015), vol. 1, Rosh Hashanah, 154; vol. 2, Yom Kippur, 34 and 190.

141. Goldberg et al., *Mishkan Hanefesh*, vol. 2, Yom Kippur, 190.

142. *Kol Haneshamah: Shabbat Vehagim* (Wyncote, PA: Reconstructionist Press, 1996), 67.

REFLECTION

# How Civic Engagement
# Recharges Jews

MEIR LAKEIN
*JOIN for Justice*

PRISONERS cannot free themselves from prison.
If civic engagement afforded Jews an opportunity to do what needs to be done, support people we care about, and live out our values, that would truly be reason enough. But, within civic engagement, if we look closely at its long, winding path, we can also find a route to our own transformation. It derives through the interplay of community and freedom.

In one of the first stories recounted in the Babylonian Talmud, we learn:

> Rabbi Chiya bar Abba fell ill and Rabbi Yochanan went in to visit him. He said to him, "Are your sufferings welcome to you?" He replied, "Neither they, nor their reward." He said to him, "Give me your hand." He gave him his hand and he raised him.
>
> Rabbi Yochanan once fell ill and Rabbi Chanina went in to visit him. He said to him, "Are your sufferings welcome to you?" He replied, "Neither they nor their reward." He said to him, "Give me your hand." He gave him his hand and he raised him.
>
> Why could not Rabbi Yochanan raise himself? They replied: "The prisoner cannot free themself from prison." (Babylonian Talmud, *B'rachot* 5b, translated by Meir Lakein)

The Gemara moves beyond questions of accepting suffering or working miracles to the most practical question: We see that Rabbi Yochanan has the power to heal. So why doesn't he just heal himself?

Why does he have to languish, waiting for Rabbi Chanina?

  Because prisoners cannot free themselves from prison.

  And neither can we.

  We all know it's possible to feel alone, even in a crowd. We know that whether we feel society's brokenness every minute of every day or live in relative comfort, we can still feel not only isolated, but impotent to push back against a day-to-day reality that hurts people we care about and mocks our values. The genius of community organizing is in its recognition that we cannot address inequality, injustice, and suffering without also addressing isolation. Because no one, no matter their level of comfort, can free themselves from prison.

  A Jew's sense of imprisonment may stem from being a person of color, disabled, or LGBTQ in America or from not making as much money as other Jews. It may come from struggling to care respectfully for elderly parents or to tend to kids who have learning disabilities, or who are harming themselves to push back against the stress they feel every day, or who are just imbibing a dominant culture that encourages them to value people for what they have, not who they are. It may come from remembering how their family came to the United States, as they read about efforts to restrict immigration and refugee resettlement, not being sure where to direct their eyes as they walk past homeless people, or knowing the struggles that decent, hard-working families whom they have never met endure only miles away from where they live. In all these circumstances, these challenges can breed a feeling of impotence, of cynicism, and of isolation, since modern culture does not look kindly on people who struggle, so we tend to keep it to ourselves. It's a very American inclination to want to work things out on our own, but the problems facing civil society that gnaw at us are too large for any of us by ourselves to do anything about—the more we try to just work it out on our own, the deeper we sink, and the easier it becomes to just be cynical, writing off hope as romanticism.

  This combination of impotence, cynicism, and isolation can make it hard to live as a Jew. As an Orthodox Jew, I willingly hand over parts of my freedom to God—the freedom to decide what I eat, what I do on Saturday, when I pray, and countless other things— restricting my freedom to get a much greater freedom, the freedom that comes from being connected to the transcendent. However, that exchange requires freedom. That is why the halachah says that slaves are not obligated to keep the mitzvot. I need to be free to offer up part of my freedom to God. If I look at the world around me and just feel hopeless and impotent, then I won't have the freedom to offer up to God. And I'll be alone, feeling too wretched to connect to God or to the people around me.

Organizing for civic engagement and social change transforms private pain into public action, and it does so by tapping another very American instinct. Alexis de Tocqueville wrote, "In a democracy, knowledge of how to combine is the mother of all forms of knowledge: on it depends all others."[143] When people combine, when they organize, they not only build the power to make a difference; they learn the art of being free.

This instinct is not only American, it is also very Jewish— obviously not exclusively Jewish, but very Jewish nonetheless. Community organizers do not have to be liberal; in the month after President Barack Obama's election, Freedom Works began building the infrastructure that supported the Tea Party and immediately sent to its operatives hundreds of copies of *Rules for Radicals*, the organizing tome by Saul Alinsky, one of the founders of modern American community organizing. But organizers cannot be absolute individualists; organizing inherently believes in the collective. While it prizes the individual, it does not fetishize individualism, because it asserts that individuals need community.

Similarly, Jews can be politically liberal or politically conservative—Torah is far too complex to be boiled down to a mortal political ideology. But Jews are not absolute individualists. In our texts, our tradition, our history, our very DNA, we hold and value "the knowledge of how to combine."

I serve as the director of organizing for JOIN for Justice, the Jewish Organizing Institute & Network, the primary organization charged with training American Jewish leaders, organizers, rabbis, young people, and organizations in the fundamentals and arts of community organizing so that they can act on their values in the public square and build communities ready not only to act, but to be the types of communities we dream of having. Every year, we help hundreds upon hundreds of people learn how to bring people together around a common cause and observe them not only making a difference, but becoming more hopeful, more relational, more free, more powerful.

When people organize in the public square, they organize their people, their resources, and their strategy in order to have the power they will need to have an impact on the issues that concern them. If we build a power premised not on a desire to dominate, but on a desire to weave people together so that they can be larger than the sum of their parts, that power can transform us. In a lecture, Rabbi Donniel Hartman of Israel's Hartman Institute addressed American Jews' shock that Israel was willing to free many prisoners convicted of violence against Israelis in order to secure the freedom of Israeli soldier Gilad Shalit in 2011. How could they take that kind of risk when they were so vulnerable? Hartman explained:

> When you have power, you have the ability to take a risk for the sake of your values. You have the ability to ask yourself, "What type of life do I want to live?" not just whether I'm going to live, but "Who do I want to be?" ... [That power] gives us the opportunity to say, "We can be better than who we are."[144]

The more we feel imprisoned by helplessness to change the world around us or live out our values, the more we feel cynical and hopeless, the more we are restrained in our ability to live as citizens or as Jews. The more we have the power to move beyond lamenting a world that doesn't conform to our values to acting to change the world, the more we can be free people and the more we can thrive as hopeful, transformed Jews. That transformation is predicated on our ability to combine—to come together not only across Jewish communities but with other communities that hold similar values, across lines of religion, race, ethnicity, and class. That organizing will not only afford us the power to act, but it will also push back against our isolation.

Prisoners don't free themselves—but, if they combine with others, they often find that we can all free each other.

## Notes

143. Paraphrased from Alexis de Tocqueville, *Democracy in America* (Indianapolis, IN: Liberty Fund, 2012), ProQuest ebrary, vol. 2, 902. The Henry Reeve translation from the original French is "In democratic countries the science of association is the mother of science; the progress of all the rest depends upon the progress it has made."
144. Donniel Hartman, "Israel, The Challenge of Power," *Jewish Thought Leaders*, podcast audio, December 6, 2011, http://www.marinjcc.org/clientuploads/directory/CJL/podcast/Donniel%20Hartman%20on%20Israel%20The%20Challenge%20of%20Power.mp3.

PART III

# *Your Guide to Plugging into Civic Engagement*

# CHAPTER 7

# Rabbis, Lay Leaders, and Congregations
## A Threefold Cord Is Not Readily Broken

Two are better off than one, in that they have greater benefit from their earnings. For should they fall, one can raise the other; but woe betide the one who is alone and falls with no companion! Further, when two lie together they are warm; but how can one who is alone get warm? Also, if one attacks, two can stand up to the attacker. A threefold cord is not readily broken!
—Ecclesiastes 4:9–12

T HE THREEFOLD CORD OF ECCLESIASTES reminds us of our col- lective power. One person may speak out against injustice, but that voice needs to be amplified to create systemic change. Two in partnership can persist with greater conviction and courage while gaining the life-affirming warmth of a personal relationship. And three together have yet more strength to endure the challenges of dissent.

Just as there is strength in the threefold cord, a partnership of three—the rabbi, lay leaders, and congregants themselves—can powerfully propel a synagogue forward. This holds true for virtually every synagogue initiative, but especially for civic engagement.

The rabbi is often in a more visible position to lead than others in the community by virtue of her position, training, and pulpit. The rabbi is the public face for the synagogue, whether joining with congregants at a public forum, speaking at a community podium or standing beside interfaith clergy. In many instances, the rabbi is best equipped to inform and inspire a congregation and commu- nity—in sermons, newspapers, blog posts, and beyond. And the rabbi can stand behind the lay leaders championing a cause, articulating the religious imperative and providing the moral support they need to succeed. In some congregations, a cantor may also be well-positioned to serve in this role.

By contrast, lay leaders are the navigators, guiding the congregation to where it aspires to go. They know the history, culture, potential pitfalls, and politics of the community. They are the managers of the process—selecting issues, creating educational forums, and delineating effective forms of advocacy. They establish policy for the process of a congregation's civic engagement and resolve crises when frustrations or disagreements emerge. Often, they are the ones who hold the rabbi and the congregation accountable to fulfill their commitments to social justice.

Finally, the congregants choose the issues of civic engagement for the synagogue, not only in voice but also in action. The problems of our communities cannot be solved from a distance, interacting only with information gleaned from television and computer screens. Gaining understanding and embracing solutions to the problems that disturb our sleep require the personal engagement of our congregants, hearing two sides of the argument with our own ears, seeing inequity with our own eyes, and embracing paths forward with our hearts. There are many examples in this book demonstrating how the collective power of congregants has changed their communities.

The social, economic, and civic problems that afflict our world are exceedingly complex. The solutions are equally complex, requiring a cycle of listening, educating, strategizing, acting, and evaluating. Moving forward with effective civic engagement is arduous, but increasingly manageable and certainly more fulfilling as we bind ourselves together in a threefold cord, as Ecclesiastes bids us. When the rabbi, lay leaders, and congregants work together, lives can be saved and more just communities can be created.

## A Guide for the Rabbi Who Enters the Arena

It is not the critic who counts; not the man who points out how the strong man stumbles, or where the doer of deeds could have done them better. The credit belongs to the man who is actually in the arena, whose face is marred by dust and sweat and blood; who strives valiantly; who errs, who comes short again and again, because there is no effort without error and shortcoming; but who does actually strive to do the deeds; who knows great enthusiasms, the great devotions; who spends himself in a worthy cause; who at the best knows in the end the triumph of high achievement, and who at the worst, if he fails, at least fails while daring greatly, so that his place shall never be with those cold and timid souls who neither know victory nor defeat.[145]

For the rabbi, venturing into the arena of social justice is not easy. Like Roosevelt's man in the arena, "marred by dust and sweat and blood," rabbis who engage in the social justice issues of our day open themselves to criticism from within their congregations, across their community, and, in these days of Internet interconnectedness, around the globe. Yet rabbis who step into the ring of civic engagement and "strive valiantly ... while daring greatly" can be profoundly impactful. The network of connections at their fingertips enables rabbis to rally support locally and worldwide, as well as garner guidance, wisdom, partnerships, and power from the movements with which they are affiliated.

A strong theme that emerged from the Reform clergy and lay leaders we interviewed was their desire to renew a social justice tradition that was rooted in the historical work of their congregational rabbis—the "prophetic Judaism" that is the solid foundation upon which Reform Judaism was built. Rabbis and lay leaders at these synagogues, as well as at some Conservative synagogues, reminisced about an almost idyllic time when their congregational rabbi showed a strong passion for justice. The example most frequently cited was when their rabbis stood on the right side of history during the civil rights movement, getting politically involved and protesting publicly through words, deeds, and marches. Clergy and congregants are inspired today by the actions of their rabbis from five decades ago— many of whom they never personally knew.

We know that those actions of clergy seeking justice did not

transpire without controversy. Mike Rosen, who grew up at Temple
Emanu-El in Dallas, recalls a story from his childhood about his
then congregational rabbi: "Rabbi Levi Olan in the 1960s was housing Freedom Riders. Some congregants went to his house and said
there were threats, he should stop. He said, 'If you want me to stop,
you have the wrong rabbi.'"

Some of the rabbis who were active in the civil rights movement
lost their pulpits as a result of their social justice positions. Such
was the case of Rabbi Seymour Atlas, who was serving an Orthodox
congregation in Montgomery, Alabama, when his photo with an
African-American reverend and a Catholic priest appeared in the
*Life* magazine issue of March 5, 1956, during National Brotherhood
Week—a concept created by the National Conference for Christians
and Jews and practiced from 1934 through the 1980s.[146] The caption
under the photo read, "Talking Tolerance, a boycott leader, Rev.
L.R. Bennett (center), joins Father Michael Caswell, Rabbi Seymour
Atlas on radio panel."[147]

Rabbi Atlas was already under pressure for driving his African-American housekeeper to and from her home during the bus
boycott and for teaching Hebrew to a young Martin Luther King Jr.
The rabbi was rebuked by his board members, many of whom were
on the White Citizens Council, which actively supported racial seg-
regation, and he was ultimately forced to resign from his pulpit.[148]

Today, rabbis need not risk losing their jobs by stepping into the
public arena. Rabbi Atlas's noble act of seeing a common humanity
and building true relationships across lines of difference was radical in his day, especially in the traditional Jewish setting in which
he lived and worked. But today's synagogues are more likely to seek
moral leadership from their rabbis. To be sure, there are still risks, in
part because congregants often feel an ambivalence—or even uneas-
iness—about where, when, and how that leadership is exerted. But
contemporary clergy who are reflective and intentional before acting
will be better prepared to respond to diverse voices in their congregations, and they will have fostered the necessary support among
their board leadership.

Many problems may be anticipated and avoided with thoughtful preparation. We offer the following ten steps to success for rabbis leading congregations in civic engagement.

## Ten Steps to Success for Rabbis Leading Congregations in Civic Engagement

### 1. Do your homework.

Before speaking out on a controversial issue, write a position statement for your temple president and board leadership. Include the scope of your intended involvement, Jewish sacred texts that support this action, relevant positions of the Jewish movement with which your congregation is affiliated, and the history of congregational action on this issue. Though clergy may clearly grasp the justification to work on an issue of civic engagement, the constantly changing lay leadership may not have the same degree of comfort with an issue nor the language to defend a position to the congregation. For some rabbis, discussing this position statement in person or in a conference call is essential to building and maintaining relationships with their board leadership; others may have sufficient shared history to send it by email.

### 2. Take congregants with you.

When Rabbi Dena Feingold arrived at Beth Hillel Temple in Kenosha, Wisconsin, her congregation was only modestly involved in volunteerism. Congregants served in the local soup kitchen to relieve the Christian staff on Christmas and Easter, and they partnered with other congregations in a community walk to raise funds and awareness to alleviate hunger and poverty. After a few years, however, Rabbi Feingold realized that she was the only temple representative still participating in the CROP Hunger Walk, and she concluded that it was time to stop walking and start regrouping.

"If a rabbi is walking alone," said Rabbi Feingold. "She shouldn't be walking." Indeed, rabbis should not march alone when representing the temple.

Walking together with congregants in petition or protest is an opportunity for you to build stronger relationships with them and harness the power of the minyan on the move. Or, if you are speaking on a community panel, invite some congregants to accompany and support you. Those who would argue that social justice work takes rabbis away from their primary work of pastoral care make a hollow claim when clergy-congregant relationships are deepened outside the synagogue walls.

### 3. Use social media to share your work.

Communicating with a blog—while you are outside your synagogue in your community, state capital, or perhaps Washington, DC— allows you to speak to interested members of your congregation. Share your perspective on social justice issues by telling stories and posting photos that connect your congregants intellectually and emotionally to an issue. The rabbi of today is unconstrained by the walls of the traditional *beit midrash* (house of study) and can use the modern platforms created by the web to preach, teach, and ultimately reach those minds, hearts, and souls not physically with them.

If you don't blog, find another platform that works for you and is easily accessible for your community. Write articles in your bulletins or reflections that can be posted on your congregational website. Even more effective, at times, are brief videos shared via YouTube or Facebook that capture a telling moment that helps people see what you see.

In September 2016 after the controversial shooting death of Keith Lamont Scott, an African-American man, Rabbi Schindler walked the Charlotte streets with her fellow clergy. She posted ten photos and a video of a gospel choir, all capturing moments of proud, passionate, and peaceful protest. In a world where media shapes what we see—often through a negative lens—congregants were grateful to again see the heart of their city as a source of pride, even as many of them were still too fearful to go uptown themselves because of the initially violent protests.

*4. Make your work an inter-congregational experience.*
When you partner with churches, mosques, or other Jewish congregations, you create more momentum for change. In addition, you make yourself less vulnerable to the often harsh and intimidating criticism from extremists.

Clergy from Temple Beth El, Piedmont Unitarian Universalist Church, and Holy Covenant United Church of Christ joined together to charter a fifty-person bus from Charlotte to Washington, DC, to legally marry seven gay couples in 2011. This trip was repeated again in 2014 with six more couples. The clergy, the couples, and the congregants who made these journeys celebrated the weddings and, through media coverage, promoted same-sex marriage in North Carolina. In this instance—as is often the case when standing up for justice—the criticism and demonization on social media was scathing. But no individual person nor house of worship was singled out because there were multiple congregations and clergy on each trip, and the large contingents countered the online attacks, posting positive words affirming equality.

*5. Develop strong partnerships with other rabbis and
non-Jewish clergy.*
Developing strong interfaith clergy relationships is essential to the civically minded rabbi and cantor. Invest time to connect regularly with your colleagues across congregations and faiths, not just in moments of crisis. Meet for coffee, study a text, attend a fellow minister's celebration, create a pulpit exchange on MLK weekend, plan an interfaith Thanksgiving service, or create a comparative religion study program.

Each time you connect and stand with other clergy, you strengthen your mutual trust. These experiences build a shared history that fosters relationships to enhance your successes and sustain you in hard times, enabling you to lead more reflectively and collaboratively. These interfaith partnerships create such valued religious leadership in the community that addressing critical issues without them becomes unimaginable.

Even when your interfaith work fails to meet its stated goals, the relationships you build can sustain you. Such was the case for Rabbi Asher Knight, then associate rabbi at Temple Emanu-El in Dallas, and now senior rabbi of Temple Beth El in Charlotte. Reflecting on the process of traveling to Austin, Texas, for a lobbying trip, he commented:

> Even in moments of loss, you can pivot into a win because of the clergy relationships . . . because we are sharing an experience, because we know each other, recognize the needs of our congregants, and the true calling of our faith traditions which we had tested out with each other in writing our positions. Those were all public relationships that became quite personal.

### 6. Weigh carefully whether to act independently as a rabbi or to lead your congregation to collectively take a stand.

An issue that will divide your congregation or cause members to leave is rarely worth pursuing. These may be instances when you are better served by inviting congregants to join you as individuals and not as representatives of the congregation. For example, despite its long history of supporting LGBTQ rights, the leadership of Temple Beth El in Charlotte opted to allow then associate rabbi Jonathan Freirich to join the 2014 federal district court case for marriage equality as an individual clergy member instead of in his official capacity at the temple. Board support for this action was uncertain, and comparable results could be achieved through this path.

If you find that you are repeatedly acting alone, it likely is a sign to start building a process to engage your congregation. Rabbi Jonathan Sacks comments on the necessity for Jewish leaders to gauge the pace of their followers, citing a passage from Numbers in his article published in the *Jerusalem Post*:

> A leader must lead from the front: he or she must "go out before them." But a leader must not be so far out in front that, when he turns around, he finds no one following. He must "lead them out," meaning, he must carry people with him. He must go at a pace that people can bear.[149]

**7. Create a clear policy on civic engagement for your congregation.**

Most synagogue policies explicitly affirm the right of clergy to express their opinions on social justice issues as individuals, separately from the institution. The challenge is to determine when rabbis are authorized to speak on behalf of their synagogue and represent it on controversial issues. Agreeing on frameworks and processes in advance expedites your clergy's and your synagogue's responses to community or national crises. The next chapter of this book provides four choices of blueprints to serve as a foundation for congregations moving forward with this work.

To be sure, there is no one-size-fits-all master plan for addressing community concerns as a congregation. With each new issue come new realities, new community players, and new congregants. Yet, having a blueprint for civic engagement enables you to keep your eyes on the bigger picture and not get lost in the details or mired in controversy.

**8. Emulate the House of Hillel by respecting opposing opinions.**

The lessons from the debates of the House of Hillel and the House of Shammai discussed in chapter 3 are powerful ones. Despite its overwhelming history of success, the House of Hillel remained "agreeable and forbearing, showing restraint when affronted . . . [teaching] both their own statements and the statements of Beit Shammai" (Babylonian Talmud, *Eiruvin* 13b). Even if you are certain that you are on the right side of history, those in your congregation who argue with you merit respect and a voice in the process.

Sister Simone Campbell, a nun and activist, has decades of experience in advocacy on Capitol Hill, where speaking out can be exceedingly contentious. For there to be justice, she teaches, everyone must be welcomed at the table. Through her experience, she developed the concept of "radical acceptance." Rather than fighting with your opponents, she advocates that you embrace them and fight for a collective goal that reflects common values.[150]

This approach creates stronger congregations and a stronger democracy. Through deliberative dialogue—aimed at listening and understanding while suspending judgment and emotion—you can find common ground that will engage everyone. Dialogue on a deeper level is a reminder that there can be more than one truth and helps you understand your own and others' values as you work to influence your congregation's and your community's collective future. The title of Rabbi Brad Hirschfield's book captures this theme well: *You Don't Have to Be Wrong for Me to Be Right.*[151]

### 9. Educate.
In instances such as community crises requiring immediate responses, there may be insufficient time to get an advocacy position approved through your synagogue process. If that is the case, you can organize educational forums or online FAQs to promote awareness of an issue along with strategies for individual action and advocacy. It is hard for someone to argue against educating the congregation, especially when both sides are presented fairly.

Sometimes this effort is not only about sharing facts and figures, but also about making an issue personal. The *Souls* social justice documentaries (co-produced by Temple Beth El, the interfaith agency MeckMin, and a variety of other partners) told stories of homeless families, minority students in public schools, and teachers in high-poverty schools. This approach allowed viewers to empathize with the "other" that they might not personally encounter. Highlighting personal stories has the power to change opinion by turning "those people" into individual faces that can be seen and human voices that can be heard.

As part of the process of educating the congregation, focus on the underlying Jewish principles that guide your synagogue. When you educate around and ultimately advocate for principles rather than politics, your work is stronger and the risk of controversy is diminished.

### 10. Balance the topics of your sermons.
A common mantra of religious activists is that their job is to afflict the comfortable and comfort the afflicted, a phrase that originally referred to the role of newspapers[152] and echoes the words of the

Psalms (Psalm 119:50). That was the role of the biblical prophets, and that remains the role of both newspapers and rabbis today. But be mindful that congregants face a myriad of pressures at work, at home, at school, in their communities, and as they follow national and global news. As a result, they often need the respite and spiritual renewal that Shabbat has to offer. While current events may require a response from the bimah, focusing only on issues of justice limits the richness of what Judaism has to offer.

Rabbi Alexander Schindler had a formula for his High Holy Day sermons. He would give a sermon focused on a national or international issue of pressing concern on Rosh HaShanah and a spiritual sermon on Yom Kippur. Consciously choosing such a balance among sermons is essential for Shabbat worship; the weekly lessons of Torah that clergy share should vary between civic and spiritual. Clergy have many methods of sharing their call to work for justice beyond the bimah. We need to use them all, varying the times, spaces, and places.

Rabbis are teachers sharing the wisdom of Torah in all its manifestations. Rabbis are preachers articulating words that inspire action. Rabbis are leaders crafting a vision for a brighter future. Rabbis are pastors shepherding congregants through their life cycles. And rabbis are also human beings who cannot lead alone.

## The Five *P*'s of Successful Lay Leadership

Rabbis need partners who share their passion to bring justice to our world. Moses could not hear every case of justice himself and instead found capable, trustworthy individuals with integrity to share the burden of leadership. Today's vision and implementation of civic engagement should also be shared. Moses learns this lesson from his father-in-law, Jethro, who tells him, "The thing you are doing is not right; you will surely wear yourself out, and these people as well. For the task is too heavy for you; you cannot do it alone" (Exodus 18:17–18).

Matters of social justice are too heavy for any one person—rabbi or lay leader—to carry alone. Jethro tells his son-in-law that not only will Moses wear himself out, but the people who are with him also will tire. Perhaps they will tire of waiting for Moses to hear their own cases. Perhaps they will tire of Moses tending to the needs of others, leaving themselves feeling diminished or ignored.

One could easily imagine similar complaints being registered about contemporary clergy. Congregants are not happy when they need a pastoral presence, only to learn that their clergy is otherwise engaged with a community issue. Our clergy are pulled in many directions—from the classroom to the pulpit to hospital bedsides to officiating at baby namings, *b'nei mitzvah*, and weddings. Rabbis cannot prioritize community needs over congregational needs; rabbis do not have the time or strength to do both full-time. This is why Jethro's words ring true today: the rabbi will exhaust himself and others if the burden of leadership is not shared.

This was indeed part of Rabbi Dena Feingold's motivation when she chose not to walk alone in Wisconsin and sought a congregant with a passion for social justice. That person was Harriet Lavin, a new member at Beth Hillel Temple. At the rabbi's request, Lavin attended the regional biennial with the temple president, where they were inspired hearing Rabbi David Saperstein speak about social justice. The two lay leaders then went to the 2005 Consultation on Conscience, which Lavin describes as a "life-changing event." Together, these educational experiences connected Lavin more deeply with her congregation, her Judaism, and her passion for social justice, providing a foundation for her newly identified lay leadership role. It was a critical moment for Lavin—and for Beth Hillel Temple.

Rabbi Feingold sought and found *passion* in Harriet Lavin. Generally, rabbis recruiting lay leaders for civic engagement also need to be mindful that these congregants have the *personality* to draw others into their work. Lay leaders require *proficiency* in the content of an issue, understanding both the details of the problem and the nature of the solutions. Lay leaders also need to work in *partnership* with clergy, founded on a relationship of mutual trust and reliability. And finally, a *pipeline* of lay leaders needs to be nurtured to sustain future work. These "Five P's"—Passion, Proficiency, Personality,

Partnership, and Pipeline—summarize the qualities to seek in lay leaders who can guide the congregation effectively on its civic engagement journey.

### Passion

Passion is so critical for lay leadership that a sponsoring congregant is required for every new social action or justice initiative at Temple Beth El in Charlotte; experience has demonstrated that projects flounder without a champion. The authors recall the Social Justice and Action Committee receiving a letter from two congregants saying that "the temple should" start a particular project. The group aptly noted that "the temple" doesn't start projects; congregants do.

Julie Weinberg, board vice president of social justice at Temple Emanu-El in Dallas, Texas, affirms that passionate lay leaders are the critical component for synagogues to be successful, saying, "My advice to congregations is to attempt to go down the most authentic path that you can, the one that is authentic to your congregation, your members, and your community. That is where we have seen the best and most successful work happen. Having a champion or several champions is key."

Steve Fox of Temple Isaiah in Los Angeles describes his Environmental Committee as small in number but great in passion. When their arguments get heated, Fox jokes, the committee members tell him to take his blood pressure. He adds, "Sister Mary Beth Larkin, a nun with whom we have worked says, 'If you are in the social justice business, you need two things: a sense of passion and a sense of humor.'"

### Proficiency

Proficiency can easily be found in large congregations, which often are rich with talented professionals in areas of expertise relevant to social justice issues. Temple Isaiah in Los Angeles is one of those congregations, with tremendous internal resources among its 850 member families. Debra Silverman, who serves on the temple's Board of Trustees, comments on the talents of its lay leadership, "Our organizing work is run by a core team of congregants. We are a diverse group—lawyers, entertainment executives, social workers, beauty industry executives, parent activists, and writers, to name a few."

Temple Israel in Boston, a congregation defined by its social justice work and located in the medical district of the city, draws congregants who are committed to civic engagement, including many medical professionals. Dr. Nick Morse, a lay leader in the second Massachusetts health care reform movement in 2011-12, commented on the importance of physicians like himself to the success of that advocacy initiative, saying, "There was a huge amount of work requiring insiders who understand the real drivers in really nuanced issues."

Congregations of any size would be wise to canvass their members to uncover the hidden experts. A solid resource is often available among retired professionals with the time and aptitude to research new issues and build public relationships. This strategy worked for Temple Beth El, who found in Stephen Phillips a lay leader to advocate on aging issues. When asked why he thought Rabbi Schindler tapped him to lead the congregation's foray into addressing issues for aging adults, Phillips said, "Somehow she spotted something in me. She said I asked interesting questions in the SPICE [seniors group] meetings."

Phillips spearheaded two transportation programs for seniors in the community and drafted a resolution on aging for the Reform Movement to consider for the 2017 Biennial, earning an award from the Charlotte Mecklenburg Aging Coalition along the way. He commented, "My involvement with issues of the aging has allowed me to move from success in life to a life of significance, and for that I will be eternally grateful to Temple Beth El."[153]

Absent an internal resource to develop viable, systemic solutions, collaborations outside synagogue walls become essential. CBCOs, the RAC, and national organizations such as Bend the Arc provide content expertise necessary for successful civic engagement.

## Personality

Personality makes the difference between launching a project based on one congregant's personal mission and a broader effort that achieves momentum in the congregation. We all have encountered single-issue activists whose focus is so narrow that they can neither compromise nor draw others into a collaborative effort. Finding lay leaders with the personality to draw others into the work is critical for mobilizing the congregation.

Lay leaders may lack official power, but they can move people to action through their influence in the congregation and the community. Rabbi Jonathan Sacks insightfully comments on the power of personality among Jewish leaders when he writes, "Judaism prefers the leadership of influence to the leadership of power. Kings had power. Prophets had influence but no power at all. . . . Influence lifts the people above their former selves. Influence respects people."[154]

## Partnership

Successful partnerships between lay leaders and clergy are marked by mutual trust. Clergy rely on lay leaders to identify wise solutions and represent the temple responsibly. Conversely, lay leaders count on their rabbi to defend them from critics both inside and outside the synagogue walls. We found many synagogues in which the depth of these relationships is profound, as seen in these three examples:

- Neil Silverston, at Temple Beth Elohim in Wellesley, Massachusetts: "It's incredibly empowering to know your clergy has your back. I have a standing conference call with Rabbi [Rachel] Saphire and Sandy Aronson (our Social Justice Fellow) every week, and both Rabbi Saphire and [Senior] Rabbi Joel Sisenwine . . . stand up publicly on the issues we all care about."
- Sara Albert, at Temple Emanu-El in Dallas, Texas: "Every one of us who has worked with Rabbi Knight would walk through fire for him if he needed it. He built such a strong relationship with each of us."

- Susan Drucker at BJBE in Deerfield, Illinois: "I went to DC with my rabbi [Karyn Kedar], I went to Israel for the Women of the Wall. I told her, 'I will follow you anywhere, just let me know where you need me.'"

The authors of this volume, ourselves a rabbi–lay leader team, have also built that relationship of trust. Judy Seldin-Cohen remembers her feelings of gratitude when, as a new social justice chair, she was asked an incendiary question in a public forum, prompting Rabbi Schindler to walk across the stage, take the microphone, and defuse the moment. Similarly, Rabbi Schindler recalls extolling the dream of a housing endowment to the Charlotte Mecklenburg Housing Coalition based on Seldin-Cohen's discussion with her of that vision. The relationship built through experiences such as these led to the authors' collaboration on this book.

### Pipeline

Synagogues with sustainable success in civic engagement create a pipeline for future lay leaders. Some lay leaders are "lifers," leading social justice initiatives for years or even decades. Yet even in those situations, replacements are eventually required because of either age or a need for new ideas and approaches. Identifying and recruiting future lay leaders is a responsibility shared by clergy, temple staff, committee members, and lay leaders themselves. In some instances, this includes finding and training one's own successor.

As part of her social justice portfolio, Rabbi Rachel Saphire is consciously developing this *pipeline* of lay leaders with *personality* and *passion* among her congregants at Temple Beth Elohim in Wellesley, Massachusetts. She begins by developing relationships with her congregants so that she knows their passions and their skills. Then, she or the synagogue's full-time community organizer follows up with each person who attends a meeting to discover why they came and how they would prefer to help—their *proficiency*; often meetings conclude by identifying these lay leaders and their commitments to fulfill the next steps. Finally, she empowers these congregants to grow into leadership roles, in some instances, making formal training available to them. As Silverston noted, Rabbi Saphire makes the time to build the *partnership* needed for leadership. By intentionally creating this *pipeline*, Rabbi Saphire now finds that passionate lay leaders approach her to share their interest in a particular issue.

The words of the rabbi from the bimah, the presence of clergy at community gatherings, and statements of a social action committee on a website are not enough to create community change. This requires strong lay leadership. The "Five *P*'s"—Passion, Proficiency, Personality, Partnership, and Pipeline—guide us to find and develop the lay leadership necessary for our congregations to be truly effective in the important work of civic engagement.

## A Covenant for the Congregation to Stand Together

The final partner in the threefold cord that will ensure the strength of our civic engagement efforts is our congregation. When members of the congregation stand together—with the rabbi, the lay leadership, and one another—civic engagement creates powerful sources of energy for recharging our synagogues, ourselves as Jews, our communities, and our country.

On Yom Kippur, the day when the largest number of Jews come to synagogue to express their commitment to their faith, Reform congregations read Moses's final words to the Israelites. In this text, Moses declares that we stand together as we commit to the covenant with God and with one another as a people:

> You stand this day, all of you, before the Eternal your God—you tribal heads, you elders, and you officials, all the men of Israel, you children, you women, even the stranger within your camp, from woodchopper to water drawer—to enter into the covenant of the Eternal your God. . . . I [God] make this covenant, with its sanctions, not with you alone, but both with those who are standing here with us this day before the Eternal our God and with those who are not with us here this day. (Deuteronomy 29:9–14)[155]

This covenant (in Hebrew, *b'rit*) connotes a more enduring commitment than a contract. As part of this covenant, modern Jews circumcise their newborn sons on the eighth day of life in the covenant of circumcision (*b'rit milah*), and they similarly celebrate their daughters' places among our people through a blessing and Hebrew naming.

Moses's words describing our covenant with God and with one another as the Jewish people offer us guidance on how we can stand together as a congregation in the covenant of civic engagement. This text inspires us to mobilize our congregation using modern organizing principles of listening to one another and engaging everyone from our children to the non-Jewish spouses in our synagogue community. The biblical consequences of failing to keep the ancient covenant may present theological challenges to many of us. Yet through our involvement in civic engagement, we can indeed prevent the negative consequences that inevitably occur when an individual, business, community, or government focuses solely on its own needs to the exclusion of others. When we do this work in relationship with one another, our congregation is strengthened.

### "You stand this day, all of you . . ."

We stood together with Moses at Sinai to affirm our covenant before entering the Promised Land; the Torah passage begins, *Atem nitzavim hayom*, "You stand this day, all of you." But there are two Hebrew words for standing as a group. The first, *omdim*, means getting up from our seats and being on our feet—as in the word with the same root, *Amidah*, the central prayers of our daily worship that require us to rise. However, a second word for standing, *nitzavim*, is used in this passage. The word *nitzav* (singular form) connotes greater intention than merely being on our feet. *Nitzav* is an active commitment to stand, firmly grounded.

Mobilizing the congregation to actively stand together today with this level of intentionality begins by involving members in identifying their passions, a critical component for community change. We discern congregational concerns through one-on-one conversations, parlor meetings, analyzing congregant volunteer hours, and tracking financial and in-kind gifts; these are ways to assess congregational commitment so that we actively stand together on an issue before moving forward in civic engagement. Congregations often mistakenly assume that hearing a voice from the pulpit is enough to inspire action or that a well-attended lecture is a sufficient indicator of support—misinterpreting *omdim* for *nitzavim*.

Although some congregants may have professional experience in organizing, the vast majority who are passionate about an issue don't know how to engage others to effect social change. This requires training, a point echoed by many we interviewed. Janet Hirsch, from Temple Isaiah in Los Angeles, reflected on learning even the basic dynamics of when and how to listen, speak, and end the conversation:

> I am starting one-on-one conversations with congregants interested in Am Tzedek [Temple Isaiah's internal name for their CBCO work with One LA]. It doesn't come naturally, knowing when to share your story and when to shut up, and when to end the conversation after thirty minutes. You don't have to be friends with everyone. This is hard.

Barbara Hyman and Sara Albert, two lay leaders from Temple Emanu-El in Dallas, talked about their struggles to grasp the concept of listening campaigns:

> I went to the first meeting and just couldn't get it, it was such a different way of doing things. It was a circle and not a line. I didn't understand it, but kept coming back until I got it and enrolled in training. (Barbara Hyman)

> I had no experience in community organizing. Frankly I had to put aside my firm beliefs about how things get done. I was very used to the leadership model, you decide what needs to get done and you go do it. This whole process of getting to know your neighbor, talking and talking, coming up with consensus, meeting after meeting—it was very hard for me to appreciate

that. I don't think I'm alone, although others learned the lesson
faster than I did. (Sara Albert)

The difficulty of shifting your synagogue to this approach should not
be underestimated. Fran Godine, a lay leader at Temple Israel in Boston, laughingly confesses to being impatient with the initial process
necessary to engage the entire congregation with the work of GBIO
(Temple Israel's CBCO). She recalls, "We did a year of discerning
what we would focus on and brought together diverse groups in the
congregation to think this through. I was bad—I would speak up
and say, 'Let's just get going.' I was given permission not to attend
all those meetings."

Susan Drucker, at BJBE in the northern suburbs of Chicago,
talks about how she ensures that members of the congregation will
stand with her: "I use one-on-ones differently; I keep it personal. I
use conversations to get people to come to an action, not an email.
That's why one-on-one is so important, not just to find leaders but
also to find out who will come when you call."

A primary principle of community organizing is the idea that
people will respond to calls for involvement when they are engaged
in the process of selecting the issues, feel passionately about the
values underlying them, and are in relationship with those others
who stand with them. Providing opportunities for members of the
congregation to be trained in leadership skills and organizing techniques enables them to mobilize the congregation so that everyone
can indeed actively stand together in civic engagement.

### "...you children..."

The inclusion in the Torah passage of "children" as active parties to
the covenant is particularly meaningful. Our children can inspire
us with their unrestrained passion for justice, especially as they act
without the hesitance, or even paralysis, that we have acquired as
adults as we weigh the pros and cons of every possible action and
reaction. One story (intentionally anonymous) shows the power of
our children: Teens at a regional youth convention were so outraged
by the passage of discriminatory state legislation that they studied

the issue and publicly made a statement as a region protesting the bill, leading the way for many congregations to follow their bold action. Many of the waves that would have been created by adults raising these issues were defused when the youth acted first. Synagogue boards may be far more forgiving when activism arises from the children in the congregation.

Temple Israel in Boston celebrates the advocacy achievements of its youth. Its commitment to incorporating civic engagement into the educational program nurtures students to understand their roles and responsibilities in democracy. Dr. Nick Morse cites two examples:

> A bill was passed allowing teenage homeless people to have their own addresses even though they were minors. That was initiated by our teen temple organization. Another bill passed about animal advocacy and rights that was initiated by a fifth grader. There's a picture of her and Governor Patrick signing the bill. These experiences set up a lifelong advocacy commitment. And it's fabulous for the congregation, too.

The fact that the word *tapchem*—meaning "young children"—is used instead of the word *b'neichem* (meaning "your children," which is typically used in the Torah) is worth noting. Commentators believe that the experience of being present at Sinai would no doubt have a powerful impact on every person, even toddlers too young to comprehend the meaning of the covenant. This teaching lives today in the widely practiced Mitzvah Day programs of our synagogues, which include every age group, even toddlers and babies in strollers.

### . . . you women, even the stranger within your camp, from woodchopper to water drawer . . ."

Specifying all the elements of society that were standing together reiterates the personal nature of the covenant—that each of us is individually and collectively a party to this enduring contract. A congregation stands together for a cause when it is inclusive and its engagement with an issue extends across its demographics, from the preschool to the seniors, as well as across its socioeconomic

boundaries, from those requiring dues subsidies to the most gener-
ous donors.

The covenant at Sinai included the non-Israelites living among us,
"even the stranger within your camp." For congregations in which
non-Jewish spouses are also members, this message of inclusion
is particularly meaningful, as many of our non-Jewish members
provide strong and capable congregational leadership in our social
justice and action work. While we never asked the question of conversion in our interviews, two lay leaders volunteered that it was
Judaism's ethic of social justice or the temple's commitment to this
work that had inspired them to become Jews-by-choice.

This exhaustive listing of all segments of society is repeated two
chapters later in Deuteronomy (31:10–13) in the passage identifying
the individuals required to listen to the public reading of the Torah
every seventh year (*Hakheil*). Just as the covenant and the Torah reading during the Sabbatical year had to be community-wide, so too
should this directive for inclusion be heeded for civic engagement to
be firmly rooted in the congregation.

### "... with its sanctions ..."

Entering the covenant carries both rewards for fulfilling our obligations and consequences for falling short. While the liberal Jew justi-
fiably struggles with this system of blessings and curses, these texts
still have lessons to teach the civic-minded congregant. The litany of
repercussions for failing to maintain the covenant is painstaking:

> Cursed shall you be in the city and cursed shall you be
>    in the country.
> Cursed shall be your basket and your kneading bowl.
> Cursed shall be the issue of your womb and the produce
>    of your soil.
>
> (Deuteronomy 28:16–18)

The list of curses continues, including hemorrhoids, madness,
blindness, fear of our enemies, and losing our homes and families.

Similarly, we suffer consequences today for not fulfilling those
covenantal responsibilities that require us to create societies built

upon the foundation of justice and equality. Today's consequences could read:

> Cursed shall we be in our cities with protests and riots.
> Cursed shall we be in our rural areas with discontent and disconnectedness.
> Cursed shall we be in our country's food pantries with more than 42 million hungry.[156]
> Cursed shall be our produce tainted by environmental damage.
> Cursed shall be our offspring with little hope of economic mobility.
> Cursed shall be our parents without a safety net of social services.

Not only does our failure to bring the values of our religion to life in our community have societal, economic, and personal consequences, but according to the text, it also threatens the security of our faith community. Deuteronomy notes what will happen if we abandon our covenant: "The Eternal will put you to rout before your enemies; you shall march out against them by a single road, but flee from them by many roads; and you shall become a horror to all the kingdoms of the earth" (Deuteronomy 28:25).

Especially because the American Jewish community knows tremendous security, historical realities place upon us a twofold obligation. First, we must speak out for the oppressed and the stranger because we have been the oppressed and the stranger. Stosh Cotler, chief executive officer of Bend the Arc, a leading Jewish social justice advocacy institution, posits the paradox that challenges American Jews today: "We must remain committed to the fight of the underdog—not *because* of our current status in American society but now *in spite* of it."[157]

Second, we must support the stranger because we know that an exclusionary environment will negatively impact us all. Allowing racism, Islamophobia, and unethical deportations to proceed without our civic engagement violates our covenant as Jews. Our fate will be determined by the society we create and sustain. If we disengage, we will face curses in our own time, many of our own making.

**". . . with those who are standing here with us this day . . ."**

Collective responsibility was part of Moses's message. Commentators teach that the promise we made at Sinai when we first became a people committed us both to a covenantal relationship with God and also to be in relationship with the hundreds of thousands who stood with us. Miraculously, we have maintained this covenantal relationship with one another throughout the millennia.

The relationships that bind us together as a people also serve us as we do the work of civic engagement as congregations. Linda Glazner is a lay leader at Mount Sinai Congregation in Wausau, Wisconsin, a congregation of fewer than one hundred families spread across seven counties. She says, "I am a committee of one. But when I need help, I put it in the [temple] bulletin and they come. People say, 'Linda, if you need us, call us, and we will walk with you.'"

Creating those relationships can be more difficult at larger synagogues, where one sees different faces in the building every time. In response to this and other factors, Temple Emanu-El in Dallas, Texas, with twenty-five hundred families, created the Sh'ma Emanu-El groups to help congregants connect to one another outside of the synagogue. Then-staff member Diana Einstein explains the concept: "You can have a Jewish life, a Temple Emanu-El Jewish life in your home. If you create meaningful relationships with other congregants in your home, then you will all come back to temple together. It's truly fascinating how it all works."

This power of relationships is compellingly illustrated in a story about Freedom Summer in 1964, when busloads of northern college students (including a disproportionately large number of Jews) traveled to Mississippi to register voters and teach in black communities. Sociologist Doug McAdam researched the differences between the one thousand volunteers who traveled south and the three hundred "no-shows" whose applications were accepted but who changed their minds when it became clear that the work would be difficult and dangerous. He explained, "The volunteers [who participated] also had stronger and more extensive ties to other project participants [prior to the summer] than did the no-shows. In fact, no other item of information on the applications proved to be a better predictor of participation in the project than this."[158]

Commenting on the power of relationships in this work, Meir Lakein says, "Injustice may spark organizing, but relationship sustains it."

### ". . . and with those who are not with us here this day . . ."

The inclusion in Deuteronomy of the words "those who are not with us" reminds us that the covenant applies to those who were not yet born and those who would join the Jewish people through conversion in the centuries and millennia to come. All future Jews would be bound by the covenantal commitment made at Sinai.

Our civic engagement work today is a fulfillment of commitments made long ago by our ancestors on our behalf. These obligations were made in the midst of community as a reminder that the teachings of Torah apply not only to the individual but to the institutions we create that support our society. Similar to this covenantal commitment, our words and actions today impact and obligate future generations.

Standing as a people at Sinai more than three thousand years ago, we were given the Torah as a metaphoric *ketubah*, a marriage contract, specifying our responsibilities to God, one another, society, and our world. The power of that Sinai moment transcended time and space. As a result, both secular and observant Jews today feel a strong and often inexplicable, even mystical connection to the Jewish people, as well as a powerful commitment to the principles of justice upon which the Torah stands.

### In Conclusion

Like a parent sending a child out into the world, Moses seeks to impress instructions from both himself and God upon the Israelites before they enter the Promised Land without him. He tries one last time to instill in them the teaching that their actions have consequences: "I have put before you life and death, blessing and curse. Choose life—if you and your offspring would live—by loving the

Eternal Your God, heeding God's commands, and holding fast to [God]" (Deuteronomy 30:19–20).

Choosing life as God commands us means becoming civically engaged. By addressing systemic racism, we are providing the next generation with the equity, equality, and access that all deserve. By creating affordable housing, we are ensuring that our "wood-choppers and water drawers"—today's minimum wage workers—are lifted up. By addressing gun violence, we are saving innocent lives and preventing senseless tragedies.

Moving our congregations, communities, and country forward is challenging. Acknowledging the barriers in our lives, Ecclesiastes calls us to find strength in one another: "Two are better than one ... a threefold cord is not readily broken." We find strength and support in our relationships with others. The rabbi, lay leaders, and congregation working together solidly anchor the work of civic engagement so that the inevitable storms that come our way can be withstood and remarkable change can be accomplished.

## Cautionary Tales

We would be wise to learn from those congregations that were un-aware of the necessity of creating the threefold cord or fell short in that effort. The cautionary tales cited in this section emerged from the authors' interviews, although the identifying characteristics are changed and some of these synagogues are not otherwise cited in the book.

What happens when clergy are not involved in the civic engagement work of the lay leaders? In one congregation in which this work was lay led without support from the pulpit, the efforts never achieved momentum and ultimately caused the lay leader to consider affiliating elsewhere. The lay leader reflected:

> Love the synagogue, they appreciated and valued me, but the board didn't want to do the harder things that took more money and other congregants wouldn't volunteer their time. Our biggest

struggle is not getting support from the pulpit. The rabbi spoke
on the issue once. I couldn't inspire and lead congregants. I am
probably switching synagogues, but with a heavy heart.

What happens when congregants are not involved in the vision for
social justice? The clergy or the social justice committee may become
isolated from the congregation and miss the opportunities for the
wisdom and involvement of congregants. In the words of one lay
leader:

> We hopped on board a CBCO campaign without doing our re-
> lational work in the congregation, just defaulted to committee
> mode. An expert in the field who was in our congregation told us
> that the unintended consequences of what we were proposing
> were far worse.

At another congregation, a lay leader commented on the challenges
of shifting to a new approach:

> The [lions and] lionesses of social justice ran the social justice
> committee for decades. The philosophy of the committee was
> that they would decide what the temple cared about. [Their atti-
> tude was:] We don't have time for all this listening. We act.

What happens when lay leaders are not skilled or trained? Projects
may flounder or other congregants become discouraged, as the following reflection demonstrates:

> Leadership is critical. One of the things we have done is allow
> people to self-identify as leaders. There are many good values
> associated with that process, but you need to find a balance
> between that and finding strong leadership. . . . Good heart and
> eagerness [are] not enough, and some people can be detrimental
> to the process.

What happens when the members of the congregation act alone,
independently of the synagogue? The work is done by Jews but may
be neither informed by Jewish tradition nor contributing to building
Jewish community. In one temple, for example:

Hundreds of people turned out for the first actions. But when change didn't move fast enough, interest waned. A group of congregants solved [the pertinent problem] for their own families but not for the community or even the whole congregation. It was a classic white, wealthy approach. Now there's this tension in the congregation [between those families and the others left behind].

In the work of civic engagement, as in so many other synagogue activities, missteps will happen. Our task is to learn each step along the way. The beauty of standing together with both our own congregation and also with other synagogues across our country is that we can learn from others who share our passion for justice and are already engaged in this important work.


## Notes to Chapter 7

145. Theodore Roosevelt, "Citizenship in a Republic," speech delivered at the Sorbonne, in Paris, France, April 23, 1910, http://www.theodore-roosevelt.com/trsorbonnespeech.html.

146. Ed Nickow, "National Brotherhood Week: Gone and Forgotten," *Chicago Now* (blog), *Chicago Tribune*, February 20, 2103, http://www.chicagonow.com/not-for-jews-only/2013/02/national-brotherhood-week-123/.

147. "A Bold Boycott Goes On," *Life*, March 5, 1956, 41.

148. Seymour Atlas, *The Rabbi with the Southern Twang: True Stories from a Life of Leadership within the Orthodox Jewish Congregations of the South* (Victoria, BC: Trofford, 2007), 66–67.

149. Jonathan Sacks, "Seven Principles of Jewish Leadership," *Jerusalem Post Magazine*, June 4, 2012, http://www.jpost.com/Magazine/Opinion/Seven-principles-of-Jewish-leadership. Quotes in Sacks's article are from Numbers 27:16–17.

150. Sister Simone Campbell of NETWORK Lobby for Catholic Social Justice, "Building Bridges: Faith and the Call to Action" (lecture, Queens University of Charlotte, Charlotte, NC, November 3, 2016).

151. Brad Hirschfield, *You Don't Have to Be Wrong for Me to be Right: Finding Faith without Fanaticism* (New York: Three Rivers Press, 2007).

152. "Observations," *Findlay [Ohio] Morning Republican* (August 13, 1928), 4.

153. Tzedek Council Proposal on Issues of Aging Adults, Temple Beth El, Charlotte, NC, December 12, 2016.

154. Sacks, "Seven Principles of Jewish Leadership."

155. This text is translated as "you tribal heads, . . . you children, you women" to be clear that Moses was speaking to each demographic; he was speaking to the children and the women directly, and not through their fathers and husbands, respectively.

156. Alisha Coleman-Jensen, Matthew P. Rabbitt, Christian A. Gregory, and Anita Singh, *Household Food Security in the United States in 2015*, ERR-215, U.S. Department of Agriculture, Economic Research Service, September 2016, 6.

157. Stosh Cotler, "Discontinuing Jewish Continuity," JDOV Talk, filmed at UJA Federation of New York, September 4, 2014, video, 14:53, http://jdov.org/talk/discontinuing-jewish-continuity/. Italics are as shown in visual aid on video.

158. Doug McAdam, *Freedom Summer* (New York: Oxford University Press, 1988), 64.

CHAPTER 8

# Blueprints of the Tabernacle
## God Is in the Details

THE BLUEPRINTS for our first sacred space were given at Sinai. The Tabernacle (*Mishkan*) stood at the center of our tribal formation as a portable dwelling place for the Divine Presence. As we marched through the wilderness, it was this *Mishkan* that held us together and renewed our faith when we faltered.

In the Book of Exodus, God calls us to build this *Mishkan*, a home for God on this earth: "And let them make Me a sanctuary that I may dwell among them" (Exodus 25:8). We are called to be co-creators, co-architects, and co-builders in establishing structures to allow God's presence to exist among us—whether in the wilderness of Sinai, in our own dwelling places, or in contemporary society.

Building a physical *mishkan*—a sanctuary—in which we can feel shelter and serenity is far easier than building a metaphoric *mishkan* of social structures and policies to protect the most vulnerable of our society. The blueprints for the creation of our metaphoric tent are not as precise, though strands of sacred teachings about social justice are woven throughout the Torah—calls to love the stranger as ourselves and to protect the widow and the orphan, as well as a foundational premise of human equality and human rights affirming that all human beings are created in the image of God. Yet, details are critical to helping congregations successfully make the journey of civic engagement. Built with intention and planning, the metaphoric *mishkan* creates holy places where more synagogues are recharged, more Jews find meaningful and relevant expressions of their faith, and more American communities find healing.

How do we build this *mishkan* that will center and ground our synagogues on their journeys of social justice? What are the tent pegs, fabric, curtains, clasps, and other components that hold up the framework of synagogue civic engagement? How do we generate the confidence to persist despite doubts and complaints?

There is no one-size-fits-all blueprint that applies to every synagogue. While your congregation will need to find its own path in light of the depth and breadth of its resources, its comfort in stepping outside synagogue walls is also a pivotal factor. We offer four models to illustrate the broad choices for this journey and explain each with examples from real congregations ranging in size from 130 to 1,200 families and located across liberal and conservative states. A framework is provided to help you then select the model that is best for your synagogue as you embark on your path.

Just as the *Mishkan* in the wilderness was repeatedly disassembled and reassembled as the Israelites set up camp on each stage of their journey, so too does civic engagement require deconstruction and reconstruction as congregations proceed on their metaphoric journey of social justice. As Michael Gecan subtitles his book on congregational organizing: "All organizing is dis-organizing and re-organizing."[159] A congregation may start with one of the models below and then shift to a different model as its work evolves or its leadership changes.

These models are intended as a guide to help you think through the issues and build upon the experiences of those already engaged in this work.

## Four Models of Synagogue Civic Engagement
The four models of synagogue civic engagement are:

1. The Resolution Model creates a public position through a board vote on a specific issue.
2. The Agenda Model sets an annual plan on specific issues, with experienced lay leaders managing the process under the board's authority.

3. The Coalition Model connects congregations, leveraging collective resources to address issues of common concern.
4. The Traction Model allows a group of congregants to pursue any issue for which they can mobilize sufficient interest.

### Resolution Model

The Resolution Model creates a public position through a board vote on a specific issue. This model is used by Beth Hillel Temple in Wisconsin, located roughly halfway between Milwaukee and Chicago. Rabbi Dena Feingold leads this Reform congregation of fewer than 150 families.

The temple's civic engagement centered around two referenda that had been placed on the November 2006 ballot in Wisconsin—a constitutional amendment to ban both civil unions and same-sex marriages and a referendum for the legislature to reinstate capital punishment. The Leadership Council of Beth Hillel Temple voted unanimously to establish the criteria for taking an advocacy position in the community:

### Beth Hillel Temple Social Advocacy Policy

- The Social Action Committee has the right and responsibility to bring issues for consideration before the Leadership Council. The Leadership Council may then vote to adopt a resolution or take a public position on this issue. The Leadership Council will then speak on behalf of the congregation in support of the issue. The Social Action Committee only needs to seek approval from the Leadership Council when it is asking Beth Hillel Temple to make a position public.
- The subject matter of a proposed resolution must have a bearing on the congregation, the Jewish community, or an issue of society at large that implicates Jewish values.
- The Union for Reform Judaism Resolutions will be used as guidelines for all national issues.
- The Leadership Council will not take any action that will result in disqualifying the temple for favorable tax treatment

pursuant to Internal Revenue Code 501(c)(3) concerning non-profit organizations.

- It is the responsibility of the Social Action Committee to provide sufficient information and educational resources about the issue to the Leadership Council, and to use such means as the newsletter, posters, and the *Tikkun Olam* resource table to educate the congregation at large on the issue.

- The Leadership Council shall adopt a resolution or position when at least two-thirds (2/3) of all voting council members, present or not, vote in favor of it.

The Leadership Council voted to take public positions on both issues, successfully passing its first temple resolution opposing the reinstatement of the death penalty and a second opposing the constitutional ban on same-sex marriages and civil unions.

Beth Hillel Temple's success adopting these two board resolutions was facilitated because there was ample time for both sufficient education and congregational discussion before public action was needed. The process began with a well-attended congregational retreat in September 2005, a full fourteen months before the state referenda. The theme of the retreat focused on *tikkun olam* and was entitled "The Shofar Calls: We Can Make a Difference." The retreat incorporated reflection and action opportunities on several social justice issues, including same-sex marriage. An educational forum launched the synagogue's campaign to garner votes against these two referenda. The result of this deliberative foundational work was a congregational affirmation that the temple has an obligation to share its voice with the broader community, perhaps even sounding an alarm like the shofar to awaken others to an injustice.

A successful civic engagement process was enabled by a powerful combination of advance planning, rabbinic and lay leadership, and congregational education, in addition to collaboration with other community organizations working against the referenda. The work was grounded in Jewish values and non-divisive, while weaving the synagogue more strongly into the fabric of the community.

Despite the temple's diligent work opposing the reinstatement of the death penalty and the constitutional ban on same-sex marriage, the Wisconsin electorate voted in favor of both referenda. Even well-planned processes can lead to profound disappointment and deep frustration, if not a sense of futility.

The *nechemta* (the consolation) is that ultimately the Wisconsin legislature did not restore capital punishment, despite the referendum, and the state ban on same-sex marriage was overturned eventually by federal courts in June 2014. With this federal ruling, Wisconsin citizens were able to enjoy the benefits of same-sex marriage a full year before the United States Supreme Court made marriage equality legal in all fifty states.

### Agenda Model

The Agenda Model sets an annual plan on specific issues, with experienced lay leaders managing the process under the board's authority. This model is used by Temple Beth El, a Reform congregation of eleven hundred families in Charlotte, North Carolina, led by senior rabbi Judith Schindler, at the time that this social justice policy was created.

Temple Beth El began its advocacy journey by passing board resolutions in 2007 and in 2010. Unlike the example from Wisconsin, neither of the issues (domestic abuse and affordable housing) was prompted by or concluded with a city or state ballot initiative. Instead, the issues surfaced from congregants who were volunteering their time addressing the symptoms of these problems and eventually sought more systemic solutions.

As congregants and agencies in the larger community became aware of the impact of the synagogue's advocacy, calls for action on other issues increased. From taking a stand on a North Carolina referendum to ban same-sex marriage, to working to reverse state budget cuts to teacher pay, to participating in the Moral Monday protests at the state legislature, the clergy and many temple members became more vocal on these and other social justice issues. Sometimes these positions were taken under the mantle of the synagogue name and sometimes as individual citizens.

Eventually, a board task force was appointed to codify and bring clarity to the advocacy process and to mitigate the divisiveness that had arisen. The outcome was the creation of an annual social justice agenda, grounded in congregational education, Reform Jewish values, and existing congregational commitments. The 2014 guiding document put the primary responsibility of overseeing the annual agenda on the Tzedek Council, a group of lay leaders experienced in running social justice and action projects at the temple. One indicator of the success of this model in affirming the temple's commitment to social justice is that the temple board asked the Tzedek Council to develop an advocacy plan on racial inequity after the controversial 2016 police shooting of an African-American man in Charlotte.

As activity on each advocacy issue waxes and wanes, the Tzedek Council manages the complexity of supporting multiple efforts. The group screens and funds new social justice and action issues and projects using preestablished criteria, including whether there is lay leadership commitment, traction within the congregation, alignment with the Reform Movement, and minimal potential for divisiveness. The reality of finite financial and human resources is always a consideration. The Tzedek Council also decides when to retire an issue—as lay leaders shift focus, a significant success is achieved, or realistic opportunities for change appear elusive.

Some examples of Temple Beth El's advocacy work to date include educating the Charlotte Jewish community's clergy on domestic abuse, catalyzing a public/private endowment to subsidize rents for homeless families on the path to financial independence, and registering voters in conjunction with the North Carolina NAACP. Advocacy projects addressing environmental change, aging, state teacher pay, and racial inequity are in the early stages of development.

### Coalition Model

The Coalition Model connects congregations, leveraging collective resources to address issues of common concern. This model is used by B'nai Jehoshua Beth Elohim (BJBE), a Reform congregation of eleven hundred families in the northern suburbs of Chicago, led by senior rabbi Karyn Kedar. BJBE has a strong relationship with United Power, a CBCO affiliated with Industrial Areas Foundation. This is the only non-Jewish organization to which BJBE pays dues, which it has done for more than twenty years. The synagogue is one of many dues-paying houses of worship that comprise United Power's membership roster.

Through its relationship with United Power, BJBE congregants have helped change the greater Chicago community and the State of Illinois. Their victories include creating the first-ever state housing trust fund and expanding health-care coverage to include more families and young adults.[160]

The BJBE lay leaders for each of the various United Power issues embraced by the synagogue have built networks within the congregation so that a delegation of synagogue members is always available to attend key actions. These have included showing the governor the impact of funding housing rehabs and demonstrating for smart guns at the International Association of Chiefs of Police convention. Ted Busch, a lay leader at BJBE, explains, "Our approach to advocacy is all about relationship-building, both within temple and through United Power."

Membership in United Power provides critical resources for BJBE. Lay leader Susan Drucker is especially enthusiastic about the training United Power makes available, such as how to put an action together on short notice. While collaborating in a metro area the size of Chicago can be logistically inconvenient, the resulting mutual support outweighs the challenges. Drucker comments on the energizing effect of working in coalition with others:

> In the car on the way to the meetings, I'll think, "What the heck am I doing this for? An hour and a half to go downtown." But I'm always happy when I come home. Always glad I went. It is hard, but then the people I go with and meet there re-energize me. Literally the passion and energy in the room energize me to continue the work.

Synagogue liaisons to United Power have a voice choosing the issues in which the CBCO will participate, as do the other member congregations. Hence the synagogue chooses to passionately engage on some United Power issues, while refraining from others. Drucker explains, "Certain battles you just decide not to fight. You have to listen to your congregation and not fight those battles. . . . Although most of [United Power's] actions we do support."

In this model, the power of one congregation is amplified by collaboration with congregations of different faiths, usually through a CBCO. Another way to apply this model is through joining a Jewish coalition of other synagogues, such as Reform California, a collaboration of Reform congregations in that state.[161]

### Traction Model

The Traction Model allows a group of congregants to pursue any issue for which they can mobilize sufficient interest. This model is used by Temple Beth Elohim, a large Reform synagogue of twelve hundred families, led by senior rabbi Joel Sisenwine and associate rabbi Rachel Saphire, in Wellesley, Massachusetts. This model allows a critical mass of congregants who share a passion for a Jewish social justice issue to move from hearing the call to gaining enough traction to advancing an issue themselves.

Temple Beth Elohim crafted a program called Shabbat Reflection to move congregants from text study to civic engagement. Described by Rabbi Saphire as their "home-grown way of organizing house meetings," Shabbat Reflections convene congregants who care about an issue, share personal stories, surface a few leaders, and then break into small groups to pursue immediate next steps.

Initially, the clergy led the Tikkun Olam Team to expand into community organizing so that congregants would be encouraged to explore their passions and speak out collectively. They adopted names like "Koach B'yachad" (strength together) and "Temple Beth Elohim Congregants to Prevent Gun Violence," rather than taking a stand as an institution, acknowledging the diversity of opinions among the congregation. While the board is informed about the ongoing work, it does not vote on the positions taken or events sponsored.

This grassroots approach allows groups to form and dissipate based on who shows up and is willing to work, without waiting for board approval or formal resolutions. This is especially useful when issues are time-sensitive. This process has been successfully used at Temple Beth Elohim for advocacy on climate action, mental wellness, Syrian refugee resettlement, and the prevention of gun violence.

## Choosing Your Blueprint

These examples illustrate how four synagogues manage their advocacy campaigns to put the challenges of process behind them and focus their energies on the social justice issues ahead. Which model is most appropriate for your synagogue? Answering "yes" or "no" to the questions in table 4 may help you define which model best fits your congregation or guide you to a hybrid model that addresses your unique situation.

**Table 4.** Say "Yes" to Your Blueprint for Civic Engagement

| RESOLUTION | YES | NO |
|---|---|---|
| a) Is your board hesitant to embark on the civic engagement journey? | ☐ | ☐ |
| b) Is your congregation new to speaking out in the community? | ☐ | ☐ |
| c) Is there a single issue already galvanizing the congregation? | ☐ | ☐ |

| AGENDA | YES | NO |
|---|---|---|
| a) Would your board delegate setting public positions to a lay committee with an annual review process? | ☐ | ☐ |
| b) Are there five to ten experienced lay leaders willing to manage the agenda? | ☐ | ☐ |
| c) Does your synagogue or clergy already speak out on multiple issues? | ☐ | ☐ |

*Continues next page*

| COALITION | YES | NO |
|---|---|---|
| a) Would your board invest the financial resources to pay dues to an outside organizing group, allowing the temple's name to be listed as a member? | ☐ | ☐ |
| b) Are there other congregations engaged in advocacy in your area as part of an active congregation-based community organizing (CBCO) group or other coalition? | ☐ | ☐ |
| c) Are you uncertain about which issue you should address or how, but feel an obligation to not stand idly by? | ☐ | ☐ |

| TRACTION | YES | NO |
|---|---|---|
| a) Would your board let multiple, and potentially conflicting, voices speak from the congregation? | ☐ | ☐ |
| b) Is there depth of public policy expertise in your congregation? | ☐ | ☐ |
| c) Is there sufficient energy around civic engagement to sustain multiple issues? | ☐ | ☐ |

In examining your results, more "yes" responses for a given model indicate a better match for your synagogue, though it is possible for more than one model to emerge as a potential blueprint. Drilling down into the details of implementing each model—the clasps and curtains of the metaphoric *mishkan*—may help you draw up your own blueprint.

The Resolution Model is ideal for congregations newly embarking on the civic engagement journey and for which a critical issue has already emerged—for example, in response to a local or national tragedy or a legislative initiative contrary to Jewish values. Temple boards that are hesitant to stand on the public stage of civic engagement retain control over defining the scope of the work through the resolution approval process. The challenge of the Resolution Model is to allow sufficient lead time for education, communication, and action.

Successfully implementing this model relies on writing a resolution that articulates core Jewish values, the position of the movement with which your synagogue is affiliated, and your congregation's track record devoting time and resources to relevant volunteer projects. The resolution must clearly identify what actions the congregation is authorized to take.

Creating forums to educate the congregation on the topic of your resolution is essential. Outside experts can be helpful to outline the problem and identify the landscape of achievable goals. Consulting with congregants whose professional work is relevant builds credibility for the campaign and limits the potential for naïve mistakes. These discussions are also an opportunity to solicit congregational input on your draft resolution and assess the potential for divisiveness prior to the board vote.

### Analyzing Your Responses: "Yes" to Agenda

**Yes / No**   a) Would your board delegate setting public positions to a lay committee with an annual review process?

**Yes / No**   b) Are there five to ten experienced lay leaders willing to manage the agenda?

**Yes / No**   c) Does your synagogue or clergy already speak out on multiple issues?

Perhaps your synagogue has already passed one or more advocacy resolutions or your clergy are respected voices on community issues. In addition, your lay leaders may have demonstrated competence and strong stewardship in leading the temple's civic engagement work, and the board accepts this work as part of the synagogue's array of programs and services. If so, your synagogue is likely recognized in the community for its good work, and a parade of issues has already found its way to your congregation in search of funding and volunteer support. An advocacy agenda managed by a lay committee is an ideal way for your synagogue to respond appropriately and effectively to these demands.

To be successful, the committee that sets the annual agenda requires a group of experienced lay leaders with sufficient perspective to assess issues, both for social action and social justice projects. Given the expansive nature of the model, the committee requires enough bench strength so that lay leaders can rotate on and off the committee, a challenge that may eliminate this model for many congregations. Each new effort also requires its own temple lay leader with the requisite "Five *P*'s" to shepherd the project (see p. 163). Such deep pools of lay leaders are more typically available in larger congregations, simply because of their size. Contrast this to the Resolution Model, in which a single lay leader can partner with clergy to lead the congregation into civic engagement.

The criteria used for setting the agenda should reflect the same principles as in the Resolution Model. Issues should be grounded in Jewish values, your synagogue's movement, and congregational interests as uncovered through listening campaigns or other participatory processes. Emphasizing community partnerships (e.g., through a CBCO or other interfaith collaboration) and focusing on fewer, deeper initiatives will enhance your synagogue's impact.

This model should incorporate a measure of board engagement. Ideally the person chairing the committee that sets the agenda would also serve as an officer on the executive board. It is recommended that the agenda be presented to the board for review annually, acknowledging that community crises may require items to be considered at other times of the year.

Successfully implementing this model requires the committee to weave itself into the fabric of the congregation to mitigate the risks of isolating civic engagement work from the congregation. Invite representatives from other synagogue groups (e.g., sisterhood, brotherhood, teens) to join the committee or periodically attend its meetings. Presenting issues on the agenda to other demographics and committees of the congregation provides opportunities for their involvement. Official temple communications are one way—not the only way—to recruit others.

### Analyzing Your Responses: "Yes" to Coalition

*Yes / No*  a) Would your board invest the financial resources to pay dues to an outside organizing group, allowing the temple's name to be listed as a member?

*Yes / No*  b) Are there other congregations engaged in advocacy in your area as part of an active congregation-based community organizing (CBCO) group or other coalition?

*Yes / No*  c) Are you uncertain about which issue you should address or how, but feel an obligation to not stand idly by?

If your synagogue wants to embark on the civic engagement journey but lacks some of the tools needed to move along that path, we recommend joining a coalition of synagogues or an interfaith organizing group such as a CBCO. This process involves familiarizing yourself with your nearby coalitions and their leadership, understanding the issues with which they are engaged and how those issues are selected, and building bridges of relationship and trust between your congregation and other member congregations.

This model is ideal if your congregation has the commitment to social justice but lacks content proficiency or organizing expertise among its lay leadership. CBCOs give you that necessary professional guidance. If you have a committee of passionate lay leaders that your board wants to support, this model channels their energy and provides a path for moving their issues forward successfully. In employing the Coalition Model, your leadership may choose to view it like other temple program offerings. Not everyone comes to Tot Shabbat, Torah study, or Shavuot services, but the synagogue is committed to offering those, too, in order to fulfill the fundamental functions of the congregation.

Whether your synagogue is large or small, in an urban or rural setting, or in a predominantly conservative or liberal community, you can comfortably make a home for those who have a heart for social justice through joining a coalition. Joining a CBCO or other coalition magnifies your impact and creates compelling actions and expanded platforms to engage your congregants. When your congregation shows up with one hundred congregants, other congregations grow the crowd to a thousand. As an added benefit, there are many examples from our research of Jews with a passion for justice whose temple engagement blossomed through the doorway of civic engagement, ultimately leading them to become board members and even board president.

While the challenges of paying dues to another institution and establishing a public profile may present seemingly insurmountable barriers to some congregations, the benefits should not be minimized. Consider the perspective of Temple Emanu-El in Dallas, a member of Faith in Texas, which is a CBCO affiliated with People Improving Communities through Organizing (PICO). In its "Social

Justice Task Force Report," the temple affirms, "A budget is a moral document, and [our] Temple's values are reflected through our budgets."[162]

The work of coalitions is built upon relationships, and that always requires compromise. One CBCO (remaining anonymous) agreed to eliminate abortion from any future platform in order to welcome a local Baptist church. They decided that the benefit from gaining the congregation was greater than utilizing the CBCO platform for this issue, leaving members who cared about reproductive rights to address the issue separately. Likewise, we heard cases of CBCOs making accommodations for synagogues, shifting assemblies from Saturday to Sunday and changing the religious language used in opening prayers. Entering a coalition is entering a relationship; it entails a willingness to be in partnership, make a commitment, learn and grow, lead and follow, challenge and be challenged, and recognize that ultimately alliances, coalitions, and networks will take us further than we could ever travel alone.

### Analyzing Your Responses: "Yes" to Traction

| | |
|---|---|
| **Yes / No** | a) Would your board let multiple, and potentially conflicting, voices speak from the congregation? |
| **Yes / No** | b) Is there depth of public policy expertise in your congregation? |
| **Yes / No** | c) Is there sufficient energy around civic engagement to sustain multiple issues? |

If the challenge is not choosing among issues but rather encouraging those with passion to organize themselves, we recommend the Traction Model. In this model, the board accepts civic engagement as part of the synagogue's array of responsibilities and acknowledges that congregants may speak in the synagogue's name on issues without specific board permission. This lack of board control may be unacceptable to some congregations whose leadership is hesitant about advocacy. But other boards may appreciate the agility of their congregation responding without emergency conference calls and endless editing of documents.

Like the Agenda Model, this blueprint requires many lay leaders skilled in advocacy and organizing. Otherwise, actions may be unproductive in achieving progress because the goals are not meaningful or the plan is not implemented successfully. Like the Coalition Model, this blueprint benefits from a CBCO or another institution organizing in the community to magnify the impact of the congregation's work.

The core of this model is studying an issue in the context of Jewish teachings and contemporary responses and then allowing congregants to decide whether to pursue a solution. You may need to offer several of these study sessions before identifying issues that resonate with your congregation.

### Say "Yes" to a Blueprint for Civic Engagement

We have shared four models, knowing that there are many workable variations and hybrids that can be created. Each congregation must find its own path, even as it looks to others for direction. Recognize, too, that the needs of your synagogue will change as it evolves or as new issues are addressed in your community. For example, Temple Beth El in Charlotte started with the Resolution Model and then evolved to Agenda Model. Temple Beth Elohim in Wellesley uses the Traction Model, but also belongs to a CBCO, using the Coalition Model to address other issues. With Torah and Talmud as guides, and case histories of other synagogues paving the way, synagogues can indeed find their way forward.

Just as the tent pegs and curtains of the ancient *Mishkan* are not enough to create a divine connection, and the bricks and mortar of the modern synagogue are not enough to create a dynamic congregation, selecting the right blueprint for civic engagement work is only the start. Once we have built our civic engagement *mishkan*—the appropriate congregational structures to support our advocacy—we begin to focus on the *avodah*, the work within it.

## Notes to Chapter 8

159. Michael Gecan, *Effective Organizing for Congregational Renewal* (Skokie, IL: ACTA Publications, 2008).

160. "United Power Impact," United Power, http://www.united-power.org/content/united-power-impact.

161. "Reform California," Religious Action Center of Reform Judaism, http://www.rac.org/reform-california.

162. "Temple Emanu-El Social Justice Task Force Report," Dallas, TX, board approved March 4, 2010, 9.

# CHAPTER 9

# The Cycle of Civic Engagement
## The Work That Fills the *Mishkan*

T HE *KOHANIM* (meaning "priests") were a family dynasty within the tribe of Levi charged with the day-to-day responsibilities of worship and rituals in the *Mishkan*. Each Yom Kippur, their leader— the High Priest—entered the Holy of Holies, the inner sanctuary, and approached the Divine. There he would offer sacrifices and seek atonement for any wrongdoing for himself, his household, and the whole House of Israel.

While doing his sacred work, the High Priest wore an ornate breastplate with four rows of three engraved gems, representing the twelve tribes. Each of the twelve gems was different: turquoise, lapis lazuli, emerald, and so on. According to the text, "The stones shall correspond [in number] to the names of the sons of Israel: twelve, corresponding to their names. They shall be engraved like seals, each with its name, for the twelve tribes" (Exodus 28:21).

The leader of this sacred work always had the names of the Isra- elites before him. These twelve unique stones also represented the diversity of the Israelites—their passions, daily labors, families, blessings, and sins. Those of you responsible for leading civic en- gagement should similarly see yourselves as representing all the diverse members of your congregation.

Consider trying this activity as you embark on your journey, whether it's your first social justice issue or one of many:

Use the grid on the next page as a modern breastplate for your congregational leadership. Write in each of those twelve boxes a demographic or interest group of your congregation. (Think about demographics such as age, gender, marital status, race, sexual orientation, ability/disability, family composition, interfaith households, or political affiliations. Consider interest groups such as lifelong learners, regular worshipers, care teams, environmentalists, or choir members.)

**Figure 4.**
Breastplate of Congregational Diversity.

Keep these groups in mind as you do your sacred work—as you write your congregational communications, plan your programs, and speak publicly. Hear each of their voices and be sensitive to them as you choose your words. Be mindful to include a representative from each of these groups as you assemble leadership teams for your synagogue's civic engagement work.

Many congregations already recognize the diverse interests among their congregants in how they recruit members to their board, conscientiously nominating members of different ages and interests and sometimes including a standing representative from such pillar groups as sisterhood and brotherhood. Reflecting this wisdom, Temple Beth Sholom in Miami Beach, Florida, has assembled its social justice network to intentionally represent each demographic in the congregation. The committee includes representatives from such varied groups as the young adults and religious school parents, as well as members-at-large. Only with your entire congregation close to your heart can you maximize inclusion and minimize divisiveness.

### The Heart of the Matter

Rabbi Ben Bag Bag taught, "Turn it and turn it again, for everything is in it" (*Pirkei Avot* 5:22).[163] While this first-century rabbi with the odd name was making reference to the study of Torah, the same principle holds true for the cycle of civic engagement. It requires a continuing process of intentional listening and learning.

Many helpful guides support congregations of all faiths in creating social change. The *Social Justice Empowerment Program Handbook* created by the Unitarian Universalist Association[164] and *Lirdof Tzedek: A Guide to Synagogue Social Action* created by the Religious Action Center of Reform Judaism[165] are two resources rich with wisdom. B'nai Jeshurun in Manhattan has assembled a "how-we-did-it" manual entitled *"Panim el Panim": Our Story*, with guidelines and sample forms for other congregations to use as a resource. We also encourage you to find a training program that will steep you in the details of organizing. For example, JOIN for Justice offers organizing training for clergy and lay leaders across the spectrum of Jewish movements.[166]

The guide that follows maps the work ahead of you into five broad stages, citing examples from congregations to illuminate your journey. Though you are undoubtedly eager to repair the world (as we all are), remember that order matters—you need to listen first, educate before you strategize, strategize before you act, and then reflect after you act but before you start the cycle over again.

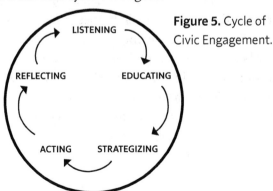

**Figure 5.** Cycle of Civic Engagement.

## Listening

People with different political views are genuinely heard when every-one's opinions are solicited and space is created for respectful discussion. Modern-day communication is increasingly a function of technology, and many of us are guilty of retreating into an echo chamber, hearing only those who share our perspective. When congregants listen with intention to each other's stories, they uncover shared concerns and thereby create authentic moments of connection. Listening is a critical first step for synagogues in the cycle of civic engagement, ultimately empowering the synagogue to move forward with consensus.

While at Temple Israel in Boston, Rabbi Jonah Pesner, now director of the Religious Action Center of Reform Judaism, created the synagogue listening campaigns that he later crafted into the model of the Just Congregations program at the Union for Reform Judaism. In the words of Rabbi Matt Soffer, a current rabbi at Temple Israel, "Stories became the fuel that would harness and build power."

Using Temple Israel's model as its starting point, B'nai Jeshurun (BJ) in New York City has incorporated listening campaigns into the synagogue's culture since 2003. An unaffiliated congregation with a venerable tradition of social justice, BJ calls its listening campaigns "Panim el Panim." *Panim el panim* means "face to face"—the way in which Jacob is said to have communicated with God during a sleepless night of struggle, from which he emerged with a new name (Israel), a new understanding of himself and his role in the world (Genesis 32:28–31).

BJ's initial campaign consisted of 613 one-on-one formally structured conversations in homes and at the synagogue (613 is the number of commandments in the Torah). More recent campaigns have been modified into "community cafés" in the synagogue or as parlor meetings in congregants' apartments, with invitations based on city neighborhoods or other commonalities. Judith Trachtenberg, a lay leader at BJ, explained, "We are changing it so people don't feel, 'Ugh, here they come again for the conversations.' We want them excited."

In Tallahassee, Florida, Barry Moline at Temple Israel acknowledges the challenges of conducting one-on-one conversations in
the thirty houses of worship in TEAM, Temple Israel's CBCO. He
shared the details of the process, saying, "At every house of worship, someone is responsible for convening the groups or talking to
people individually in their congregation. Talking to people is more
effective, but convening the group is faster and easier. Like touching
an elephant, everyone sees things differently."

BJ's report on its community cafés couched issues in terms of
congregants' personal feelings, mitigating the political overtones.
The headings in the article were "We heard you say," "You are angry
about," "You are worried about," "You care about."[167] Regardless of
format, listening campaigns seek to reveal those issues that interest a
critical mass of congregants while identifying passionate leadership.

Trachtenberg points out the heightened commitment that was
necessary before establishing BJ's "Aging in New York Hevra."
(*Hevra* is Hebrew and Yiddish for "close-knit group" and the name
BJ has given to its advocacy campaign working groups.) She noted,
"We tried something [on aging] seven or eight years ago, and congregants were interested but not enough to work on it. About five years
ago, people were very ready." Over the years, BJ has helped to achieve
impressive results on many fronts, including addressing mold in
public housing, achieving same-sex marriage in New York State,
and passing the New York State Domestic Workers' Bill of Rights.
Manhattan Together (part of Metro IAF) has been BJ's CBCO partner on some issues, although not all. But each issue found its roots
in a listening campaign.

As the synagogue embarked on strategic planning in 2017, the
listening campaign became a tool to discern congregants' connections to BJ itself. This is an emerging trend among both Jewish and
Christian congregations. Using the listening campaign strengthens
congregants' connections to one another and to their houses of worship. The issues that surface in the meetings—which may include
social justice—determine the institution's future direction.

While one-on-one listening campaigns are powerful for a

congregation, they are difficult and labor-intensive and may even cause frustration among the many lay leaders eager to act immediately. The essential objective of this stage in the cycle of civic engagement is to ground the selection of your issues in your congregants' passions. More and more congregations across the country are choosing to hold parlor meetings, recognizing that even a handful of gatherings will uncover more valuable insights than a social justice committee alone can imagine in a conference room.

These gatherings take many forms: Beth Hillel Temple in Wisconsin used its previously mentioned family retreat weekend, and Temple Beth Elohim in Wellesley holds Shabbat Reflections. Temple Beth Sholom in Miami Beach holds "Justice Jams" in congregants' homes seven to fourteen times each year, with the synagogue relying on the host to fill the room. Rabbi Gayle Pomerantz of Temple Beth Sholom elaborates:

> We create a comprehensive and interesting presentation that is sometimes experiential and sometimes frontal. . . . I weave in Jewish values, texts, and themes. At the end of Justice Jams we have an evaluation and ask, "What issue is urgent to you right now?" We hear what's on people's minds, discuss it at the social justice network meeting, and that is how we determine what to focus on in the year ahead.

Conducting surveys is a tempting way to quickly assess congregational interests. That process can be a precursor—but not a substitute—for in-person gatherings where genuine connections are made that energize the community and drive the process forward. One congregation was so eager to be inclusive that the rabbi gave a High Holy Day sermon on social justice and then passed out surveys to solicit participation on a spectrum of issues. Although the sermon was well-received and the individual follow-up to the surveys was thorough, this process did not create the desired momentum—even with peak High Holy Day attendance and the liturgy's powerful call for personal accountability.

Another tool for helping you either engage participants or make the final decision among competing issues that surfaced through the listening process is to tally how many individuals are already involved in your congregation's social action projects, whether through volunteering or making donations. Seeing where congregants already give time and money will reveal where they are more likely to climb to another rung on the ladder of civic engagement.

In the case of a synagogue choosing to support an issue previously selected by its CBCO, the synagogue needs to be especially conscientious to create listening opportunities for its congregants. Examples surfaced of divisiveness that was averted when congregations chose not to engage on issues that would have publicly pitted the CBCO against businesses owned by congregants. On the other hand, when CBCO issues were selected without proper vetting, the conflict rose to the board level. In situations where some congregants feel a passion for a divisive issue, congregants and clergy should act as individuals, not as representatives of the synagogue. Failing to listen properly and gain the support of your congregation may threaten the willingness of the board to support any civic engagement, eliminating the potential for much good work in the community.

### Educating

Once you have selected your issue, the next critical step will be educating yourselves—learning the language, meeting the players, identifying the barriers, and researching best practices both in your community and elsewhere. Sessions with nonprofit or business professionals, university professors, civic leaders, and especially individuals most impacted by the issue will enable you to deepen your understanding. As part of each meeting or program, be sure to ask, "What do you think we should advocate for?" Keeping a running list of recommendations will help you refine your specific goals. As you gain knowledge and experience with an issue, focus on building relationships and not just gathering research. Not surprisingly, you may find partners through this process with whom you can brainstorm and collaborate.

Lara Ettenson, chair of the Tzedek Council at Congregation Emanu-El in San Francisco, described how the working group on homelessness engaged in an intentional process of education prior to choosing partnerships. In order to better understand the issues and engage directly with the homeless population they intend to help, the group started a variety of projects on homelessness. Through this work, they built partnerships with two agencies focused on ending homelessness for families in San Francisco.

To educate himself on issues related to aging, Stephen Phillips, from Temple Beth El in Charlotte, set up meetings and attended conferences with such groups as the Catholic Diocese, the North Carolina Baptist Aging Ministry, the South Asian Senior Center, and the Charlotte Mecklenburg Aging Coalition. He found that the single biggest problem for aging adults was transportation and that it was difficult for seniors to access the special needs services provided by the Charlotte Area Transit System (CATS). At a subsequent meeting at Providence United Methodist Church, Phillips met the head of CATS, who was enthusiastic about the prospect of an outreach program for seniors. That conversation paved the way for Phillips to explore a pilot program at houses of worship with a one-stop process replacing the existing bureaucracy consisting of four steps (filling out an application, obtaining medical authorization, visiting CATS for an evaluation, and then waiting for notification).

Educating your congregants, and not just your social justice committee, builds a stronger case for taking on an issue. Dr. Nick Morse, at Temple Israel in Boston, talks about how its ad hoc aging committee sees issues resonating with the congregation in its education process:

> Right now our ad hoc advisory board on aging comes up with topics and seminars, the temple helps us advertise, and then amazingly thirty to fifty people come. We are just now [early 2015] thinking about it as a permanent part of the temple. . . . In parallel, GBIO [their CBCO] is right now deciding what some of their next big things are, and likely to choose challenges of aging and end-of-life care.

Education is critical even for those congregations joining an existing community organizing initiative. In addition to local CBCOs, national Jewish social justice organizations, such as those who are members of the Jewish Social Justice Roundtable, may provide educational resources, training, and support to help you on your journey. Through education, you gauge your congregants' interest while giving them the tools they need to understand the complexities of the issue.

## Strategizing

Having developed an understanding about an issue, you are ready to set your goals. As you strategize, consider the following questions:

- Is your priority to change policy in your local community, in your region, or nationally?
- What goals are actionable and winnable?
- Who has the power to make those changes?
- What are the means to exert pressure on those decision-makers?
- With which organizations can you partner to magnify your power?

## Local versus Statewide versus National

The Stan Greenspon Center for Peace and Social Justice, a new organizing enterprise led by Rabbi Schindler at Queens University of Charlotte, chose to explore refugee advocacy as its first issue, beginning with an eight-week educational course that attracted 130 participants from within the university and across the community. Speakers included refugees themselves, along with professors, lawyers, and nonprofit leaders. The Queens students and community members engaged in the program kept a running list of potential areas for advocacy that surfaced. Later, they considered the possibilities of each advocacy initiative and then voted to set the agendas for their local, state, and national advocacy working groups, which guided their subsequent work.

While the Queens initiative chose to pursue local, state, and national goals simultaneously, you may find that local goals make your work more manageable and tangible, often with more immediate results. In order to sustain momentum and manage burnout, the team of Rabbi Saphire, Temple Beth Elohim's community organizer, and its lay leadership evaluates the prospects for a success within the first eighteen months of each effort. Barry Moline, at Temple Israel in Tallahassee, also espouses a strategy of seeking achievable goals, noting, "It's always better to try good ideas and take small bites of the apple."

A local focus proved to be an effective path for teaching teens about the power of advocacy. Boston's Jewish Community Relations Council (JCRC) uses synagogue organizing as an expression of their Jewish mission as it relates to secular concerns. The Jewish teens at Temple Emanuel, a Conservative congregation of twelve hundred households in Newton, Massachusetts, had expressed dismay about their synagogue's lack of a recycling program to Joy Friedman, then a JCRC organizer. With Friedman's encouragement to explore the issue, the teens learned that their congregation's failure to recycle was not a result of apathy, but of the city's policy to exclude nonprofits.

Abby Flam, a Temple Emanuel member and board officer, remembers the pride of the congregation in seeing their teens take action. She recalls, "It was tremendous. There was an assembly with four hundred people, and the teens came in carrying one week's worth of bags of recycling and then spoke with such clear understanding of the issues and commitment to help change the options." When the recycling contract for the City of Newton (Massachusetts) was up for renewal, the teens successfully organized to pressure the city to expand the contract to include nonprofits and small businesses.

Expanding your scope to the state level requires both a deeper understanding of the political process and broader partnerships. Temple Beth Elohim in Wellesley collaborated with many other congregations to lobby the Commonwealth of Massachusetts to pass legislation in 2014 to reduce gun violence. Four of the coalition's task force recommendations were included in the law in some form: mandated universal background checks for all gun purchasers, compliance with federal laws on sharing data on mental health and substance abuse rulings, expanded police chief discretion to include rifle and handgun buyer suitability, and greater use of a database tracking gun owners and sources.[168]

Changing national policy calls us to find organizations beyond our own communities that share our goals. Achieving nationwide marriage equality took decades of work across many states before reaching the United States Supreme Court. Through a combination of shifting public opinion, some legislative successes, and victories in state courts (including Massachusetts), marriage equality became the norm in an increasing number of states. These gains helped shape and inform litigation in the federal courts that ultimately resulted in nationwide success. The political realities of each state led to different marriage equality strategies—lobbying for legislation, filing lawsuits, or seeking a voter referendum.

The same holds true as we work on other issues, from immigration reform to living wages to racial justice. Synagogues and coalitions in each state work in their own way to change public opinion, apply pressure on their representatives, campaign for a referendum, or provide assistance to legal efforts, while at the same time learning from the successes and the failures of others across the country.

## Picking up a Meaningful Piece of the Puzzle

Most of the social justice issues that keep us awake at night are complex and overwhelming. Our challenge as Jews and as Americans is to not allow the sheer magnitude of these problems to paralyze us or, conversely, leave us tilting at windmills.

Community solutions to homelessness in Charlotte have been persistently stymied by a variety of factors. Serving on a newly formed city-county commission charged with implementing a "ten-year plan to end homelessness," Rabbi Schindler preached a strategy of taking steps that were actionable and winnable, saying, "Homelessness is a puzzle. It is impossible for any one of us to solve it as a whole. But it is possible if each of us picks up one more piece of the puzzle."[169]

While many communities and states have been successful creating affordable housing trusts to fund and build housing for low-income residents, Charlotte's strategy of funding new construction was repeatedly frustrated as higher-income neighborhoods fought against one proposed affordable housing development after another. A campaign to change these "not in my backyard" (NIMBY) attitudes failed to shift public opinion.

Community volunteers from multiple houses of faith became determined to tackle the unmet need for low-income housing. Two distinct efforts emerged, both of which required tremendous volunteer leadership and community support. These concurrent and unrelated housing initiatives addressed two critical pieces of Charlotte's puzzle to end homelessness, ultimately creating sustainable housing solutions for two different segments of the homeless population. The first initiative evolved from a series of breakfasts at a local deli, and the second from the chance encounter of a soup kitchen volunteer.

Frustrated by the lack of coordination across congregations and convinced that current efforts were treating only the symptoms of homelessness, lay leaders from different faith communities started meeting in 2009 in what became informally known as the "Phil's Deli Group." Over a year of monthly breakfasts, they developed a creative idea that would provide affordable housing and social services for families that put participants on a path to self-sufficiency. The core of this approach featured rental subsidies for apartments scattered around the city, thereby dodging neighborhood backlash while garnering broader city council support.

The group met with the Foundation For The Carolinas, the local community foundation, which embraced the plan and created A Way Home, a $20 million public/private endowment. In its third year, at only partial capacity, A Way Home was already housing ninety-nine families. The fund was not only providing stable housing but also coordinating the county supportive services the families needed to increase their wages and build more sustainable budgets. As an endowment, the A Way Home principal remains untouched, and the program is expected to move a new cohort of families from homelessness to financial self-sufficiency every two years.

A second piece of the puzzle was solved by Kathy Izard, a dedicated volunteer at Charlotte's Urban Ministry Center, which provides daytime services and meals for people experiencing homelessness. While escorting a guest speaker on a tour of the facility, Izard was discomfited by his question "Where are the beds?"[170] In her book, *The Hundred Story Home*, Izard describes her journey to build Moore Place, which houses eighty-five chronically homeless, single adults who were among the most vulnerable to dying on the streets. After a two-year community campaign to raise awareness, the NIMBY response to the project was muted, in part because the site had previously hosted a junkyard, and ultimately cost only one vote on the city council.[171]

While neither A Way Home nor Moore Place has ended homelessness in Charlotte, they created solutions that have moved a few hundred people from homelessness to stable housing. They have provided measurable outcomes in a sector that evaluates success by the number of people served. Just as putting a few puzzle pieces in place starts to inform the bigger picture, these two initiatives created the basis for broader solutions: Moore Place expanded to serve ninety additional single adults, and A Way Home catalyzed more collaborative programs among the agencies serving people experiencing homelessness.

Parsing the puzzle into smaller pieces also makes it more manageable. As you set your goals, view the larger issue that you have selected as a puzzle, and think about a significant piece on which you could work. As you identify goals that can make a real impact, ask yourself: Does your plan change the underlying source of injustice? Will you impact enough people to make a difference? What has been achieved in other states? Who are the opponents, and what are the barriers? How can you defuse opposition? Where can you find common ground? Is there a reasonable path to success?

**Power, Pressure, and Partnerships**
Discerning who has the power to make the changes you seek will inform your strategy. You may have the expertise to sort through these issues on your own, but there is no prize for reinventing the wheel. Solicit partners who have political or organizing experience

and who can join with you—more hands, more minds, more voices, and more impact.

Power usually resides with money or people. Companies are more likely to be moved by the choices of their customers that affect the bottom line. Elected officials care about voters and also about the funders of their political campaigns. While colleges and universities care about the opinions of their students and faculty, they are also influenced by their board of trustees, alumni, and donors. Understanding these power dynamics will lead you to a strategy to exert pressure on key decision-makers. Rarely is public opinion powerful enough on its own.

Building relationships and credibility with your legislators creates power, a lesson learned at BJ through its connections with legislators in both New York City and New York State. BJ lay leader Rochelle Friedlich elaborates, "We did meetings with elected officials, and did trainings on how to meet with elected officials and why they should be interested in our particular issue. BJ has become an important voice after all these years of meeting with elected officials. I believe we carry some weight."

Rabbi Sydney Mintz, at Congregation Emanu-El in San Francisco, recognized both the responsibility and responsiveness required for public partnership. Rabbi Mintz reflected on how civic engagement made the synagogue an essential partner in progress, saying, "We recognized that in order to be successful, we needed to become part of a movement for change and not stand alone. One night I received a phone call inviting me to be at the table the next day with California governor Jerry Brown on the subject of immigration reform." To be counted as a player, she knew that you have to be part of the team both in preparation and on gameday.

Rabbi Matt Soffer, at Temple Israel in Boston, differentiates between advocacy and a sustained expression of commitment for a cause. He sees advocacy as one-way, even one-time communication, but finds success instead in strategic relationships. These relationships require showing up both in numbers and over time.

> Advocacy is so one-way. It is not relational. It is not just a singu-
> lar meeting. It is not just a singular action. It's building strategic
> relationships. How are we developing those relationships? We
> get a thousand people in the sanctuary and say [to elected offi-
> cials], "Will you commit to this?" It's not lobbying or advocacy;
> it is holding our public officials accountable.

The 2016 Pomona letter from college and university presidents illustrates how to build a power base to exert pressure on a national level. In 2012, President Obama used his executive authority to create DACA (Deferred Action for Childhood Arrivals), which protected a limited category of undocumented students. Preparing for the Trump administration and its anti-immigration agenda, these academic institutions set the goal of publicly affirming their commitment to their undocumented students. The strategy involved maximizing the number of college president signatures to a statement urging that DACA be "upheld, continued, and expanded."[172] Highlighting that these students were already an established part of their campus communities and engaging a broad network of students, professors, and alumni helped deflect opposition from university stakeholders.

With which organizations can you align to magnify your power? In Charlotte, A Way Home gained a community voice with an ad hoc group of Christian and Jewish lay leaders from influential congregations. In Massachusetts, congregations achieved success with the Massachusetts Coalition to End Gun Violence. Nationally, the Pomona letter relied on college and university presidents to pressure the U.S. president, and marriage equality was advanced with the Civil Marriage Collaborative. Change rarely happens with one institution alone.

You can create partnerships for your causes with other Jewish congregations on a regional or national level or through interfaith coalitions, particularly CBCOs. Some issues are led by single-issue organizations and may be faith-based. "The Power of Partnerships" section in this chapter explores partnership opportunities in greater depth. Whether your congregation is initiating an issue or joining a preexisting organizing effort, partnerships will broaden the base of influence and move the cause forward.

Strategizing requires that you are already educated on the issues. With that knowledge, you are better equipped to define the sphere of your work, pick up a meaningful piece of the puzzle, analyze the power dynamics, and develop partnerships.

## Acting

Once you have identified your issue, educated yourselves, and developed your strategy, you are finally ready to act. But this *avodah*, the work of social change, is tough stuff. Like the many rituals detailed in Leviticus, the work is complex, makes daily demands upon us, and requires both sacrifice and skill. Campaigns are not straightforward, but take twists and turns that require thoughtful planning at the outset and responsiveness along the way.

The challenge of engaging in action is to focus on results. It is not enough to collect names for a petition unless it opens the door to prospective change, puts an issue on the ballot, or forces negotiations to ensue. The question to ask before you act is, "If we are successful with this action, what will change?" If an action does not have the potential to move your strategy forward, why pursue it? Low-profile meetings constituted the actions in the Charlotte examples. For both homelessness initiatives, these meetings were with prospective donors, agencies serving the homeless, and institutions that would own the solutions. In the case of the Pomona letter, Queens University of Charlotte professors and the Stan Greenspon Center met with their president to share their fears for undocumented students and the legitimate threats to their safety.

Not every step in the path toward change needs to make headlines; intentional conversations can move you along the journey. Conversely, mass media moments mark the beginning rather than the end goals; we may feel better marching with like-minded people, but we need to use those rallies to build the relationships that will enable us to take the longer and harder journey of systemic change.

Sometimes the challenge is to find actions that engage the

congregation. Only so many people can—or will—travel to the state capital to meet with legislators. B'nai Jeshurun tries to broaden its actions beyond lobbying to include more congregants. When the BJ Economic Justice Hevra worked on passing the New York State's Domestic Workers Bill of Rights in 2010, it wanted to make the issue tangible to congregants who were not lobbying in Albany. Lisa Zucker from BJ explains, "Legislation is hard. Albany is far away."

For BJ, actionable meant not only changing legislation but engaging in conversations that enabled congregants to realize the implications of their homes being workplaces for their housekeepers or nannies. Paula Galowitz from BJ elaborates, "A smaller piece was getting people at BJ who employed domestic workers to commit to have a conversation and do a few different things, not just money [wages]."

Fortunately, you do not need to invent your own actions, because there likely are other communities around the country working on these same issues with already proven techniques and tools. Note that acting is where you reap the benefits of the relationships that you have taken the time to build, using your collective power to create meaningful change.

## Reflecting

In Exodus 31:17, "On the seventh day [God] ceased from work and was refreshed," the word used for "refreshed" is *vayinafash*, which has as its root the word for "soul," *nefesh*. Since God doesn't tire, what are we meant to learn from God being "refreshed" as part of the cycle of Creation? Rashi, the esteemed eleventh-century French commentator, explains that this text exists "in order to make comprehensible to the human ear what it can understand." He notes further, "The idea is that one calms one's soul and takes breath when one reposes after the toil of labor." While God, who creates only through words, does not need to rest, we, as human beings who create through effort, need that pause to replenish ourselves (Rashi on Exodus 31:17).

Those of us working in the cycle of civic engagement can similarly refresh our own souls by periodically pausing and taking a breath.

Like the practice of using Shabbat to reflect on the week gone by as we prepare for the week ahead, we can find renewal in the work of civic engagement by allocating time after each series of actions to evaluate our efforts. Are our partnerships effective and positive, and if not, how can we improve our relationships and collaborative process? Are we communicating clearly and frequently with our stakeholders and congregation? Are we still moving the needle on our issue, or has the time come to retire it?

Rabbi Matt Soffer of Temple Israel, a Boston congregation known for its long-standing social justice engagement, commented on the difficulty of sustaining campaign cycles: "How do we engage the community at whatever level they want, and then uphold this method for getting work done? It's keeping people energized, recharging, and celebrating the little wins. . . . If we don't constantly work [on engaging the congregation], we slip back, and it's hard to rebuild."

Consider how other congregations have addressed the following key questions in this stage of the cycle.

### Is it time to codify our story?

We are often tired after the hard work is done. But to be able to continue this work, we have to inform our communities of its value and impact. We need to share our progress with our board, congregants, and partners.

Janet Goldenberg, of Temple Beth Elohim in Wellesley, Massachusetts, wrote a two-page letter to her congregation while state gun legislation was pending. The letter, entitled "In Deep Appreciation of TBE Congregants to Prevent Gun Violence," read in part:

> Leviticus 19:16: "Do not stand idly by the blood of your neighbor."
>
> Nine months ago, in the wake of the Newtown tragedy, a group of TBE congregants came together for a Shabbat reflection of contemplation, consolation and support. At the end of the afternoon, we came away determined to make a difference. . . .

Since then, we met and organized and reached out to others. We joined with congregants at Temples Isaiah and Emunah, Sinai and Israel. We educated ourselves about the problem and set out to educate others. . . .

We collaborated with diverse communities and organizations engaged in the same fight. . . . Partnering with the coalition we helped to build, we attended and testified before legislative hearings in Worcester, Springfield, and Boston. . . .

Our work has made a difference, and we are far from done. . . . To fellow TBE members who would like to learn more or to join our efforts, we welcome you! Reach us at . . .

. . . A personal note to all our TBEPGV [Temple Beth Elohim congregants to Prevent Gun Violence] leaders. Simply put, you are AMAZING. . . . To quote Neil Silverston, "One day when future generations look back to see when the movement to end gun violence first took hold, I believe they will look to the faith-based community—to you—with gratitude."[173]

Goldenberg's letter is particularly notable because it started with the Jewish text that inspired many of the volunteers and then touched on all the stages of the cycle of civic engagement—how the congregation identified the issue, the education that ensued, the strategy of legislative change with the partnerships built, the actions taken, and the gratitude expressed in reflecting on the progress made. But it also acknowledged that the work was not yet complete. By codifying the story while it was still in progress, the letter also served as a recruitment tool for additional congregants.

### Is it time to retire the issue?

Each *hevra* at BJ in New York City weaves evaluation into its work. Without these moments of reflection, the leadership believes that opportunities to pivot may be missed. BJ makes the decision to retire an issue when a break is needed or an effective path for change does not emerge. Rabbi Felicia Sol at BJ explains:

We had a Panim el Panim Retreat every year where we would evaluate. After a campaign has been won or lost or completed they [the advocacy working groups] have to make a decision about whether they move forward. There was a Women's Hevra that was working on issues of voter engagement. Following the election . . . it concluded its work. . . . [Similarly, the] Marriage Equality [Hevra] worked on advocating locally and then state-wide to pass New York's Marriage Equality Act in 2011, then closed up.

Work on issues also needs to be responsive to new realities. Changing administrations on local, state, or national levels, achieving significant systemic successes, and unexpected community crises can all alter our plans.

Like the learning that is deepened with the annual cycle of studying Torah, so too, does one grow through the cycles of civic engagement, even after a defeat. Rabbi Jack Romberg, at Temple Israel in Tallahassee, Florida, chaired TEAM, his local CBCO, from 2005 to 2007. He credits the strong and well-organized work of an initiative that failed with creating the foundation of TEAM's next success:

> We had a pretty decent number of people who were involved in TEAM—going to rallies and participating—and they would sit together and review what happened. We worked to pass a half-cent sales tax to provide health care for the working poor of the county [and the referendum failed]. . . . We put TEAM on the map. The way they did the campaign got them on the map. The next year, when we met with the school superintendent and associate superintendent, we didn't need to apply pressure. There was no resistance. They respected their [TEAM's] recommendation and made close to all their changes. . . . The organization won because politicians all had a new level of respect, so that when we came back to them, there was a whole new atmosphere.

### Is it time to celebrate?

> L'chayim—to life, to light, to love, and most of all, to equality. (Rabbi Schindler's Shabbat toast to her congregation just moments after marriage equality was won in her state.)

It was a Friday afternoon, October 10, 2014, when marriage equality was won in North Carolina. Based on arguments of religious discrimination, the federal district court overturned North Carolina's "Amendment One" that had banned same-sex marriage. The appeal had been filed jointly by three sets of plaintiffs: religious denominations embracing marriage equality, clergy who wished to marry same-sex couples, and same-sex couples seeking marriage. These plaintiffs included Temple Beth El congregants Joel Blady and Jeffrey Addy—a couple seeking to marry—and Temple Beth El associate rabbi Jonathan Freirich, who wished to marry them, although participating as an individual clergy.[174] Along with many other national religious organizations and clergy, the Central Conference of American Rabbis later joined the suit—the first suit that the CCAR joined as a plaintiff, rather than filing a friend of the court brief.

Shortly after news of the legal victory flashed across phone and computer screens, champagne was hastily purchased, and Temple Beth El congregants were invited to a toast before Shabbat services. The next Shabbat, all the same-sex couples at Temple Beth El who had been legally wed in other states—including on the temple's two Washington (DC) Wedding trips—were invited to the bimah as part of a special wedding blessing, as were couples just married under North Carolina's new legal standard. The bimah was filled with couples who had dreamed that their home state would acknowledge the equality of their love. Prayers had been answered as a result of decades of sustained sacrificial acts of civic engagement, not unlike those offered in Leviticus on the altar of the ancient *Mishkan*, our sacred sanctuary.

The response from the congregation to the bimah blessing was powerful. Eyes filled with tears and applause broke out spontaneously among congregants more accustomed to snapping their fingers in approval than clapping on Shabbat. This was a profoundly moving moment of celebrating civil rights.

Stopping to celebrate these successes is essential. The road to securing human and civil rights will always be long and there will always be more work ahead of us, and we speak from experience, living in North Carolina.

Evaluate your *avodah*, your work. Celebrate your wins. Analyze your losses. Document your story. Communicate to your congregation and share on your website. Write your thank-you notes. Reinforce the relationships that helped you achieve your goals. Take a deep breath and then reorganize to start the cycle of civic engagement again.

## In Conclusion

We listen to each other's stories to find common ground for healing our communities. We educate ourselves and our congregations so we can wisely engage in social change. We strategize how to be successful, whether in our city, state, or country. We act responsibly and effectively, as a congregation and in partnerships. We reflect on our work, celebrate our successes, and learn from our failures, which in so many cases lay the foundation for future gains.

The *avodah*, the sacrifices of Leviticus, were offered with the goal of making connections. In ancient times, these rites drew the Israelites closer to one another and to God. In fact, the root of one of the biblical words for "sacrifice," *korban*, is *k-r-v*, which means "drawing close." Through the civic engagement cycle, our work—our *avodah*—similarly draws us closer to each other and to our faith. Today, thankfully, our sacrifices are not animals, but rather time, treasure, and talent. Connections are made among congregants, between congregants and their synagogues, among faith communities, across racial and economic boundaries, and perhaps even between Jews and God.

## The Power of Partnerships

As the Israelites traveled through the wilderness, the *Mishkan* (the Tabernacle) was at the center of the procession. To the east were the tribes of Judah, Issachar, and Zebulun. To the south trooped Reuben, Simeon, and Gad. To the west of the *Mishkan* marched the tribes of Ephraim, Manasseh, and Benjamin, and to the north were Dan, Asher, and Naphtali (Numbers 2:3–30). The wilderness of Sinai could be harsh, but we had each other to ensure that we endured and that the *Mishkan* was protected on all sides.

Moving the *mishkan* of civic engagement forward also requires intentional collaboration. To create a powerful movement for change, we need more than one—more than one person, one synagogue, or one faith. Building partnerships outside the synagogue yields a multitude of other benefits. Forming relationships across religious, ethnic, racial, and class lines humanizes those "others" who differ from ourselves and shapes how those others view us as Jews. Collaborating with those who are more impacted by the issues we address than we are helps us work *with* those in our community, and not *for* them. Finally, collaborations with Jewish organizations may ease the discomfort of our boards and congregations to move forward in the cycle of civic engagement.

### Congregation-Based Community Organizing (CBCO)

Many synagogues involved in civic engagement find partnerships through joining a CBCO, which is a model grounded in the work of Saul Alinsky, the founder of community organizing. Alinsky's professional life was devoted to empowering the poor and the powerless, values no doubt inculcated in him through his Orthodox Jewish upbringing. We heard many compelling stories from lay leaders at synagogues active in CBCOs. These stories recounted how cross-cultural understandings were built, allowing these synagogue members to work with, instead of for, those most affected by the issues with which they have chosen to engage.

## CROSS-CULTURAL UNDERSTANDING

Temple Isaiah in Los Angeles belongs to One LA, a CBCO that is part of IAF, the Industrial Areas Foundation. Honey Kessler Amado, Temple Isaiah's then-incoming board president, describes her experience changing a Latino man's preconceptions about Jews through a one-on-one meeting outside her synagogue:

> We would start with telling each other our stories, meeting one-on-one. In one meeting, I met with a Hispanic man, and in our conversation, he told his story of a heartbreaking loss from fire. I shared that my grandmother lost friends in the Triangle Shirtwaist Factory fire in the early 1900s, and he was shocked to hear that my family were immigrants.

Amado created two points of connections between the Latino man and herself through these personal stories—their families shared the experiences of immigration to America and the tragedy of fire.

Janet Hirsch, also at Temple Isaiah, echoes Amado's experience. Hirsch is intentionally building relationships with the African-American and Latina women at St. Brigid Catholic Church, another member congregation of One LA. She invited a group of these women to join the Temple Isaiah women's seder. She said, "Afterwards, one of the women from St. Brigid, an extremely well-educated woman, said to me, 'I never realized Jews had been slaves.'"

Likewise, Judith Trachtenberg, at B'nai Jeshurun in New York City, is the temple's liaison to its CBCO, Manhattan Together, which is also part of IAF. Trachtenberg has become friendly with the Latino pastor at a Pentecostal church, an evangelical Christian movement with few commonalities with liberal Judaism. Despite their opposing religious beliefs across many issues, Trachtenberg and the pastor have built bonds of friendship. Trachtenberg reflects on their personal closeness, "He would be there for me. If I were in trouble and needed his personal help, he would be there."

We enlighten others about ourselves when we tell them our stories and are enlightened when we listen to theirs, finding commonalities that surprise those who thought they knew the other. In an increasingly polarized America, intentionally establishing these relationships across boundaries of faith creates the possibility of unity in our community, state, and even nation. These new relationships establish a cross-cultural foundation that strengthens the community both in peaceful times and also in times of crisis.

## WITH, NOT FOR

Partnerships can be powerful mechanisms for changing how we view ourselves and how we view others. Amado talked about the impact of building relationships across class boundaries and then encountering her fellow activists out of context. She shared, "[The CBCO] opened us to other communities, especially Hispanic and Catholic. It's an interesting kind of mixing—I ran into a housekeeper in the supermarket whom I know from organizing, and we greeted one another as activists and friends."

Hirsch emphasizes the power of the organizing process to elicit leadership from those most affected by an issue, saying, "One LA is really about leadership development. Issues and actions are secondary, really they are teaching people how to fix their own problems. It's not charity. It's amazing to watch . . . someone like myself who eight years ago could not speak in front of people."

Hirsch reflected on how the Jews involved in this work realized that the problems are not ones that they can fix by themselves. She commented, "Jews like to fix things, like to pick up the phone. It's really interesting to see the light go off, that in order to get this particular issue resolved, we need this [other] constituency to act with us . . . politicians only respond to their own interests and the interests of their [own] constituents."

Rabbi Felicia Sol, at B'nai Jeshurun in New York City, comments on the limitations of building relationships with the elected officials only from her congregants' precincts, saying, "The Upper West Side is a progressive community in general, as are [its] elected officials. The ones we've elected are not the only people who need the pressure." Partnerships in civic engagement take us out of our bubbles of religion and race, and sometimes even class.

### Single-Issue Alliances

Because Charlotte lacks a CBCO, ad hoc alliances of interfaith congregations have formed around single issues. For example, Temple
Beth El connected with the Catholic diocese and the North Carolina
Baptist Aging Ministry, and together with other faith organizations,
congregants wrote letters to the state legislature, successfully rein-
stating medical deductions on state income taxes. Likewise, the Phil's
Deli Group addressed affordable housing in a collaboration of lay
leaders at Temple Beth El, Christ Church, Myers Park Baptist Church,
Myers Park Presbyterian Church, and Myers Park Methodist Church.
And, to work toward marriage equality in North Carolina, Charlotte's
liberal clergy formed an alliance including faith leaders from Temple
Beth El, Myers Park Baptist Church, Piedmont Unitarian Universalist
Church, Holy Covenant United Church of Christ, Caldwell Memorial
Presbyterian Church, and Holy Trinity Lutheran Church, among many
others.

Many synagogues align themselves with national advocacy groups
that focus on a single issue. Interfaith Power & Light, for example,
describes itself as "a religious response to global warming" and is
promoting "energy conservation, energy efficiency, and renewable
energy."[175] Temple Isaiah in Los Angeles is active in the California Interfaith Power & Light chapter, and Temple Beth Elohim in Wellesley is
in the Massachusetts chapter. Among the other national groups that
congregations have accessed are HIAS (refugees), Human Rights
Campaign (LGBTQ rights), and the NAACP (racial equality).

### Jewish Alliances

Given the Jewish community's passion for justice, many organizing
efforts have emerged among synagogues and clergy. These collaborations may be regional, such as Reform California or Tzedek Reflection
in Boston, or national, such as the Religious Action Center of Reform
Judaism or Rabbis Organizing Rabbis.

Aligning with other synagogues can also be an effective means to
convince hesitant board members to take on advocacy issues. Rabbi
Sydney Mintz, at Congregation Emanu-El in San Francisco, describes
"many starts and stops" in the synagogue's organizing efforts that

finally coalesced with Reform California, a collaboration of the Reform Movement. She noted that Reform California gave her congregation's leadership the confidence it needed because the partners were other Reform synagogues and therefore more familiar to them. She explained:

> The rabbis were speaking a common language and, as a result, the synagogue leadership felt a sense of belonging and shared values. As a result, organizing became more clearly understood and less of a fiery point for congregants, which was very important. The last thing we wanted was to be divisive.

Outside of the congregational world, many Jewish organizations address ethical issues in our country. The Jewish Social Justice Roundtable connects fifty-seven Jewish organizations engaged in the work of social justice. It provides a platform for collaboration among national organizations such as the American Jewish World Service, Bend the Arc, Hazon, HIAS, JOIN for Justice, the National Council of Jewish Women, T'ruah, and rabbinic organizations from the Reform, Conservative, and Reconstructionist Movements, along with many local Jewish organizations as allies.[176]

## In Conclusion
However constructed, partnerships create the power to make change in our country. Tufts University professor Peter Levine aptly names his book *We Are the Ones We Have Been Waiting For: The Promise of Civic Renewal in America*. He writes, "A combination of deliberation, collaboration, and civic relationships is the core of citizenship. If we had much more of this kind of civic engagement, we could address our nation's most serious problems."[177]

When we complete reading a book of Torah, we say *Chazak, chazak, v'nitchazeik,* "Be strong, be strong, and let us strengthen one another." Torah is not read in isolation, but in the community created by a minyan. Social change is the same. We need one another, and we are strengthened by one another. When we want to move forward with an issue, we should stop and ask, "From whom can we learn? With whom can we work as allies and partners? Whom can we strengthen, and who can strengthen us?"

## Notes to Chapter 9

163. Translated by the authors.

164. *Social Justice Empowerment Program Handbook*, Unitarian Universalist Association, http://www.uua.org/sites/live-new.uua.org/files/documents/aw/sje_handbook.pdf.

165. Evelyn Laser Shlensky, *Lirdof Tzedek: A Guide to Synagogue Social Action*, ed. Marc D. Israel (New York: UAHC Press, 2001), http://www.rac.org/sites/default/files/Lirdof%20Tzedek%20-%20no%20cover.pdf.

166. JOIN for Justice, www.joinforjustice.org.

167. Marcy Einhorn, "Panim el Panim Community Cafés Lead Us in New Directions," July 2011, B'nai Jeshurun, https://www.bj.org/Articles/panim-el-panim-community-cafes-lead-us-in-new-directions/.

168. Massachusetts Coalition to Prevent Gun Violence, accessed March 1, 2017, https://mapreventgunviolence.org/projects/.

169. Rabbi Judith Schindler, Solve the Puzzle Charlotte Website Launch, Main Library, Francis Auditorium, Charlotte, NC, February 15, 2012.

170. Kathy Izard, *The Hundred Story Home: A Journey of Homelessness, Hope, and Healing* (Charlotte, NC: Grace Press, 2016), 98.

171. Izard, *The Hundred Story Home*, 247.

172. "College & University Presidents Call for U.S. to Uphold and Continue DACA," Pomona College, November 21, 2016, https://www.pomona.edu/news/2016/11/21-college-university-presidents-call-us-uphold-and-continue-daca.

173. Janet Goldenberg, "In Deep Appreciation of TBE Congregants to Prevent Gun Violence," Temple Beth Elohim, Wellesley, MA, September 2013.

174. General Synod of the United Church of Christ v. Cooper, Case 3:14-cv-00213 Document 1, filed March 28, 2014.

175. Interfaith Power & Light, http://www.interfaithpowerandlight.org, accessed March 1, 2017.

176. "We Are 57 Organizations Pursuing Social Justice from a Jewish Perspective," Jewish Social Justice Roundtable, accessed March 1, 2017, http://www.jewishsocialjustice.org.

177. Peter Levine, *We Are the Ones We Have Been Waiting For: The Promise of Civic Renewal in America* (New York: Oxford University Press, 2013), Kindle edition, 3.

REFLECTION

# How Civic Engagement Is Good for America

RUTH MESSINGER
*American Jewish World Service*

TIME WORKS in strange ways. I spent twenty years in local politics in New York City (1977–97), serving as a council member and as Manhattan borough president. Much of my time and energy was focused on urging greater public participation in government, whether through voter registration, campaign work, lobbying of elected officials, or local community mobilizing and organizing.

I did much of my work in partnership with local community-based organizations, often teaching them the best ways to get and stay involved, to collaborate with each other, to seek an ever-louder voice in decisions about city policy, law, and budget. I spoke regularly to how essential such participation was if we wanted to ensure that government worked in the public interest.

Then I spent another two decades with American Jewish World Service. My focus switched from local to global, but I continued to work with community and grassroots organizations to help them pursue their visions of justice.

I was increasingly enmeshed in making the case to Jews—individual donors, rabbis and lay leaders, organizations—that Jews are called to work for social justice, that this is an enduring and text-based obligation, that we are told to pursue justice and reminded that study is good not only for its own sake but because it leads to action.

That case is, in my opinion, brilliantly made in this book. It speaks to the what, the why, and the how of increasing our commitment to social justice—or, as it is described here, civic engagement. The authors speak to the importance of Jews doing this work as Jews, often in and with their congregations, respecting and responding to our text, our history, our life experience, and our values.

So, too, is the case made with many examples from across the country, that encouraging Jews to do this work as Jews in their congregations and communities strengthens those congregations and communities. It provides interested Jews with additional reasons for getting involved, and it offers a new portal into Jewish life for persons interested in community engagement who might not, on their own, think of a congregation as the best place to pursue such interest.

Now, at a moment when it is more imperative than at many other times in our history for more of us to be involved, I speak to another aspect of the issue, an aspect that resonates totally with my earlier career. I speak to make the case that increased civic engagement is good for America.

Civic engagement by more people on a broader array of issues with a greater degree of informed intensity is essential right now. Without this kind of civic engagement, we ignore our American history as a nation of immigrants. We disregard our democratic tradition of working across lines of difference for the common good. We unwind long-standing American policy positions that were forged with wisdom.

This is a time when we must resist, when we must organize and push back, when we must strive to grow our numbers to ensure that we are heard, when we are determined to stand up for what we believe in and make a difference.

That brilliant commentator on America, Alexis de Tocqueville, made this very point in the nineteenth century when he wrote:

> It is therefore most especially in the present democratic ages, that the true friends of liberty and greatness of man ought constantly be on the alert to prevent the power of government from lightly sacrificing the private rights of individuals to the general

execution of its designs. At such times no citizen is so obscure that it is not very dangerous to allow him to be oppressed—no private rights so unimportant that they can be surrendered with impunity to the caprices of government.[178]

De Tocqueville speaks across the ages to tell us to be vigilant, to remind us that such involvement is good for America, good for a country in which voter registration is low, election turnout often appallingly small, and too few people participate in any of the ways that are open to them. It is precisely this kind of a country in which candidates who do not reflect the public will can get elected and can wreak havoc on public policy and international relations.

The *Washington Post* has adopted a new slogan for these times as it ramps up coverage of the administration: Democracy Dies in Darkness. We might similarly say: Democracy Is Not a Spectator Sport. It requires citizens who know their rights, who step in and speak up, who are prepared to work over the long haul to ensure that their point of view is not only heard but followed. Or, as de Tocqueville warned, "Nothing is more wonderful than the art of being free, but nothing is harder to learn how to use than freedom."[179]

And here is a guide that teaches us how to use our freedom to fight back, that urges Jews to act on our values and to fulfill our obligation to pursue justice, and that tells us how. Imagine as you read the final section of the book what it means in these various jurisdictions across the United States for ever-larger numbers of citizens to know how to do a power analysis, mobilize support for a position, lobby their representatives, and demand accountability.

We have seen the effectiveness of this work already. Citizens enraged at threats to their values have raised their voices by phone, by email, and at marches. They show up at town hall meetings during congressional breaks, augmenting the all-too-familiar dozen "regulars" with organized crowds of several hundred constituents. It is clear that there are representatives who, as a consequence, are thinking twice about congressional votes that might further anger and engage these constituents.

Having individuals and organizations in a district committed to civic engagement, ready to teach others, is a vision of our democracy that has been absent for a while. It is coming alive again now at a time when America desperately needs such engagement. Our congregations should be one of the central places where people are being taught how to work together over the long haul to stake a claim for greater democracy.

And, to go full circle, think of the broader implications of Jews doing this work in and through their congregations. As they learn the tactics of civic engagement, they become a "go to" group for other faith groups to partner with, to learn from. In the interfaith collaborations that are recommended within these pages for amplifying our voices on an issue, it would be Jews who would be seen not only as a people determined to pursue justice, but as an informed group with knowledge to share across faith lines so that others could do this work as well.

We respond to the challenges of the time, we respond as Jews, in our Jewish institutions, and we end up strengthening our democracy, doing work that is good for the future of America.

**Notes**

178. Alexis de Tocqueville, *Democracy in America*, vols. 1–2, trans. Henry Reeve (optimized for Kindle, 2007), 243, loc. 13858.
179  de Tocqueville, *Democracy in America*, 139, loc. 5185, paraphrased from "It cannot be repeated too often that nothing is more fertile in prodigies than the art of being free; but there is nothing more arduous than the apprenticeship of liberty."

**AFTERWORD**

*Moving Forward*

*CHAPTER 10*

# *Vayisu*
## And They Journeyed . . .

T HE WORD *vayisu*, which means "and they journeyed,"[180] appears forty-two times in the final portion of the Book of Numbers. This portion—*Mas'ei*, meaning "journeys"—recounts each time that the Israelites stopped and started as they traveled from enslavement in Egypt to the Promised Land. Forty-two times the Israelites found the strength and the faith to resume their march forward.

Leading our synagogues on the journey of civic engagement requires us to find this same strength and faith. We need strength to redefine our Jewish institutions, though we can be encouraged by the increasing numbers of synagogues across the United States that have successfully made this journey already. Our tradition teaches that Judaism is all-encompassing, involving study and action, prayer and practice, the weekday and Shabbat, and the sacred and the secular. When congregants accept civic engagement as a fundamentally Jewish obligation—alongside Torah study, communal prayer, and acts of loving-kindness—then we have successfully transformed our synagogues into institutions that will heal our souls, both when we are inside and outside those walls. As we accomplish the work of civic engagement through our synagogues, but not necessarily inside our synagogues, we also connect the loosely affiliated Jew more meaningfully to our Jewish community.

As congregations across the country bring Jewish values of human dignity, equality, and equity to their communities, they are also teaching congregants an expression of Judaism that is relevant to their modern lives. The lay leader who has been unable to articulate why this work is Jewish becomes empowered to find her Jewish voice when the church members alongside her speak so freely about their faith. The Jewish activist who joins with other Jews under the leadership of his synagogue will advocate for social justice with a more powerful voice and communicate the Jewish call for justice to the next generation. Caring for the earth as it sustains us all will become a pillar of faith for the Jewish people, not just for the Jewish environmentalist, gardener, or vegetarian. Civic engagement enables Jews and synagogues alike to recharge themselves.

But this work is not solely for our individual or institutional benefit. The challenges that face our country today call us to respond as Jews and as Jewish institutions, to literally lift and save lives. The issues in America today—from health care to human trafficking, from gun violence to exploiting our environment, from the global refugee crisis to racial justice—these are at the heart of who we, as Jews, are called to be. Reflecting on our responsibilities as both Jews and Americans, Rabbi Peter Stein blogged about walking on the Journey for Justice with the NAACP and nearly two hundred other Reform rabbis: "And we did it all carrying a Torah scroll, proudly, alongside the American flag."[181]

The Talmudic sage Rabbi Tarfon urges us forward: "The day is short and the work is much. . . . It is not your responsibility to finish the work, but neither are you free to desist from it" (*Pirkei Avot* 2:15–16). Living our faith requires us to respond to America's problems, even if we cannot solve them completely, nor solve them all. As we each shoulder some responsibility—as American Jews and as synagogues woven into the social fabric of our communities—we garner liberty and justice for more Americans, even if not yet for all.

We find strength to continue our journey of civic engagement by building bridges across boundaries of faith and race. We maintain momentum by working on multiple rungs of the ladder of civic engagement. We remain motivated to move forward because, as Jews, we are called upon to repair the world in which we live and, as Americans, democracy empowers us to do this work. We say *hineini* as individual Jews and *hineinu* collectively as congregations—"here I am, here we are" as modern links in the chain of our prophetic tradition that instructs us to pursue justice.

## Using Our Faith as a Bridge of Cooperation

Eboo Patel, founder and president of Interfaith Youth Core, reflects on the ways that religion can cause hurt and the ways it can heal: "Faith can be a bunker of isolation, a barrier of division, a bludgeon of domination or a bridge of cooperation. There are lots of forces in the world investing in bunkers, barriers, and bludgeons. We are doing our best to lift up the builders of bridges."[182]

We can find the strength to journey on by finding communities that are sympathetic to the causes about which we care, and we can find strength by partnering with those who have endured similar struggles. The African-American parents fearing for their son's safety find commonalities with the Latin American workers who fear deportation. Victims of Islamophobia and targets of antisemitism share sympathy and voice. African-Americans and Jews are again marching together as we did in the civil rights era, linked by our histories as American minorities and perhaps even by our respective histories as African slaves in America and Hebrew slaves in Egypt. The increased visibility of organizations supporting white supremacy is thus countered by the loud voices of a broad alliance.

Charles Barkley, televised basketball analyst and retired NBA player, spoke eloquently about shared experiences of discrimination while he was commentating for CBS Sports during the first round of 2017 March Madness. NCAA college basketball games that would typically have been played in North Carolina were scheduled elsewhere because of the state's discriminatory legislation against transgender individuals. After thanking Duke University coach Mike Krzyzewski for his on-air criticism of the law, or as Barkley called it, "standing up for my gay friends," Barkley went on to say:

> Now, my point, as a black man, I am against any form of discrimination whether you're gay, Muslim, Hispanic, Jewish, whatever. . . . All these other groups are getting to feel what black people feel like now. With the Muslim ban, they're

deporting these immigrants. White folks are actually getting an opportunity to feel what black people have always felt. And discrimination is wrong in any shape whatsoever.[183]

Barkley uses his own experience as a black man to publicly defend other victims of discrimination. But as we saw with the examples of LGBTQ Jews and Jews of color in chapter 3, some people identify with more than one minority community. A professor of law at the University of California, Los Angeles, Kimberlé Williams Crenshaw coined the term "intersectionality,"[184] acknowledging that these more complicated social identities lead some individuals to experience intersecting systems of disadvantage. For example, intersectionality calls us to look more closely at African-American women—discriminated against both as women and as African-American, but in different ways than either African-American men or white women. Recognizing intersectionality helps synagogues be more welcoming to diverse Jews, whether LGBTQ Jews, Jews of color, or Jews with disabilities. Intersectionality also guides us to find common ground with other minorities as we build partnerships outside our sanctuaries, finding shared experiences as immigrants, as women in the workforce, or as simply being the "other."

Listening leads to empathy, moving us as Americans from isolation to connection. Building relationships inspires compassion and a shared commitment to create a safer society for all. Asking questions and analyzing the ways in which the struggles of our day impact us help us create stronger and more sustainable solutions—building power that can bring about change. As Jews committed to civic engagement in our synagogues, our faith becomes the bridge that connects us both to our own communities and to others that desire a safer and more equitable world.

## Climbing Ladders

When Jacob left Canaan, fleeing for his life to Haran, he stopped and slept at a place he later named Beit El (House of God). He had a famous dream there: "A ladder was set on the ground, with its top reaching to heaven, and lo—angels of God going up and coming down on it" (Genesis 28:12).

The biblical text, noting that the angels were ascending and descending the ladder, has two relevant lessons for our work. First, angels dwell on earth; if these angels had been based in heaven, they would be descending first. And second, angels are constantly in motion, moving upward and downward. This metaphor also applies to our ladder of civic engagement, which was originally introduced in chapter 1.

Just as the biblical angels dwell on earth, those of us who volunteer our time and talent are doing lifesaving work on the rung of the ladder closest to earth. And just as these angels are always in motion, congregations committed to systemic change occupy multiple levels of the ladder. As we enter into a covenant of civic engagement with

**Figure 6.** *The Ladder of Civic Engagement.*

| |
|---|
| Join a Movement |
| Connect with Community Organizing |
| Engage in Advocacy |
| Invest in Solutions through Philanthropy |
| Embark on Education |
| Give Time through Social Action |

our congregation, we must continue to climb up and down the ladder, sustaining the volunteerism that may have led us to recognize the need for social change.

The congregation that continues to occupy multiple rungs recognizes that different congregants may gravitate toward different tactics for achieving social justice. Some congregants appreciate the personal contact and immediate gratification of social action; others value the relationships built through grassroots organizing. Some may be motivated to participate through philanthropy, donating essential funds; others are drawn to becoming educated about the nature of societal challenges and illuminating the path toward solutions. Providing opportunities for congregants to match time, talents, and treasure with the needs of the civic engagement journey is critical, as we stand together with others and fulfill our covenantal obligations as Jews.

### Good for the Jews, Good for America

We do this work because we are Jews; our faith requires us to take responsibility for our community and those within it.

We do this work because we are Americans; it is our obligation as citizens in a democracy.

How fortunate we are that the values of equality, justice, and liberty are both American and Jewish and that we have the right and the responsibility to speak out. In order to maintain a democracy, we need to fulfill our own obligations as citizens—by voting, holding our elected officials accountable, and engaging in the civic life of our communities. But, democracy is also the tool by which we create an America that fulfills the ethical mandates of our faith, ensuring protections for the neediest, affirming the equality of all its citizens, and respecting the dignity of all who live here.

Some clergy and synagogue board members are fearful of the risks of engaging in this work. But what are the risks of standing idly by? What lessons are we teaching our children if we do not act on our beliefs? How meaningful are our prayers if we leave them behind in our sanctuaries? What will our future look like if the millions of students from impoverished rural and inner-city neighborhoods remain undereducated, trapped in the cycle of generational poverty? Who, in fact, will be left to speak for us if we fail to protect Muslim targets of religious discrimination and Latin Americans victims of xenophobia?

We want to create the best America we can. In our increasingly partisan country, we can start with conversations in our own congregations about our shared values and goals for the communities in which we live. If we cannot find common ground discussing such challenges as homelessness or immigration among the Democrats, Republicans, and independents within our own synagogues, how can we possibly expect to overcome our divisiveness as a country and make progress toward our American ideals?

Stosh Cotler, of Bend the Arc, speaks eloquently of why civic engagement is the right path for synagogues and for American Jews:

> I would contend that . . . we are having a profound crisis of Jewish communal purpose. . . . So the American Jewish community is one of the most affluent, educated, integrated, and safe Diaspora communities our people have ever known. And at the very same moment, we are at risk of losing our core identity as empathizers and prophetic actors. And this is so painful and ironic because if we were to act as empathizers and prophetic actors, we now have more power in American society so that if we leveraged that power for the common good it would make a real difference. . . .
>
> If we are not leveraging our community's tremendous resources for the common good, who are we, what do we stand for, what has our history taught us, and among all of the identities one can choose to be in the world right now, why choose to be Jewish in America today?[185]

As American Jews, we are living in a unique period of history. We are part of a democracy that provides us with incomparable freedoms—freedoms that must be embraced and freedoms that must be protected.

## Call to Action

Moving forward on this journey is challenging. Lessons on taking bold steps can be learned from syndicated author Dan Savage and his partner Terry Miller, who started the It Gets Better Project in 2010 to communicate a message of hope to despondent LGBTQ teens. Recording a YouTube video about their personal life was a particularly bold step for Miller, who wrote about why he breached his own principle of privacy:

> My rule has always been that Dan could write whatever he wanted to about us, and say whatever he wanted to say on TV, so long as I didn't have to go on TV or do any interviews or pose for

any photographs. But I agreed to make this video. I wanted to reach out to the kids I was reading about—kids who were being bullied, sometimes to death, because they were gay or perceived to be gay—because I knew that not every LGBT kid is lucky enough to have parents as loving and supportive as mine would turn out to be.[186]

The first lesson that Miller models is that justice requires us, at times, to step out of our comfort zone. The second lesson is that only in stepping forward ourselves can we bring others along. Savage and Miller's goal was for another hundred LGBTQ adults to upload videos, two hundred if they were wildly successful. In less than a week, one thousand others recorded and shared inspiring videos, each with the hope that some LGBTQ teen would choose to persevere into adulthood instead of committing suicide.[187] The project would eventually elicit videos from people across the boundaries of sexual orientation, gender identity, faith, race, occupation, and nationality, including such disparate groups and individuals as Orthodox Jews, Latinx,[188] African-Americans, an Episcopal bishop, a United States Marine, Ellen DeGeneres, President Barack Obama, and British prime minister David Cameron.

Savage and Miller bravely took the first step. Seven years later, fifty thousand YouTube videos are available on itgetsbetter.org, and these have been collectively viewed more than fifty million times. We can only imagine how many lives have been saved and how many spirits uplifted by this bold project. We learn from Miller that it does not get better until we, with moral courage, make it better.

At the National Cathedral in Washington, DC, in 1968, the great Rev. Dr. Martin Luther King Jr. spoke about the challenges of answering the call to action, saying:

> On some positions, cowardice asks the question, is it expedient? And then expedience comes along and asks the question, is it politic? Vanity asks the question, is it popular? Conscience asks the question, is it right? There comes a time when one must take the position that is neither safe nor politic nor popular, but he must do it because conscience tells him it is right.[189]

We wrote this book to help synagogues make the journey to civic engagement in ways that would be more pragmatic, more politic, and more popular among their congregants. Congregations will not reach consensus on every issue that arises, but they will be able to address many of today's critical issues, energizing themselves as synagogues and as Jews while moving our country forward. In choosing to guide their synagogues along this path, clergy and lay leaders can overcome the questions raised by Dr. King and the complaints of their skeptical congregants, heartened to know that this decision is right—fulfilling our responsibilities both as Jews and Americans.

*Vayisu*, "and they journeyed forward."

Abraham was called to journey forward. God wanted him to argue for the innocent as a way to teach those who would follow him to work for justice and righteousness.

Moses was called to journey forward. He was compelled to confront a tyrannical leader and redeem an oppressed people. He was called to convey a vision of a society built upon the principles of justice and equality.

Jeremiah was called to journey forward and proclaim the dire consequences that the community would face if it did not change its errant ways.

Esther was called to reveal her Jewish identity and consequently save our people so that we could all continue the journey forward.

As Israelites in the desert, we were called to journey forward as a people bound by a covenant with God and with one another. We traveled toward a more promised place with the ancient sanctuary, the *Mishkan*, at the center of our formation. The vision for a more perfect world was not meant to be kept inside that sacred space, but shared and lived in the world. That is our obligation.

Together we, too, can find the strength to journey forward—as Jews, as synagogues, and as Americans.

## Notes to Chapter 10

180. We chose to translate *vayisu* as "and they journeyed" rather than "and they set out."

181. Rabbi Peter Stein, "Marching toward a World of Justice," Religious Action Center of Reform Judaism, August 24, 2015, http://www.rac.org/blog/2015/08/24/marching-toward-world-justice.

182. Tim Funk, "Interfaith Champion Will Speak Friday at Queens University of Charlotte," *Charlotte Observer*, March 19, 2015. http://www.charlotteobserver.com/living/religion/article15281630.html.

183. CBS Sports, March 16, 2017, links to video clips on Alysha Tsuji, "Charles Barkley Supports Coach K's Opposition to North Carolina's anti-LGBT Law," *USA Today*, http://ftw.usatoday.com/2017/03/charles-barkley-coach-k-krzyzewski-north-carolina-anti-lgbt-law-discrimination-bathroom-bill.

184. Kimberlé Crenshaw, "Demarginalizing the Intersection of Race and Sex: A Black Feminist Critique of Antidiscrimination Doctrine, Feminist Theory and Antiracist Politics," *University of Chicago Legal Forum*, vol. 1989, issue 1, article 8, http://chicagounbound.uchicago.edu/uclf/vol1989/iss1/8.

185. Stosh Cotler, "Discontinuing Jewish Continuity," JDOV Talk, filmed at UJA Federation of New York, September 4, 2014, video, 9:20 and 10:29, http://jdov.org/talk/discontinuing-jewish-continuity/.

186. Dan Savage and Terry Miller, eds., *It Gets Better: Coming Out, Overcoming Bullying, and Creating a Life Worth Living* (New York: Penguin Books, 2016), Kindle edition, loc. 4078.

187. Savage and Miller, *It Gets Better*, Kindle edition, loc. 144.

188. Gender-neutral description for Latino and Latina.

189. Martin Luther King, Jr., "Remaining Awake through a Great Revolution," National Cathedral Speech, Washington DC, March 31, 1968, entered into *Congressional Record*, April 9, 1968, http://kingencyclopedia.stanford.edu/encyclopedia/documentsentry/doc_remaining_awake_through_a_great_revolution/.

# Glossary of Hebrew Terms

*Hebrew terms are defined at their first usage.*
*This glossary includes only terms used again without a definition.*

*adat*: community

*Amidah*: central prayers of Jewish liturgy

*avodah*: literally "service," sacrificial worship (biblical), prayer or work (modern)

*bal talin*: commandment to pay workers on time

*bal tashchit*: commandment to avoid unnecessary destruction

*beit*: house of

*beit midrash*: house of study

**bimah**: pulpit

*b'nei mitzvah*: "children of the commandment," plural of *bar/bat mitzvah*, the age of religious responsibility for a Jewish boy/girl

*B'nei Yisrael*: Children of Israel

*b'rachah, b'rachot*: blessing, blessings

*b'rit*: covenant

*chilul HaShem*: desecration of God's name

*eidah*: community

*glatt*: Yiddish for "smooth" (referring to the lungs of the animal), reflecting a higher level of scrutiny for ritual kashrut

*Hakheil*: assembly every seventh year to hear the reading of Torah

**halachah**: Jewish law

*hefkeir*: ownerless

*hevra*: close-knit group; society

*hineini*: here I am

*hineinu:* here we are
*Kaddish:* prayer sanctifying God's name
kashrut: Jewish dietary laws
*k'dushah:* holiness
kosher: proper, often proper for eating
Kotel: Western Wall
midrash: commentary on Torah, encompassing both legend and law
minyan: a gathering of ten Jews required for communal worship
*mishkan:* a sanctuary
*Mishkan:* ancient Tabernacle
Mishnah: an authoritative compilation of Jewish legal teachings codified around 200 CE
mitzvah/mitzvot: commandment/commandments
Mourner's *Kaddish:* prayer sanctifying God's name recited after the death of a close relative
*nefesh/hanefesh:* soul / the soul
*nitzav/nitzavim:* stand (singular/plural), the connotation of standing firmly
*omdim:* stand (plural)
*panim el panim:* face to face
seder: literally "order"; ritual meal recalling the Exodus from Egypt that marks the beginning of the Passover holiday
Shabbat: the Jewish Sabbath; day of rest, celebrated Friday evening until Saturday night
*sh'ma:* listen, hear
*Sh'ma / Sh'ma Yisrael:* Hear / Hear O Israel; the watchword of the Jewish faith affirming the Jewish belief in one God
*Sh'mitah:* Sabbatical year
shofar: ram's horn
*shomrei adamah:* guardians of the earth
Talmud: the central text of Rabbinic Judaism capturing teachings that span approximately six centuries
*t'filah:* prayer

*tikkun hanefesh*: repair of the soul

*tikkun olam*: repair of the world

*toch*: in the midst of

**Torah:** Five Books of Moses; may refer to the twenty-four books of the Hebrew Bible; may refer to all Rabbinic literature

*tzedakah*: an obligatory gift that ensures justice

*tzedek*: righteousness

*V'ahavta*: And you shall love; the prayer following the *Sh'ma*

*vayisu*: and they journeyed

*yetzer hara*: the evil inclination

*yetzer hatov*: the good inclination

*Yoveil*: the Jubilee year; the fiftieth year

*zachor*: remember

*z"l (zichrono/zichronah livrachah)*: may his/her memory be a blessing

# *Abbreviations*

| | |
|---|---|
| AJWS | American Jewish World Service |
| AME | African Methodist Episcopal |
| BJ | B'nai Jeshurun (New York City) |
| BJBE | B'nai Jehoshua Beth Elohim (Deerfield, Illinois) |
| CATS | Charlotte Area Transit System (North Carolina) |
| CBCO | congregation-based community organizing |
| CCAR | Central Conference of American Rabbis |
| CDF | Children's Defense Fund |
| CLAL | The National Jewish Center for Learning and Leadership |
| CROP, CROP Hunger Walk | Originally, Christian Rural Overseas Program; their website states, "We've outgrown the acronym but we retain it as the historic name of the program" (https://www.crophungerwalk.org/Static/About-Us). |
| CUSH | Congregations United to Serve Humanity (CBCO of Kenosha, Wisconsin, affiliate of WISDOM/Gamaliel) |
| DACA | Deferred Action for Childhood Arrivals |
| DART | Direct Action and Research Training Center (CBCO) |
| FBI | Federal Bureau of Investigation |
| GBIO | Greater Boston Interfaith Organization (Massachusetts CBCO, affiliate of IAF) |
| HIAS | Originally, Hebrew Immigrant Aid Society; their website states, "As we expanded our mission to protect and assist refugees of all faiths and ethnicities, our name no longer represented the organization. We are now known as HIAS, the global Jewish nonprofit that protects refugees" (https://www.hias.org/FAQ/HIAS). |
| IAF | Industrial Areas Foundation (CBCO) |

JCRC       Jewish Community Relations Council
JOIN, JOIN for Justice
           Jewish Organizing Institute & Network
LGBTQ      Lesbian, gay, bisexual, transgender, queer
MLK        Martin Luther King
NAACP      National Association for the Advancement of Colored
           People
NAOMI      North Central Area Congregations Organized to Make
           an Impact (Wisconsin CBCO, affiliate of WISDOM/
           Gamaliel)
NBA        National Basketball Association
NCAA       National Collegiate Athletic Association
NCJW       National Council of Jewish Women
NIMBY      Not in my backyard
NJPS       New Jewish Publication Society
One LA     One Los Angeles (CBCO, IAF affiliate in Los Angeles,
           California)
OSHA       Occupational Safety and Health Administration (U.S.
           federal agency)
PACT       People Acting for Community Together (CBCO of
           Miami Beach, Florida, affiliate of DART Center)
PICO, PICO Network
           People Improving Communities through Organizing
           (CBCO)
RAC        Religious Action Center of Reform Judaism
TBE        Temple Beth El (Charlotte, North Carolina); also,
           when noted, Temple Beth Elohim (Wellesley,
           Massachusetts)
TBEPGV     Temple Beth Elohim congregants to Prevent Gun
           Violence (Wellesley, Massachusetts)
TEAM       Tallahassee Equality Action Ministry (Florida CBCO,
           now defunct; was affiliate of DART Center)
URJ        Union for Reform Judaism
WISDOM     Wisconsin affiliate of Gamaliel
WOW        Women of the Wall (Israel)

# Sources Consulted

Aiken, Lisa. *The Hidden Beauty of the Shema*. Brooklyn, NY: Judaica Press, 1997.

Alinsky, Saul D. *Rules for Radicals: A Pragmatic Primer for Realistic Radicals*. New York: Vintage Books, 1971.

Atlas, Seymour. *The Rabbi with the Southern Twang: True Stories from a Life of Leadership within the Orthodox Jewish Congregations of the South*. Victoria, BC: Trofford, 2007.

Baker, Katie J. M. "Here Is the Powerful Letter the Stanford Victim Read Aloud to Her Attacker." BuzzFeed News, June 3, 2016. https://www.buzzfeed.com/katiejmbaker/heres-the-powerful-letter-the-stanford-victim-read-to-her-ra?utm_term=.tgnpmRr3v#.ju8A2xVY9.

Balin, Carole B. "Making Every Forkful Count: Reform Jews, Kashrut, and Mindful Eating, 1840–2010." In *The Sacred Table: Creating a Jewish Food Ethic*, edited by Mary L. Zamore, 5–16. New York: CCAR Press, 2011.

Barkley, Charles. "NCAA Basketball Tournament: Villanova vs. Mount St. Mary's/New Orleans." CBS Sports, aired March 16, 2017.

Bartholomew, Dana. "Valley Beth Shalom Rabbi Harold M. Schulweis, World Leader, Dies at 89." *Los Angeles Daily News*, December 18, 2014.

"A Bold Boycott Goes On: Montgomery Negroes Keep Up Bus Protest as Leaders Are Arrested." *Life*, March 5, 1956, 40–43.

Bonhoeffer, Dietrich. *Letters and Papers from Prison*. Edited by Eberhard Bethge. New York: Macmillan, 1971.

Brickner, Balfour, and Albert Vorspan. *Searching the Prophets for Values*. New York: UAHC Press, 1981.

Buber, Martin. *I and Thou*. New York: Charles Scribner's Sons, 1970.

———. *Ten Rungs: Collected Hasidic Sayings*. Translated by Olga Marx. London and New York: Routledge, 2002.

Bureau of Labor Statistics, Department of Labor. "Volunteering in the United States, 2015." Economic News Release, February 25, 2016. https://www.bls.gov/news.release/volun.nr0.htm.

Calmes, Jackie, and Ashley Parker. "Obama Challenges Perry to Rally GOP Around Border Plan." *New York Times*, July 9, 2014.

Coleman-Jensen, Alisha, Matthew P. Rabbitt, Christian A. Gregory, and Anita

Singh. *Household Food Security in the United States in 2015*. ERR-215, U.S. Department of Agriculture, Economic Research Service, September 2016.

"College & University Presidents Call for U.S. to Uphold and Continue DACA." Pomona College, November 21, 2016. https://www.pomona.edu/ news/2016/11/21-college-university-presidents-call-us-uphold-and-continue-daca.

*The Complete Metsudah Siddur*. Brooklyn, NY: Metsudah Publications, 1990.

*The Condition of Jewish Belief: A Symposium Compiled by the Editors of "Commentary" Magazine*. Northvale, NJ: Jason Aronson, 1989.

Connor, Philip and Jens Manuel Krogstad. "U.S. on Track to Reach Obama Administration's Goal of Resettling 110,000 Refugees This Year." Pew Research Center Fact Tank, January 20, 2017. http://www.pewresearch.org/ fact-tank/2017/01/20/u-s-on-track-to-reach-obama-administrations-goal-of-resettling-110000-refugees-this-year/.

Cotler, Stosh. "Discontinuing Jewish Continuity." JDOV Talk, filmed at UJA-Federation of New York, September 4, 2014.

Crenshaw, Kimberlé. "Demarginalizing the Intersection of Race and Sex: A Black Feminist Critique of Antidiscrimination Doctrine, Feminist Theory and Antiracist Politics." *University of Chicago Legal Forum*, vol. 1989, issue 1, article 8. http://chicagounbound.uchicago.edu/uclf/vol1989/iss1/8.

David S. Wyman Institute of Holocaust Studies. "Wagner-Rogers Bill." Encyclopedia of America's Response to the Holocaust. http://enc.wymaninstitute.org/?p=523.

Davis, Adam, ed. *Hearing the Call Across Traditions: Readings on Faith and Service*. Woodstock, VT: SkyLight Paths, 2009.

Ehrlich, Thomas, ed. *Civic Responsibility and Higher Education*. Westport, CT: American Council on Education and the Oryx Press, 2000.

Falk, Marcia. *The Book of Blessings: New Jewish Prayers for Daily Life, the Sabbath, and the New Moon Festival*. New York: CCAR Press, 2017.

"Food Justice." Religious Action Center of Reform Judaism. http://www.rac. org/food-justice.

Friedman, Thomas L. *Thank You for Being Late: An Optimist's Guide to Thriving in the Age of Accelerations*. New York: Farrar, Straus and Giroux, 2016.

Frishman, Elyse D., ed. *Mishkan T'filah: A Reform Siddur*. New York: CCAR Press, 2007.

Funk, Tim. "Elie Wiesel Encourages Global Activism." McClatchy Newspapers, March 28, 2007. http://www.popmatters.com/article/elie-wiesel-encourages-global-activism/.

———. "Interfaith Champion Will Speak Friday at Queens University of Charlotte." *Charlotte Observer*, March 19, 2015.

Gecan, Michael. *Effective Organizing for Congregational Renewal.* Skokie, IL: ACTA Publications, 2008.

General Synod of the United Church of Christ v. Cooper, Case 3:14-cv-00213 Document 1, filed April 28, 2014.

Giving USA Foundation and Indiana University Lilly Family School of Philanthropy. *Giving USA 2016: The Annual Report on Philanthropy for the Year 2015.* Giving USA Foundation, 2016.

Goldberg, Edwin, Janet Marder, Sheldon Marder, and Leon Morris, eds. *Mishkan HaNefesh: Machzor for the Days of Awe.* 2 vols. New York: CCAR Press, 2015.

Goldman, Ari L. *The Search for God at Harvard.* New York: Ballantine Books, 2008.

Hartman, Donniel. "Israel, The Challenge of Power." *Jewish Thought Leaders.* Lecture, Osher Marin Jewish Community Center, San Rafael, CA, December 6, 2011. Podcast audio at 38:00. http://www.marinjcc.org/clientuploads/directory/CJL/podcast/Donniel%20Hartman%20on%20Israel%20The%20Challenge%20of%20Power.mp3.

Heschel, Abraham Joshua. *Abraham Joshua Heschel: Essential Writings.* Edited by Susannah Heschel. Modern Spiritual Masters Series. Maryknoll, NY: Orbis Books, 2011.

———. *The Insecurity of Freedom: Essays on Human Existence.* Philadelphia: Jewish Publication Society of America, 1966.

———. *Moral Grandeur and Spiritual Audacity.* Edited by Susannah Heschel. New York: Farrar, Straus and Giroux, 1996.

Heschel, Susannah. "God and Society in Heschel and King." Reprinted in the Shalom Center, September 8, 2001. https://theshalomcenter.org/node/64.

Hirschfield, Brad. *You Don't Have to Be Wrong for Me to Be Right: Finding Faith without Fanaticism.* New York: Three Rivers Press, 2007.

Hoffman, Lawrence A., ed. *My People's Prayer Book: Traditional Prayers, Modern Commentary.* Vol. 1, *The Sh'ma and Its Blessings.* Woodstock, VT: Jewish Lights, 1997.

Izard, Kathy. *The Hundred Story Home: A Journey of Homelessness, Hope, and Healing.* Charlotte, NC: Grace Press, 2016.

*JPS Hebrew-English Tanakh.* Philadelphia: The Jewish Publication Society, 2003.

Kaplan, Mordecai M. *Not So Random Thoughts.* New York: Reconstructionist Press, 1966.

"Kashrut & Hekhsher Tzedek." Resolution adopted by the Board of Trustees, August 2008, Central Conference of American Rabbis. http://ccarnet.org/rabbis-speak/resolutions/2008/kashrut-hekhsher-tzedek/.

King, Martin Luther, Jr. "Letter from Birmingham Jail." April 16, 1963.
———. "Remaining Awake through a Great Revolution." National Cathedral Speech, Washington, DC, March 31, 1968. Entered into *Congressional Record*, April 9, 1968.
———. *Strength to Love*, reprint edition Minneapolis: Fortress Press, 2010.
Kleinman, Kevin M. "Curb Your Consumerism: Developing a *Bal Tashchit* Food Ethic for Today." In *The Sacred Table: Creating a Jewish Food Ethic*, edited by Mary L. Zamore, 163–71. New York: CCAR Press, 2011.
*Kol Haneshamah: Shabbat Vehagim*. Wyncote, PA: Reconstructionist Press, 1996.
Kravitz, Leonard, and Kerry M. Olitzky. *Pirke Avot: A Modern Commentary on Jewish Ethics*. New York: UAHC Press, 1993.
Krohn, Paysach J. *In the Spirit of the Maggid*. Brooklyn, NY: Mesorah, 2008.
Levine, Peter. *We Are the Ones We Have Been Waiting For: The Promise of Civic Renewal in America*. New York: Oxford University Press, 2013. Kindle edition.
Lewis, David. *Hearts & Minds: The Untold Story of How Philanthropy and the Civil Marriage Collaborative Helped America Embrace Marriage Equality*. Amherst, MA: Proteus Fund, 2015. http://www.proteusfund.org/sites/default/files/upload/inline/29/files/CMC%20Case%20Study%20FIN3_pages.pdf.
Lipowsky, Josh. "Jewish Groups Ramping Up Response to Sex Trafficking." Jewish Telegraphic Agency, August 12, 2013. http://www.jta.org/2013/08/12/news-opinion/united-states/a-painful-memory-sex-trafficking-and-the-jewish-community.
Lupton, Robert D. *Toxic Charity: How Churches and Charities Hurt Those They Help (And How to Reverse It)*. New York: HarperCollins, 2011.
Marcus, Yossi. "'Rabbi, I'm a Bad Jew!'" Chabad of the North Peninsula, n.d. http://www.chabadnp.com/templates/articlecco_cdo/aid/1025039/jewish/Rabbi-Im-a-Bad-Jew.htm.
McAdam, Doug. *Freedom Summer*. New York: Oxford University Press, 1988.
*Millennials: A Portrait of Generation Next*. Washington, DC: Pew Research Center, 2010. http://www.pewsocialtrends.org/files/2010/10/millennials-confident-connected-open-to-change.pdf.
Namako, Tom. "Joe Biden Writes an Open Letter to Stanford Survivor." BuzzFeed News, June 9, 2016. https://www.buzzfeed.com/tomnamako/joe-biden-writes-an-open-letter-to-stanford-survivor?bftwnews&utm_term=.jcl4bv7bK#.comp5Oe5K.
Nelson, Geoffrey B., and Isaac Prilleltensky. *Community Psychology: In Pursuit of Liberation and Well-Being*. New York: Palgrave Macmillan, 2010.
"Observations." *Findlay [Ohio] Morning Republican*, August 13, 1928.
"1,000+ Rabbis Sign Letter in Support of Welcoming Refugees." HIAS. https://www.hias.org/1000-rabbis-sign-letter-support-welcoming-refugees.

O'Sullivan, Jim, and Maria Sacchetti. "Patrick Wants Mass. to Host Immigrant Children: Says Immigrants Detained in Southwest Deserve a Safe Haven." *Boston Globe*, July 17, 2014.

Plaut, W. Gunther, ed. *The Torah: A Modern Commentary*. Revised edition. New York: CCAR Press, 2005.

"Poll Reveals Majority Here Would Bar Doors to Refugees; View on Jews Held Static." Jewish Telegraphic Agency, March 27, 1939. http://www.jta.org/1939/03/27/archive/poll-reveals-majority-here-would-bar-doors-to-refugees-view-on-jews-held-static.

*A Portrait of Jewish Americans: Findings from a Pew Research Center Survey of U.S. Jews*. Washington, DC: Pew Research Center Religion and Public Life Project, 2013.

"Reform Judaism: A Centenary Perspective." Adopted by the Central Conference of American Rabbis in San Francisco, 1976. http://ccarnet.org/rabbis-speak/platforms/reform-judaism-centenary-perspective/.

Rittner, Carol, and Sondra Myers. *The Courage to Care: Rescuers of Jews during the Holocaust*. New York: New York University, 1986.

Roosevelt, Theodore. "Citizenship in a Republic." Speech delivered at the Sorbonne, in Paris, France, April 23, 1910, http://theodore-roosevelt.com/trsorbonnespeech.html.

Rosensaft, Menachem Z., ed. *God, Faith and Identity from the Ashes: Reflections of Children and Grandchildren of Holocaust Survivors*. Woodstock, VT: Jewish Lights, 2015.

Sacks, Jonathan. *Rabbi Jonathan Sacks's Haggadah*. New York: Continuum International, 2006.

———. Seven Principles of Jewish Leadership." *Jerusalem Post Magazine*, June 4, 2012. http://www.jpost.com/Magazine/Opinion/Seven-principles-of-Jewish-leadership.

———. *To Heal a Fractured World: The Ethics of Responsibility*. New York: Schocken Books, 2005.

Savage, Dan, and Terry Miller, eds. *It Gets Better: Coming Out, Overcoming Bullying, and Creating a Life Worth Living*. New York: Penguin Books, 2016. Kindle edition.

Schachter-Shalomi, Zalman, with Joel Segel. *Jewish with Feeling: A Guide to Meaningful Jewish Practice*. Woodstock, VT: Jewish Lights, 2013. Kindle edition.

Schwarz, Sidney. *Judaism and Justice: The Jewish Passion to Repair the World*. Woodstock, VT: Jewish Lights, 2006.

*Sefaria: A Living Library of Jewish Texts*. https://www.sefaria.org/.

"Sex Trafficking: What You Need to Know." National Council of Jewish

Women, August 2014. http://f.cl.ly/items/
1J22003f24odojoFiyoj/talking-points_sex-trafficking_final.pdf.

Shlensky, Evelyn Laser. *Lirdof Tzedek: A Guide to Synagogue Social Action.* Edited
by Marc D. Israel. New York: UAHC Press, 2001. http://www.rac.org/
sites/default/files/Lirdof%20Tzedek%20%20no%20cover.pdf.

*Siach: A Jewish Conversation on Social Justice.* Video. Hazon. http://hazon.org/
siach-a-jewish-conversation-on-social-justice/.

Snow, Luther K. "The Quick and Simple Congregational Asset-Mapping
Experience." In *The Power of Asset Mapping: How Your Congregation Can Act on
Its Gifts.* Herndon, VA: Alban Institute, 2004. https://alban.org/uploaded-
Files/Alban/Bookstore/pdf/resources/Asset_Mapping/resource2.pdf.

"Social Action Blessing Cards." Religious Action Center of Reform Judaism. http://www.rac.org/sites/default/files/social_action_blessing_
cards_2012_-_front.pdf.

*Social Justice Empowerment Program Handbook.* Unitarian Universalist Association. http://www.uua.org/sites/live-new.uua.org/files/documents/aw/
sje_handbook.pdf.

*The Soncino Babylonian Talmud: Seder Nezikin.* Vol. 3. London: Soncino Press,
1935.

*Souls of Our Students: Appreciating Differences.* Charlotte, NC: Professional Communications, 2008. DVD.

"State Advocacy Fact Sheet: Safe Harbor Laws." National Council of Jewish
Women, September 2016. https://act.ncjw.org/wp-content/uploads/dlm_
uploads/2016/09/Fact-Sheet_Safe-Harbor_Updated-2016.pdf.

Tocqueville, Alexis de. *Democracy in America.* Vols. 1 and 2. Translated by Henry
Reeve. Optimized for Kindle, 2007.

Twist, Lynne. *The Soul of Money: Reclaiming the Wealth of Our Inner Resources.*
New York: Norton, 2003.

"United States Border Patrol Southwest Family Unit Subject and Unaccompanied Alien Children Apprehensions Fiscal Year 2016: Statement by Secretary Johnson on Southwest Border Security." U.S. Customs and Border
Protection, October 18, 2016. https://www.cbp.gov/newsroom/stats/
southwest-border-unaccompanied-children/fy-2016.

United States Holocaust Memorial Museum. "Martin Niemöller: 'First They
Came for the Socialists . . .'" Holocaust Encyclopedia. https://www.ushmm.
org/wlc/en/article.php?ModuleId=10007392.

———. "Voyage of the St. Louis." Holocaust Encyclopedia. https://www.
ushmm.org/wlc/en/article.php?ModuleId=10005267.

"U.S. Immigrant Population and Share over Time, 1850-Present." Chart of
U.S. Census Bureau data by Migration Policy Institute, Washington, DC.

http://www.migrationpolicy.org/programs/data-hub/charts/
immigrant-population-over-time?width=1000&height=850&iframe=true

"Who We Really Are: A Conversation with Syrian Refugees in America."
Brookings Institution, Washington, DC, February 19, 2016. http://www.
brookings.edu/events/2016/02/19-syrian-refugees-america.

Wiesel, Elie. *One Generation After.* New York: Schocken Books, 2011.

Wolfson, Ron. *Relational Judaism: Using the Power of Relationships to Transform the Jewish Community.* Woodstock, VT: Jewish Lights, 2013.

# Index

*This index covers individuals interviewed, their congregations or institutions, and the civic issues discussed. Five individuals were interviewed but not cited. One congregation asked to remain anonymous.Congregations were involved in more civic issues than addressed in this book.*

Abundance Farm, 134–36
aging, 60, 69, 120, 166, 188, 203, 206, 224; mentioned, 48, 120, 137, 146
Albert, Sara, 167, 171–72
Allen, Rabbi Morris, 132–33
Alpert, Rabbi Thomas, 47
Amado, Honey Kessler, 222–23
Baron, Gail, 109–10
Belasco, Judith, 139
Bennett, Rabbi Allen, 113
Beth Hillel Temple (Kenosha, WI), 8, 9, 22, 157, 164, 185–87, 204
B'nai Jehoshua Beth Elohim (Deerfield, IL), 22, 168, 172, 188–90
B'nai Jeshurun (New York, NY), 19–20, 22, 201, 202–03, 212, 215, 217–18, 222, 223
Busch, Ted, 189
capital punishment, 185–87
Central Conference of American Rabbis, 32, 127, 133, 219, 225
Chabad. See under Orthodox Judaism
Chicago Sinai Congregation (Chicago, IL), 22, 40, 79–80
civil rights movement, 21, 35, 40–41, 55–56, 121, 155–56, 176–77, 235;

mentioned, 89, 93, 116, 176–77, 235
See also Heschel; King
Congregation Beth Am (Los Altos Hills, CA), 22, 107–08
Congregation B'nai Israel (Northampton, MA), 134–36
Congregation Emanu-El (San Francisco, CA), xv, 9, 90, 205–06, 212, 224–25
Conservative Judaism, 14–15, 31–32, 107, 126, 133, 225; rabbis of, 15, 40, 46–47, 107, 121, 132–33, 134–36, 143; synagogues of, 67, 134–36, 155, 208
death penalty. See capital punishment
disability, mentioned, 48, 62, 64–65, 146, 199–200, 236
domestic abuse, 104–05, 108, 187, 188;
Drucker, Susan, 168, 172, 189–90
education reform, 42, 55–56, 67–68, 79–80, 86–87, 187, 218, 238; mentioned, 18, 136, 162
Einstein, Diana, 176
environment, 125–26, 128–29, 131–41, 141–43, 208, 224, 234; men-

tioned, 5, 6, 10, 14, 109–10, 129, 175, 188, 200. See also Abundance Farm; food justice; Hazon

Ettenson, Lara, xv, 90, 205–06

Feingold, Rabbi Dena, 9, 157, 164, 185

Fine, Rabbi Jacob, 134–36

Flam, Abby, 208

food justice, 139. See also Abundance Farm; environment; Hazon; hunger; kashrut.

Fox, Steve, 138–39, 165

Freirich, Rabbi Jonathan, 160, 219

Friedlich, Rochelle, 212

Friedman, Joy, 208

Frimmer, Rabbi Dara, 9

Galowitz, Paula, 215

Glazner, Dr. Linda, 114–15, 176

Godine, Fran, 172

Goldenberg, Janet, xv, 6–7, 74, 216–17

Groner, Rabbi Yossi, 119, 121

Grow and Behold Foods, 129–30

gun violence, xv, 6–7, 79–80, 189, 190–91, 208, 213, 216–17; mentioned, 3, 6, 9, 178, 234

Hanau, Anna, 129–30

Harris, Alec, 80

Hazon, 139, 225. See also environment, food justice.

health care, 68–69, 79, 80, 166, 189, 191, 218, 224; mentioned, 3, 234

Heschel, Rabbi Abraham Joshua, 40–41, 43, 55–56, 90–91, 121; mentioned, xiii, 116

Heschel, Dr. Susannah, xiii, 40; foreword by, vii–ix

HIAS, 98–99, 224, 225, 247

Hirsch, Janet, 171, 222, 223

Holocaust, 14, 39, 55, 56–57, 58–59, 61, 91–92, 94–95, 95–99, 99 (fn80,

fn81), 111

homelessness, 7–8, 18, 24 (fn2), 86–87, 106, 110–11, 173, 205–06, 209–11. See also housing, affordable

housing, affordable, 7–8, 18, 86–87, 106, 110–11, 173, 205–06, 209–11; A Way Home, 110–11, 178, 187, 209–11, 213, 214, 224; housing trust funds, 77, 189; mentioned, 3, 113, 146. See also homelessness.

hunger, 15, 18, 35, 48, 66, 110, 125–26, 134–36, 137–38, 139–40, 157, 175; mentioned, 9

Hyman, Barbara, 171

immigrants, 80, 85–86, 96–99, 99 (fn80, fn81), 119–20, 175, 212, 213, 214, 222; mentioned, 61–62, 146, 228, 235–36, 238. See also HIAS, refugees.

Islamophobia, 61–62, 80, 85–86, 97, 98, 112, 175, 235–36, 238; mentioned, 6

Jewish Community Relations Council (Boston, MA), 208

Jewish Federation of Greater Charlotte, 35, 67–68, 136

Jews-by-choice, 63–64, 174, 177

JOIN for Justice, 12, 147–48, 201; mentioned, 145, 225

Kahn, Raizel, 33

kashrut, 126–33; eco-kashrut, 132; ethical treatment of animals, 126, 128, 129–30, 132, 133, 141; Heksher Tzedek, 133; Magen Tzedek, 132–33; paying wages on time, 130–31, 133; mentioned, 89, 115. See also Grow and Behold

Kedar, Rabbi Karyn, 168, 188–89

King Jr., Dr. Martin Luther, 3–4, 19,

33, 34, 40–41, 51–52 (fn44), 92, 94, 156, 240–41; mentioned, 33, 43, 44, 159

Knight, Rabbi Asher, 12, 73, 160, 167

Lakein, Meir, xiii, 12, 120, 177; essay by, 145–49

Lavin, Harriet, 164

LGBTQ rights, 8, 37–38, 93–94, 159, 160, 185–87, 203, 209, 217–18, 218–19, 224, 235–36; It Gets Better Project, 239–40; LGBTQ Jews, 62–63, 64–65, 159, 160, 218–19, 236; mentioned, 3, 62, 113, 146, 224, 239, 240

Linder, Rabbi John, 106

Magen Tzedek. See under kashrut.

marriage equality. See LGBTQ rights.

Messinger, Ruth; xiii; essay by, 227–30

Mintz, Rabbi Sydney, 9, 212, 224–25

Moline, Barry, xv, 74, 114–15, 203, 208

Morse, Dr. Nick, 68–69, 166, 173, 206

Mount Sinai Congregation (Wausau, WI), 22, 114–15, 176

Orthodox Judaism, 62, 126–27, 130–31; Chabad rabbis of, 115, 119, 121, 132; rabbis of, 12, 14, 39, 44, 115, 119, 120, 121, 123 (fn118), 130–31, 132, 156, 160, 167; ultra-Orthodox, 29–32

Pesner, Rabbi Jonah, xiii, 202; essay by, 77–81

philanthropy. See tzedakah

Phillips, Stephen, 60, 166, 206

Pomerantz, Rabbi Gayle, 204

racial justice (contemporary), 32–34, 35, 37, 40–42, 61–62, 62–63, 80, 93, 158, 188, 222, 223, 235–36; NAACP

Journey for Justice, 40–42; Bryan Stephenson, 37; voting rights, 42, 93; mentioned, 188, 209, 234.

rape, 109

Reconstructionist Judaism, 15–16, 143, 225

Reform Jewish Movement, 13–14, 31–32, 40–41, 127, 155, 188, 224–25; and its liturgy, 48, 88–89, 119–21, 141–43, 169; see also Central Conference of American Rabbis, Religious Action Center of Reform Judaism, Union for Reform Judaism

refugees, 61–62, 85–86, 95–99, 99 (fn80, fn81), 146, 191, 207, mentioned, viii, 6, 234; see also HIAS, immigrants.

Religious Action Center of Reform Judaism, xiii, 13–14, 40–41, 77, 119, 139, 201, 202, 224–25, 234

Renewal, Jewish, 132

Romberg, Rabbi Jack, 218

Rosen, Mike, xv, 156

Rosenn, Rabbi Jennie, 98–99

Sachs, Lesley, 31

Saperstein, Rabbi David, 13–14, 119–20, 121, 164

Saphire, Rabbi Rachel, 167, 168–69, 190, 207–08

Schindler, Rabbi Alexander, 10, 43–44, 163

Schindler, Rabbi Judith, xii, 10, 35, 43, 63, 68, 111–12, 158, 165, 166, 168, 187, 207, 209, 218

Schwarz, Rabbi Sid, 15–16, 128, back cover

Seldin-Cohen, Judy, xii, 10, 113, 115, 165, 168

Shalom Park (Charlotte, NC), 67–68,

69, 105, 136–37
Silverman, Debra, 17, 165–66
Silverston, Neil, 138, 167, 169, 217
Sims, Mike, 90
Sisenwine, Rabbi Joel, 167, 190
Soffer, Rabbi Matt, 10, 23, 74, 202, 212–13, 216
Sol, Rabbi Felicia, 217–18, 223
*Souls* documentaries, xii, 86–87, 162
Stan Greenspon Center of Queens University of Charlotte, 207, 214
Stickler, Marsha, 105, 116
Temple Beth Am (Seattle, WA), 8
Temple Beth El (Charlotte, NC), xii, 7–8, 32–34, 60, 63–64, 68, 86–87, 105, 109–10, 113, 116, 158, 159, 160, 162, 165, 166, 168, 187–88, 197, 206, 218–19, 224
Temple Beth Elohim (Wellesley, MA), xv, 6–7, 22, 74, 138, 167, 168–69, 190–91, 197, 204, 207–08, 216–17, 224
Temple Beth Sholom (Miami Beach, FL), 22, 200, 204
Temple Emanu-El (Dallas, TX), xv, 12, 22, 31–32, 73, 79, 81 (fn79), 87, 90, 156, 160, 165, 167, 171–72, 176, 196
Temple Emanuel (Newton, MA), 22, 208
Temple Isaiah (Los Angeles, CA), 9, 17, 22, 138–39, 165–66, 171, 222–23, 224
Temple Israel (Boston, MA), xiii, 10, 22, 23, 68–69, 74, 78–79, 166, 172, 173, 202, 206, 212–13, 216, 217
Temple Israel (Tallahassee, FL), xv, 22, 25 (fn28), 74, 114–15, 203, 208, 218
Temple Solel (Phoenix, AZ), 22, 106

Thull, Yonatan, 136–37
Trachtenberg, Judith, 202, 203, 222
trafficking (human, sex), 14–15, 55, 105–08, 234
tzedakah, 16–17, 18–19, 25 (fn17), 66–67, 92–93, 120, 135–36, 223, 237
Union for Reform Judaism, xiii, 32, 43, 166, 185, 202, 225
Uri L'Tzedek, 130–31
Weinberg, Julie, 165
Wolman, Jean, 107–08
Women of the Wall, 29–32
women's rights, 29–32, 36, 86, 93, 236
workers' rights, 8–9, 48, 78–79, 80–81, 119–20, 128, 130–131, 132–133, 187, 203, 215
Worrel, Sue, 67–68
Yanklowitz, Rabbi Dr. Shmuly, 130–31
Yarmolinsky, Hannah, 77–78
Zucker, Lisa, 215